Black Authors and Illustrators of Books for Children and Young Adults

4th Edition

Black Authors and Illustrators of Books for Children and Young Adults

4th Edition

Barbara Thrash Murphy
and
Deborah Murphy

Routledge
Taylor & Francis Group
New York   London

Routledge is an imprint of the
Taylor & Francis Group, an informa business

Routledge
Taylor & Francis Group
270 Madison Avenue
New York, NY 10016

Routledge
Taylor & Francis Group
2 Park Square
Milton Park, Abingdon
Oxon OX14 4RN

© 2007 by Taylor & Francis Group, LLC
Routledge is an imprint of Taylor & Francis Group, an Informa business

Printed in the United States of America on acid-free paper
10 9 8 7 6 5 4 3 2 1

International Standard Book Number-10: 0-415-97219-1 (Hardcover)
International Standard Book Number-13: 978-0-415-97219-2 (Hardcover)

Visit the Taylor & Francis Web site at
http://www.taylorandfrancis.com

and the Routledge Web site at
http://www.routledge-ny.com

Dedicated to my son, James Murphy.
                        Barbara Thrash Murphy

Dedicated to my brother, James Murphy.
                        Deborah Murphy

Contents

Acknowledgments

Initial research was conducted as an independent study by students Angelle Pryor and Candice Gruver under the guidance of Professor Ellen Detlefsen of the University of Pittsburgh School of Library and Information Sciences. Technical support was provided continually throughout this venture by Ahsan Akmal with his expertise in arranging files, establishing databases, and solving the many computer problems that occurred. We are indebted to Diane Cadwell of D & T Business Services for the completion of the manuscript preparation. Doris Mace, our remarkably patient and competent typist, deserves considerably more thanks than she has already received for her scrupulous nature and meticulous attention to detail.

Grateful appreciation is extended to the many publishers who forwarded our questionnaire to their authors and illustrators. Without this component, the dictionary would not have the personal aspect that was achieved by the individual responses.

In particular, to Nancy Hogan of Front Street Books (Boyds Mills Press) we are deeply grateful for her willingness to provide us not only with extensive help in finding and locating contributors, but her enthusiasm was most encouraging.

The Carnegie Library of Pittsburgh and its branches in the Hill District, East Liberty, and Homewood, especially librarians Gwendolyn Hawk and Jennifer Pickle kept us informed of new titles. Many thanks to Janese Frasier of Marus Books in Oakland and San Francisco, California.

Most helpful in our research was the enormous collection of books by and about African Americans from the massive acquisition of reference works by the late Professor Emeritus Wendell Wray (University of Pittsburgh School of Library and Information Sciences) housed at the Chatham College Library in Pittsburgh, Pennsylvania.

The late Toni Trent Parker provided an invaluable service to these editors and to African American authors, illustrators, parents, and children by researching, compiling, and publishing three noteworthy annotated reference volumes: *Black Books Galore! Guide to Great African American Children's Books; Black Books Galore!*

Guide to Great African American Children's Books about Boys and *Black Books Galore! Guide to Great African American Children's Books about Girls.*

We appreciate the efforts of Pat Thrash for proofreading several pages of the manuscript. Her expertise and meticulous reading of the text were most professional. Mary James Hicks gave us much encouragement during the process.

Finally, we are indebted to all of the authors and illustrators represented in this anthology who took the time and effort to complete and return the questionnaire and send a photograph.

Barbara Thrash Murphy
Deborah Murphy

Photograph Credits

Benny Andrews: *Jerry Siegel, www.jerrysiegel.com*
Tracey Baptiste: *Kevin Fox Photography, www.foxphotography.net*
Sandra Yvonne Belton: *J.S. Hammond*
Donald Crews: *Nina Crews*
Nina Crews: *Nina Crews*
Pat Cummings: *Percidia A. Norris*
Leo Dillon: *Lee Dillon*
Gwendolyn Hooks: *MotoPhoto Crossroads*
Cathy Ann Johnson: *Kelley R. Foster*
Charles Johnson: *Mary Randlett*
Janet McDonald: *Gwen Wock*
Kadir Nelson: *www.harrisonphoto.com*
Marilyn Nelson: *Doug Anders*
Gloria Jean Pinkney: *Myles C. Pinkney*
Myles C. Pinkney: *Myles Studio*
Sandra L. Pinkney: *Myles Studio*
Brenda Roberts: *Barbara DuMetz*
Synthia Saint James: *Leroy Hamilton*
Irene Smalls: *Lynn McCann*
Nicole Tadgell: *Erika Sidor*
Dimitrea Tokunbo: *D A Photography*
Eric Velasquez: *Deborah Velasquez*
Carole Boston Weatherford: *Ronald Weatherford*

Introduction to the Third Edition

BARBARA THRASH MURPHY

The parenting editor of *Essence* magazine, Joy Duckett Cain, gave me an opportunity to write a "Children's Book Guide" for Black History Month. During the course of that pursuit, I discovered *Black Authors and Illustrators of Children's Books* by the late Barbara Rollock, coordinator of children's services at the New York Public Library. Mrs. Rollock envisioned an important guide and resource to aid in the understanding of the aspirations, thoughts, and viewpoints of authors and illustrators indigenous to Black culture. This was achieved in two editions. It is my hope to continue her efforts in this volume.

This third edition contains the 153 biographical sketches from the second edition with updated information for the majority, and 121 new authors and illustrators, expanding the listings to 274. More than 120 photographs have been added. Every effort was made to ensure the accuracy of the information by checking the data against a number of reputable reference sources. The expertise of the reference department at the Schomburg Center for Research in Black Culture, especially Sharon Howard, was extremely helpful.

The Wendell Wray Collection in the library at Chatham College in Pittsburgh, Pennsylvania, provided many facts and information necessary to complete some of the biographies.

More than 150 individuals were contacted personally either as a new entry or to update a biography from the second edition. In this regard, artist/illustrator Cheryl Hanna was most helpful by putting me in touch with various people in the publishing genre, which initiated a networking process that greatly facilitated locating many elusive persons. Authors who are well known for their adult and scholarly works—such as Alice Walker, Langston Hughes, Augusta Baker, Paul Laurence Dunbar, Nikki Giovanni, and historian Benjamin Quarles among others—are included with only their children's and young adult book titles listed.

The designation of the word "Black" is used throughout the book to identify the ethnicity of not only African Americans but also of those entrants who are from other countries throughout the world. Inclusive in the listings are authors and illustrators native to the Bahamas, the British Virgin Islands, Cameroon, Ethiopia, France, Grenada, Haiti, Indonesia, Jamaica, Nairobi, Nigeria, Panama, Senegal, Sierra Leone, Tanzania, Trinidad, Uganda, and the Upper Volta.

The individuals profiled in this work are identified by their full names (when available) with their given name in parentheses. For instance: illustrator Cal Massey's name appears in his entry title as Massey, Cal(vin Levi). Individuals who use pseudonyms or pen names professionally are listed that way, with their given names in smaller print directly beneath.

Many new talents are also included, especially emerging young artists like thirteen-year-old illustrator Martin K. Riley, Jr., and author Anika Dawn Thomas, who wrote and illustrated her first published book at the age of thirteen. In quite a few instances, both talents are found in one person who conceives and creates those literary images to which Black children can easily identify.

The selection process for new entries involved mailing more than 1,287 questionnaires to 183 publishers of books of particular interest to Black children, asking that they forward them to these authors and illustrators and identify any additional names. Approximately 425 responses were received, but some were not African American authors and illustrators and therefore not included in this work.

The questionnaire requested birth year, place of birth, educational background, military service, occupations, inspirational influences, approach to writing and/or illustrating, achievements, awards, memberships, gallery and art exhibits, personal family information, a bibliography of published children's and young adult book titles, and a photograph, which formed the basis of each entry.

All of the author and illustrator book titles are not necessarily included in their bibliographies. The discretion of the authors and illustrators determined the appropriateness of the titles included. In most instances, the date of original publication is cited.

The bibliographies include titles that span the entire spectrum of literature for children and young adults to include picture books, humor, folk and fairy tales, animal stories, mysteries and adventure, science fiction and fantasy, historical fiction, poetry, drama, biography, and other nonfiction. These titles reflect the contributions of ancestral forefathers and foremothers to contemporary generations, linking past to present. With the proliferation of African American bookstores (a partial national registry can be found in Appendix 3), more books that symbolize the cultural heritage and the contemporary lifestyles that unite Black people can be selectively acquired.

Books by, about, and for African Americans have increased in number over the past decade. However, most literature for children continues to exclude the African American culture. It is important to continue to write and illustrate books of quality that express this heritage and have them available not only to Black readers, but also for the edification of all readers.

Introduction to the Fourth Edition

BARBARA THRASH MURPHY
DEBORAH MURPHY

The fourth edition of *Black Authors and Illustrators of Books for Children and Young Adults* expands and updates the last index. This new edition aims to continue the biographical research for those who have an interest in African American writers and artists of books for children and young adults.

The book (to our knowledge) is the only readily available collection of current informational biographies and bibliographies featuring African Americans and a complete informational source of reference including personal photographs, e-mail and Web addresses for students, librarians, teachers, parents, children, the general public, educators, public libraries, academia in general, and Black heritage collections.

The dictionary chronicles data ranging from infant and toddler titles to books of interest to young adults. We have made an extensive search to include, whenever possible, all of the titles for each author or illustrator listing from the very earliest publication to the most current work to span the entire writing career. It includes not only well-known, award-winning writers and artists who have a historical perspective, but also those who are less prominent and initiating a writing or artistic career with only one or possibly two published works to date.

The word "Black" is used throughout the book to identify the ethnicity of not only African Americans, but also for those entrants who are from other countries throughout the world.

Books written by Black authors and illustrated by Black artists share a feeling that every person has—a pride in their own race. There should be a deeply founded footing in one's own heritage and culture, and one way this perspective can best be conveyed is through stories, art, and literary forms. One of the best and easily accessible avenues to provide this information to children and young adults is through books.

The profiles are of authors and illustrators who have written a wide variety of literary interests with subjects such as poetry, biographical topics of famous and well-known African Americans as well as those of important status but little or few prominent recognitions, teenagers' subjects, adolescent situations, adventures, continental African themes, animals, sports, civil rights, civil wars, family and life situations, fantasy, folktales and legends, friendships, historical fiction, heritage, music, mystery, poetry and rhymes, church and religion, holiday celebrations, self esteem and self identity, slavery, and more.

Dr. Elizabeth Fitzgerald Howard, professor emerita of West Virginia University and the author of ten children's books, states the following: "All of us who are concerned with children's books are convinced of the power of literature in promoting awareness, understanding and appreciation of other people and viewpoints. Surely the most compelling need in our society is for this. With the current demand for 'multicultural' books there are undoubtedly writers who are hopping on this bandwagon because it is a 'good thing,' just as there are surely editors who are anxious to flush out their multicultural lists however they can. But I also worry that as the economics of children's book publishing begins to force publishers to cut back, so-called multicultural books may be the first to be sliced. In these times of conflicting issues (more multicultural books needed vs. too many children's books being published) there is a danger that the present real zeal to find authors and illustrators from the parallel cultures will fade away."

To help establish a prospective database, the editors of *Black Authors and Illustrators of Books for Children and Young Adults* sometimes had to rely on the selection of books they deemed of particular interest to Black children by cover illustration, subject matter, or titles. Very few books contained a photograph of the author or illustrator on the back dust jacket flap and even then ethnicity was not always discernable.

For the most part, this anthology is a compilation of information submitted by the authors and illustrators themselves as well as information obtained from a variety of published sources.

In order to compile the anthology, ever-vigilant eyes and ears were constantly attuned to someone's passing remark about a new book title, browsing through the main branch of the Carnegie Library of Pittsburgh's children's section, and periodically visiting the collections in the branches at the Homewood Carnegie Library, the East Liberty Branch, and the Hill District Branch to check out books of ethnic interest they had recently acquired. The task remains endless. Almost every reference led to several more and a voluminous amount of computer search hours following "leads" of relevant topics, consuming much time and effort, some profitable and some not.

We began the task to update prior entries from the third edition by sending questionnaires requesting additional current information of biographical data and listings of new books published.

In most cases, our first approach to locating and contacting new authors and illustrators was made through the publishing houses with a book title of particular interest to an African American child, or a cover illustration depicting an African American individual or scene. The cooperation of publishers making information available and their agreement to forward our questionnaire to the authors and illustrators publishing with their individual companies varied enormously.

Questionnaires were sent to prospective new authors and illustrators requesting information to include birth year, where they were born, education, military service, occupations, achievements, awards, memberships, recognitions, gallery and art exhibits, family, and where they are currently residing (city and state).

Those contacted were further asked to precede each autobiography with a "personal statement" regarding their thoughts on writing for children and young adults; what influenced them and how they think children can be motivated to read more. This addition to these autobiographies made the information much more personal and revealing.

A listing was requested of all their published works to have a complete record of the bibliographies regardless of whether or not some of the book(s) were currently out of print. Those with only one published title would also qualify for inclusion in the book.

Every effort was made to obtain information directly from the authors and illustrators themselves; however, biographical sources were also consulted. Further details came from published interviews, obituaries, feature stories, book reviews, etc., and we were vigilantly attuned to the most minute mention of a book of interest.

The profiles of the illustrators of children's books reflect their contributions by providing the collaboration of two distinct artistic talents with vivid imagination to form a work to be enjoyed twice as much by the equal blending of words and images.

It is the ability of the illustrator to capture the essence of the text to present the reader with an extension of the written words.

The illustrators of these children's books skillfully combine the words and thoughts of the authors to form characters and scenes that enhance the enjoyment of the story.

Verifying content information necessitated the study and research of many books, databases, special collections, exhibits, pamphlets, bookmarks, newspapers, and magazine articles.

Improvements in technology and indexing have made both library book and periodical searching incredibly faster and easier, but ultimately opens up a voluminous amount of material that has to be read, sorted, accepted, or rejected.

This anthology comprises a grouping of authors and illustrators representing four distinct categories, although the dictionary is printed in alphabetical sequence. The volume contains (1) entries of legendary authors from a historical perspective, (2) contemporary authors and illustrators who have established a long listing of publications and have won awards, (3) emerging new talents with perhaps only one or two publications to date, and (4) the inclusion of international authors and illustrators.

This fourth edition of *Black Authors and Illustrators of Books for Children and Young Adults* is therefore an extensive collection of the Black artists and authors who are prominent in the genre of literature for children and young adults.

Foreword

CARLA D. HAYDEN
Executive Director, Enoch Pratt Free Library
Past President, American Library Association

The recent fiftieth anniversary of the historic Supreme Court decision *Brown v. Board of Education* ending officially imposed segregation in public education was the occasion for numerous commemorative events and reflections. Although the resolution of this landmark federal case opened the door for the end of segregation in all aspects of life, the reality of a promise unfulfilled echoed throughout the celebrations and activities. Indeed, some commentators noted that young people of today, particularly African Americans, still need to understand their own and other cultures in order to bring about the dreams of those who labored to bring the case to fruition and the subsequent civil rights movement that followed. There was also ample evidence presented that demonstrated that despite the many achievements made since the decision, African American youth were still significantly behind in the educational arena and had not closed the gap that had played such a large role in making the case.

The passing of civil rights pioneer Rosa Parks led to further re-examination of the progress of the struggle for equity and equality. Yet again, educators, legislators, activists, citizens, and many others pointed to the need to continue the push for fairness and parity while recognizing the gains that had been made in many areas. The need for more cultural and global understanding was also highlighted with world events, from natural disasters at home and abroad to troubling instances of racial and ethnic intolerance throughout the world.

The recent passing of Coretta Scott King brings the issue to the forefront in the realm of literature for young people. Her influence and support for the award program named in her honor were extremely significant in promoting African American authors and illustrators and their works. Since its inception in 1969, the Coretta Scott King Awards have increased awareness and visibility while providing broader opportunities for numerous writers and creators of color. And in 2000, a trailblazing event occurred shortly after the publication of the last edition of *Black Authors and Illustrators of Books for Children and Young Adults*. The Coretta Scott King Award winner was, for the first time, also the winner of the Newbery Award, the most prestigious recognition in children's literature. *Bud, not Buddy* by Christopher Paul Curtis was selected by both award committees. Deborah Taylor, chair of the King Committee that year and past president of YASLA, recalled, "these were two very different committees looking at some of the same things and some different things in what they were going to recognize the book for as the best for that year." It had been nearly twenty-five years since any African American had won the Newbery Award, although a few had been honor winners along with Caldecott Award honors for picture books. Curtis was the first African American male to win a Newbery and his accomplishment demonstrated the growth in the field.

This breakthrough caused some to question the need for continuing the King Award program and even the need for reference tools such as *Black Authors and Illustrators for Children and Young Adults*. However, despite the phenomenon of 2000, there is still a need for a testament to the talent, creativity, and diversity displayed in this edition. There are only approximately one hundred books by African Americans published annually out of thousands of titles. As a result, there is a need to distinguish not isolate African Americans in literature for youth, to bring attention to them, and not risk oblivion by inclusion without notation in other sources. In addition, there is a need to have as many ways as possible to recognize and encourage quality books and to identify authors and illustrators and their works.

This edition stands not only in continuing tribute to the pioneering efforts of Barbara Rollock but to the dedication and scholarship of Dr. Barbara Thrash Murphy and Deborah Murphy who have expanded and enhanced what is acknowledged as the only resource of its kind. Their work will build on the legacies of the past and such noted scholars as Dr. E. J. Josey, and Dr. Wendell Wray of the University of Pittsburgh, as well as bring this invaluable resource into the new century with more entries and additional personal reflections from the creators.

As the new century progresses with the fast paced progression of technology affecting almost every facet of human endeavor, including publishing, we still need to inspire and motivate youth through reading and seeing themselves reflected in literature and illustrations. The influence of media of all types and formats is real and immediate and can either help advance or hinder human understanding. *Black Authors and Illustrators of Books for Children and Young Adults* is a tool for everyone concerned about our future. We owe a debt of gratitude for the commitment and vigilance of Dr. Murphy and Deborah Murphy to ensure an important part of "the world of children's books" will remain identifiable for all to see.

Bibliographical Sources

Baker, L., Dreher, M.J., and Guthrie, J.T. Why Teachers Should Promote Reading Engagement. *Journal of Early Childhood Literacy.* Vol. 6, no. 1, 5–31, 2006.

Baker, L., Mackler, K., Sonnenscheim, S., and Serpell, R. Mothers' Interaction with Their First Grade Children during Storybook Reading and Relations with Reading Activity and Achievement. *Journal of School Psychology,* Vol. 39, no. 5, 415–438. 2001.

Combs, Richard E. and Nancy R. Owens, eds. *Authors: Critical and Biographical References.* Lanham, MD: Scarecrow, 1993.

Evans, Mari, ed. *Black Women Writers, 1950–1980. A Critical Evaluation.* Garden City, NY: Anchor/Doubleday, 1984.

Hawkins, Walter L. *African American Biographies: Profiles of 558 Current Men and Women.* Jefferson, NC: McFarland, 1992.

Hine, Darlene Clark, Brown, Elsa Barkley, and Terborg-Penn, Rosolyn, eds. *Black Women in America: An Historical Encyclopaedia.* Brooklyn, NY: Carlson Publishing, 1993.

Kutenplon, Deborah and Ellen Olmstead. *Young Adult Fiction by African American Writers, 1968–1993.* Routledge: New York, 1995.

LaBeau, Dennis and Tarbert, Gary, eds. *Biographical Dictionaries Master Index.* Detroit, MI: Gale Research, 1975.

LaBeau, Dennis, ed. *Children's Authors and Illustrators: An Index to Biographical Dictionaries.* Detroit, MI: Gale Research, 1976.

Malinowski, Sharon, ed. *Black Writers: A Selection of Sketches from Contemporary Authors.* Detroit, MI: Gale Research, 1994.

Murphy, Barbara Thrash. *Black Authors and Illustrators of Books for Children and Young Adults* (3rd ed.). New York: Garland, 1999.

Nakamura, Joyce, Andrews, Shelly, and Standley, Laura, eds. *Something About the Author: Autobiography Series.* Detroit, MI: Gale Research, 1998.

New York Public Library. Office of Children's Services. *The Black Experiences in Children's Books.* New York Public Library, 1994.

Newby, James Edward. *Black Authors: A Selected Annotated Bibliography.* New York: Garland, 1991.

Silvey, Anita, ed. *Children's Books and Their Creators.* Boston: Houghton Mifflin, 1995.

Smith, Henrietta M., ed. *The Coretta Scott King Awards 1970–2004* (3rd ed.). Chicago: American Library Association, 2004.

Smith, Valerie, ed. *African American Writers.* New York: C. Scribner's Sons, 1991.

Williams, Helen Elizabeth. *Books by African-American Authors and Illustrators for Children and Young Adults.* Chicago: American Library Association, 1991.

Adisa, Opal Palmer

(1954–)

AUTHOR

E-mail: opalwrites@sbcglobal.net

Web site: www.opalwrites.com

Adisa was born in Kingston, Jamaica, the second of two girls. What she remembers fondly, and attributes to her development as a writer, are the stories she heard as a child. Adisa wrote poetry as a young girl, and had her first poem published when she was a thirteen-year-old student at Wolmer's High School for Girls in Jamaica. It was not until Adisa moved to New York City in 1970, where she attended Hunter College, that she seriously considered writing as a career and began to tell stories professionally. When she returned to Jamaica in 1976 with a bachelor's degree in communications from Hunter College, she worked at the Educational Broadcasting Corporation as an Education Officer/Director.

She has taught in numerous elementary and high schools, has anthologized more than thirty books of children's poetry, and is cofounder of Watoto Wa Kuumba, a children's theater group in Oakland, California. For her storytelling performances, she was named master folk artist in 1991–1992 by the California Arts Council. *Tamarind and Mango Women* won the 1992 PEN Oakland Josephine Miles Literary Award. In 1994 she taught playwriting and performance skills at Castlemont High School in Oakland, California, was poet-in-residence at Huckleberry House in San Francisco, California, and conducted poetry workshops at Brete Harte Middle School in Oakland, California.

The author is an internationally acclaimed lecturer and author of books for children and adults. In addition, Adisa's awards include a Creative Artist Fellowship Award for storytelling, Cultural Funding Program, Oakland, California; a Creative Work Fund Grant—Senior Citizen Oral History Project, San Francisco, California, and a Master Folk Artist award for Storytelling from the California Arts Council.

She holds two master of arts degrees, in English and Drama, from San Francisco State University and a doctorate in Ethnic studies from the University of California, Berkeley. She is the chair of the Ethnic Studies/Cultural Diversity Program at California College of Arts and Crafts, where she is an associate professor.

Adisa lives in Oakland, California, and has three children.

BIBLIOGRAPHY

Pina, the Many-Eyed Fruit. Illustrated by Jimi Evans. Julian Richardson, 1985.

Bake-Face and Other Guava Stories. Kelsey Street, 1986.

traveling women. With Deborah Major. Jukebox, 1989.

Tamarind and Mango Women. Sister Vision, 1992.

Leaf-of-Life (Poetry). Juke Box Press, 2000.

Adoff, Jaime L.

(1967–)

AUTHOR

E-mail: jaime@jaimeadoff.com

Web site: www.jaimeadoff.com

"I write for the boy in the last row who never raises his hand, but has so much to say. I write for the girl in the front row who now has pages of poems and stories for me to read, before I've even taken my coat off. I write because it is the most freeing experience I know of. I can create my own world, my own universe, create my own rules, then break them if I want to.

"I would like to think that I could make a difference in a young person's life, but that is making too much of what I do. I would settle for just being a small part in getting a young person to see themselves and to see others around them. To see how we are all the same and different at the same time, and to respect and honor those differences. Showing a teen that there can be hope, that there is always hope even in the darkest hour.

"I write because I love the fact that a book doesn't care what color you are, or what religion you are or how much money your parents make.

"Books are for everyone and should be shared like a big slice of apple pie with two scoops of ice cream on top.

"So what do you say?

"Let's dig in ..."

Adoff was born in New York City but grew up in Yellow Springs, Ohio. He received a Bachelor of Music degree from Central State University in Ohio, where he studied drums and percussion. Moving to New York City in 1990, he attended the Manhattan

3

School of Music and studied drums and voice. Adoff then went on to pursue a career in songwriting and fronted his own rock band for eight years. He released two CDs of his own material and performed extensively in New York City and throughout the Northeast.

He is the author of *The Song Shoots Out of My Mouth: A Celebration of Music* (2002), which was a Lee Bennett Hopkins Poetry Award Honor book (2003) an IRA Notable book (2003), a New York Public Library book for the teenage (2003), a VOYA poetry pick (2002), and a CCB Best Book for 2002.

The critically acclaimed *Names Will Never Hurt Me* (2004) was his first young-adult novel and was named a New York Public Library book for the teenager (2004).

His latest novel, *Jimi & Me*, was published in September of 2005.

Jaime lives in his hometown of Yellow Springs, Ohio. He is the son of the late Newbery Award-winning author Virginia Hamilton and renowned poet Arnold Adoff.

BIBLIOGRAPHY

The Song Shoots Out of My Mouth: A Celebration of Music. Illustrated by Martin French. Dutton, 2002.

Names Will Never Hurt Me. Dutton, 2004.

Jimi & Me. Jump at the Sun (Hyperion), 2005.

Agard, John

(1930–)

AUTHOR

Agard—an actor, journalist, short-story writer, and poet—was born in Guyana, South America. He and his wife contributed to the art scene of Guyana, and his poetry has appeared in *Expression*, edited by Janice Lowe; *Plexus*, edited by R.C. McAndrew; and the *Sunday Chronicle*. Many of his short stories have been broadcast.

Besides works for adults he has published five children's books.

Agard lives in England.

BIBLIOGRAPHY

The Calypso Alphabet. Illustrated by Jennifer Bent. Holt, 1989.

Lend Me Your Wings. Illustrated by Adrienne Kennaway. Little, 1989.

Life Doesn't Frighten Me at All. Holt, 1990.

A Caribbean Dozen: Poems from Caribbean Poets. With Grace Nichols. Illustrated by Cathie Felstead. Candlewick, 1994.

No Hickory No Dickory No Dock: Caribbean Nursery Rhymes. With Grace Nichols. Illustrated by Cynthia Jabar. Candlewick, 1994.

Andrews, Benny

(1930–)

ILLUSTRATOR

"I'm interested in illustrating books because it enables me to reach a much broader audience than my paintings do. As I travel through the country for my painting and drawing exhibitions, I meet people who first became aware of my work through books I'd illustrated."

Andrews approaches his works for books the same way he approaches doing fine art. Each work must stand on its own. Often people who would like to own his paintings cannot afford them but they can afford the books.

Each book he illustrates is exhibited in fine art galleries, therefore, the illustrations must stand up individually and not be dependent on the essay to make it meaningful.

Andrews has exhibited his art work at many galleries and museums since his first showing in 1962 at the Forum Gallery in New York. His most recent exhibits have been at the Breanu University Gallery in 2002 in Gainesville, Georgia; York College Gallery in New York; ACA Gallery in New York, and the Southside Gallery in Oxford, Mississippi. Several museums, art centers, and institutes hold permanent collections of Andrews' works. Among them are The Zora Neale Hurston Museum at Eatonville, Florida, The Wichita Art Museum in Wichita, Kansas, The Verich Museum in Wichita, Kansas, The Savannah College of Art & Design in Savannah, Georgia, The Philadelphia Academy of Art in Pennsylvania, The Ohio State University Art Gallery in Columbus, Ohio, and many more.

BIBLIOGRAPHY

Sky Sash So Blue. By Libby Hathorn. Simon & Schuster, 2001.

The Hickory Chair. By Lisa Rowe Fraustino. Scholastic, 2001.

Pictures for Miss Josie. By Sandra Beton. Greenwillow, 2003.

Delivering Justice. By Jim Haskins. Candlewick, 2005.

Langston Hughes: Poetry for Young People. By David Rosessel and Arnold Rampersad. Sterling, 2006.

John Lewis in the Lead: A Story of the Civil Rights Movement. By Jim Haskins. Lee & Low, 2006.

Baptiste, Tracey

(1972–)

AUTHOR

"Life is about discovery, and we discover most of what we know about ourselves and relationships when we are children and young adults. Books can be a huge part of that discovery. It's important that as authors of books for young people, we take responsibility to create literature that is inspiring and encouraging. As children read and see themselves in the pages of books, they will see the possibility for finding more positive things in themselves and their lives. I hope that I can always create stories that move readers, the way that many stories I read as a child moved me."

Baptiste was born in Trinidad, the southernmost island in the Caribbean, and grew up on fresh fruit picked straight from the tree, tropical breezes, and the love and support of her parents and older brother. Since the age of twelve, Baptiste wanted to become a writer, but she started really taking her writing seriously after reading *Friends* by Rosa Guy. At the time, Baptiste was fifteen and had recently moved to Brooklyn, New York, with her family. Later, she attended New York University where she received a BA in English Literature and an MA in Elementary Education. She taught second grade in Jersey City, New Jersey, and Brooklyn, New York, while writing picture book manuscripts. After six years of teaching, Baptiste left to work for an educational publisher in New York City. She edits Reading and Language Arts textbooks for elementary school teachers and students. Baptiste joined the Society of Children's Book Writers and Illustrators where she met other aspiring and established writers who encouraged her to continue writing. After trying unsuccessfully to market her writing for very young readers, Baptiste decided to try her hand at writing a novel for young adults. The result of this effort was *Angel's Grace*, published by Simon & Schuster in January 2005.

Baptiste lives in Englewood, New Jersey, with her husband and daughter, where she is at work on her second novel.

BIBLIOGRAPHY

Angel's Grace. Simon & Schuster, 2005.

Barnwell, Ysaye M.

AUTHOR

E-mail: ymb@mindspring.com

Web site: www.ymb@ymbarnwell.com, www.sweethoney.com

Barnwell is a native of New York, now living in Washington. D.C., where since 1979 she has performed with the internationally acclaimed a cappella quintet, *Sweet Honey in the Rock*. She is a vocalist with a range of over three octaves and appears on more than twenty-five recordings with Sweet Honey as well as other artists. In her first year with Sweet Honey, she provided leadership in making the group's concerts accessible to the Deaf and hard-of-hearing through Sign Language interpretation.

The daughter of a violinist, Barnwell began her fifteen-year study of the violin with her father at the age of two and one half She holds both Bachelor and Master of Science degrees in Speech Pathology (1967, 1968 SUNY, Geneseo), a Doctor of Philosophy in Cranio-facial Studies (1975, University of Pittsburgh), a Master of Science in Public Health (1981, Howard University, Washington, D.C.), and the (Honorary) Doctor of Humane Letters (1998, SUNY, Geneseo). She has been a professor at the College of Dentistry at Howard University. In addition to conducting community based projects in computer technology and in the arts, she has administered and implemented health programs at Children's Hospital National Medical Center and at Gallaudet University in Washington, D.C.

After coming to Washington, D.C., Barnwell founded, and for three years directed, the All Souls Jubilee Singers where she began composing and arranging music for vocal ensembles. Barnwell composed and arranged music on more than fourteen recordings on labels including Flying Fish, EarthBeat!/Warner, Music for Little People and Rykodisc/Palm Pictures, Sony Classical. She has worked as a commissioned composer on numerous and varied projects including Sesame Street, Dance Alloy of Pittsburgh, David Rousseve's Reality Dance Company, Liz Lerman Dance Exchange, Women's Philharmonic of San Francisco, Redwood Cultural Work, The New Spirituals Project, The Steel Festival of Bethlehem, Pennsylvania, The Plymouth Music Series and numerous choirs—all outgrowths of her combined understanding of creative arts inextricably bound to society. For twenty years now, Barnwell has conducted *The Workshop: Building a Vocal Community*—Singing in the African American Tradition where throughout the United States, Canada, Great Britain, and Australia she has utilized African and African American history, values, cultural, and vocal traditions to work with singers and nonsingers alike.

Barnwell is an actress whose credits include voice-overs, documentary film narration, a principal role in an episode of the TV show *A Man Called Hawk*, and an appearance in the film *Beloved* directed by Jonathan Demme. Professional association memberships include NARAS (National Association of Recording Arts and Sciences), and SAG (Screen Actors Guild).

BIBLIOGRAPHY

No Mirrors in My Nana's House. Illustrated by Synthia Saint James. Harcourt, 1998.

UM HMM: A Feast of African American Stories and Songs for Children. Sounds True/Windhorse Prod., 2000.

Battle-Lavert, Gwendolyn

(1951–)

AUTHOR

E-mail: glavert@aol.com

Battle-Lavert was born in Texas, the first of four children. When she was a young child, storytelling, church, and music were important parts of family life. Battle-Lavert credits this training for her love of books and the motivation to become a writer.

While in elementary school and throughout her college years, she listened to stories as well as wrote them. She graduated from East Texas State University with a Bachelor of Elementary Education degree in 1974 and earned her master's in education as a Reading Specialist in 1976. She taught elementary school for thirteen years, and for five years she was a reading/writing coordinator for the Texarkana Independent School District. Her interest in multicultural education has led her to conduct reading and writing workshops in schools throughout the country.

Battle-Lavert is an African American children's author, storyteller, and performer. She has also written for *Cricket*, *Ladybug*, and *Adoptive Families* magazines. In Texas she has provided numerous presentations during Martin Luther King, Jr. and Black History month.

She is a member of the International Reading Association, the Society of Children's Book Writers and Illustrators, the Texas State Reading Association, and the Association for Supervision and Development. She is working on a series for reluctant readers.

Works in Progress are *Tabias Leads the Way, Eddie Ray and Hi Rocking Chair, The Harmonica Man, Daisy's Christmas Wish*.

A wife and mother of a son and a daughter, Battle-Lavert is currently an assistant professor of Education at Indiana Wesleyan University in Marion, Indiana.

BIBLIOGRAPHY

The Barber's Cutting Edge. Illustrated by Raymond Holbert. Children's Press, 1994.

Off to School. Illustrated by Gershom Griffith. Holiday House, 1995.

The Flying Red Tails. The Wright Group/McGraw Hill, 1999.

The Shaking Bag. Illustrated by Aminah Brenda Lynn Robertson. Albert Whitman, 2000.

Not Yet Uncle Skeet. The Wright Group/McGraw Hill, 2000.

The Music in Derrick's Heart. Illustrated by Colin Bootman. Holiday House, 2000.

Papa's Mark. Illustrated by Colin Bootman. Holiday House, 2002.

Belton, Sandra Yvonne

(1939–)

AUTHOR

E-mail: sybroo@sbcglobal.net

Web site: www.harperchildrens.com

"In the rows of library shelves I searched as a child, none of colorful, narrow volumes were written or designed to catch the eye and imagination of a young African-American girl. It was this void that sparked a strong desire to extend and enrich the reflections on those shelves—a desire further fueled and strengthened by an ever increasing knowledge of the many wonderful stories within a magnificent heritage yet to be told."

Belton's childhood was spent in the majestic hills of West Virginia. Her educational background includes a bachelor of arts degree from Howard University (Washington, D.C.), master of arts degree from George Washington University (Washington, D.C.), and a year of study at the Boston Conservatory of Music.

Belton's career in education began in Washington, D.C., where she taught first and second grades and continued in Chicago, Illinois where she taught briefly in a community college before becoming a developer of educational technology materials, including audio, video, and interactive software. Her first book for children, *From Miss Ida's Porch*, was published in 1993 and received the 1994 Friends of American Writers Young People's Literature Award.

Belton continues to live in Chicago with her husband, James Hammond. Her books continue to receive critical acclaim, including the much-reviewed *Ernestine & Amanda* series of which was written: "With the series, Belton ... has succeeded in making sure

African-American children will see themselves in her lively, well-rounded characters..."

BIBLIOGRAPHY

From Miss Ida's Porch. Illustrated by Floyd Cooper. Four Winds Press/Macmillan, 1993.

May'naise Sandwiches and Sunshine Tea. Illustrated by Gail Gordon Carter. Four Winds Press/Macmillan, 1993.

Ernestine & Amanda. Simon & Schuster/Aladdin, 1996.

Ernestine & Amanda: Members of the C.L.U.B. Simon & Schuster/Aladdin, 1997.

Ernestine & Amanda: Summer Camp, Ready or Not! Simon & Schuster/Aladdin, 1997.

Ernestine & Amanda: Mysteries on Monroe Street. Simon & Schuster/Aladdin, 1998.

McKendree. Greenwillow, 2000.

Pictures for Miss Josie. Illustrated by Benny Andrews. Greenwillow/Amistad, 2003.

Beauty, Her Basket. Illustrated by Cozbi Cabrera. Greenwillow/Amistad, 2004.

Store Bought Babies. Greenwillow/Harper Collins, 2006.

If Houses Could Sing. Illustrated by Cozi Cabrera. Greenwillow/HarperCollins, 2007.

Berrien, Todd

(1944–)

ILLUSTRATOR/ARTIST

E-mail: toddberrien@comcast.net

"It is clear to me that fine arts have a significant impact on the quality of life in our culture. My worldview, as it translates to canvas, is based on my varied life experiences and a strong value system that has enabled me to recognize that the strength and beauty of the human spirit can survive and blossom despite adversity. My paintings are visual expressions depicting the social and political concerns of the Black community as well as the human condition in general. I use my brush like a hammer to protest and comment on the conditions I see."

Harlem painter, designer, and illustrator, Berrien has been a professional artist since 1970. His paintings, depicting a broad spectrum of human emotions, have been exhibited widely in museums, universities and art galleries around the country and he is represented in several collections. He has published numerous lithographs.

He studied art at several colleges and universities, including the Art Student's League of New York, the School of Visual Arts, Parsons College of Art & Design, Indiana University, the University of North Carolina (BA), and the graduate school at the Savannah College of Art & Design. He also studied privately with established artists Daniel Greene and John Howard Sanden in their workshops.

His professional life has ranged from the jungles of Vietnam where he was a decorated combat pilot, to an airline pilot, to major advertising agencies as an award-winning creative director, to currently promoting health as the social marketing director at the Los Angeles County Department of Public Health.

Memberships: National Conference of Artists, the Distinguished Flying Cross Society, and Disabled Veterans of America.

Berrien lives in Los Angeles with his wife Dolores and is the father of three grown children, Dawn, Jenelle, and Todd David. He is the grandfather of an eighteen-month old, Jordan.

BIBLIOGRAPHY

An Old Soul with a Young Spirit: Poetry in the Era of Desegregation Recovery, with Dr. Toni Yancey. IMHOTEP Publishing, 1997.

Blackman, Malorie

(1962–)

AUTHOR

Web site: www.malorieblackman.com

"There was such a dearth of books featuring child protagonists of colour when I was growing up that, in my mid-twenties, I decided to try and do something about it. After two years and a vast number of rejection letters, I finally had my first book accepted for publication. I've been a full-time writer ever since. My aim has always been to make reading a more inclusive activity, an experience to be shared and enjoyed by all children where no child feels excluded or invisible. I write the books I missed as a child: thrillers, mysteries, whodunits, funny stories, horror stories, contemporary stories where the protagonists are Black. My greatest thrill is to receive letters from ex reluctant readers, telling me that one of my books has switched them on to reading. For me, there can be no greater compliment."

Blackman worked in computing for ten years, as a systems programmer and database manager, before deciding to become a writer of children's books.

Her first book, published in 1990, was a collection of short stories called *Not So Stupid!* Since then she has written over fifty books (many of the titles now re-issued in paperback editions) across all age ranges and won a number of awards including a BAFTA for Best Children's Drama for *Pig-Heart Boy* in 2000. The book was also short-listed for the Carnegie Medal. She has also been awarded the Red House FCBG Children's Book Award for *Naughts and Crosses* 2002 and the Smarties Silver Award for *Cloud Busting. Naughts and Crosses* was a BBC Big Read Top 100 title (number 61). Blackman was the only Black writer in the top 100.

She also is a script-writing graduate of the National Film and Television School.

Blackman is married and has one daughter. She lives in Kent, England.

BIBLIOGRAPHY

Not So Stupid. Livewire Books, 1990.

Elaine, You're a Brat. Illustrated by Doffy Weir. Orchard, 1991.

That New Dress. With Rhiah Nest James. Hodder & Stroughton Children's Division, 1991.

A New Dress for Maya. Illustrated by Rhian Nest James. Gareth Stevens (no American edition), 1992.

Girl Wonder's Winter Adventures. With Lis Toft. Orion Publishing, 1992.

Girl Wonder and the Terrific Twins. Illustrated by Lis Toft. Dutton, 1993.

Hacker. Yearling Books, 1993.

Operation Gadgetman. Transworld Publishers, 1993.

Hurricane Betsey. Illustrated by Lis Toft. Egmont Children's Books, 1994.

My Friend's a Gris-Quok. Scholastic Hippo, 1994.

Rachel and the Difference Thief. Longman Book Project, 1994.

Mrs. Spoon's Family. With Jan McCafferty. Anderson Press, 1995.

Grandma Gertie's Haunted Handbag. With David Price. Egmont Children's Books, 1996.

The Secret of the Terrible Hand. With Patrice Aggs. Illustrated by Jan Smith. Orchard Books, 1996.

Betsey's Birthday Surprise. Mammoth Storybooks, 1997.

The Computer Ghost. Scholastic, 1997.

The Mellow Moon Mystery. Illustrated by Patrice Aggs. Orchard Books, 1997.

The Quasar Quartz Quest. Illustrated by Jan Smith. Orchard Books, 1997.

Whizziwig. Chivers North America, 1998.

A Christmas Tree of Stories. With Gillian Cross, Jean Ure, et al. Scholastic, 1999.

Animal Avengers. Egmont Children's Books, 1999.

Dare to be Different. Bloomsbury Publishing, 1999.

Dizzy's Walk. Tamarind Limited, 1999.

Fangs (Pet Pals S.). Illustrated by Tony Blundell. Orchard Books, 1999.

Marty Monster. Tamarand Limited, 1999.

Hostage. Illustrated by Derek Brazell. Barrington Stoke Ltd., 2001.

Snow Dog. Corgi, 2001.

Dead Gorgeous. Doubleday, 2002.

I Want a Cuddle. Illustrated by Joanne Partis. Orchard Books, 2002.

Jessica Strange. Hodder Children's Books, 2002.

Pig Heart Boy. Corgi Childrens, 2004.

The Monster Crisp-Guzzler. Illustrated by Sam Sweeten. Corgi Books, 2004.

Checkmate. Doubleday. UK, 2005.

Cloud Bursting. Corgi, 2005.

Disabled Fables. Aesop's Fables Retold. Star Bright Books, 2005.

Ellie and the Cat. Orchard Books, 2005.

Knife Edge. Corgi, 2005.

Naughts & Crosses. Simon & Schuster Children's Publishing, 2005.

Sinclair, Wonder Bear. Illustrated by Deborah Allwright. Crabtree Children's Books, 2005.

The Deadly Dare Mysteries. Corgi, 2005.

Bolden, Tonya

(1959–)

AUTHOR

E-mail: tonbolden@aol.com

Web site: www.tonyabolden.com

"I write because as a child I fell in love with reading—with every facet of a book, from content and illustrations to the feel of a book in my hands. I write because as a child I fell in love with the art of writing (mostly small stories as a child, mostly poetry as a teen). I write, I also believe, because when I was young TEACHER was usually my response when the question was 'What do you want to be when you grow up?'"

Bolden was born in New York City and grew up in East Harlem and the Bronx, New York. She graduated magna cum laude from Princeton University in 1981 with a bachelor of arts degree in Slavic languages and literatures (majoring in Russian) and received a master of arts degree in the same discipline from Columbia University in 1985, along with a certificate of advanced studies of the Soviet Union. Before coming to writing, she worked in New York City's garment center and later for the novelist, playwright, and screenwriter James Goldman.

Bolden's early writing career included literary reviews and other articles for *Black Enterprise, Essence, Small Press,* the *New York Times Book Review,* and the 1989 and 1990 *Black Arts Annual,* among other periodicals. She served as book columnist for YSB (*Young Sisters and Brothers*) magazine from its inception in 1991 until it ceased publication several years later.

Bolden received a starred review in December 2003 from Kirkus Reviews for her book *Portraits of African-American Heroes.*

Also, from the March 1994 issue through the June 1995 issue, she served as editor of the Quarterly Black Review of Books.

Bolden's books for the young have received praise from the *Washington Post Book World, Kirkus Reviews, Booklist,* and *School Library Journal,* and won recognition from the American Library Association, Junior Library Guild, Black Expressions Book Club, and the New York Public Library.

In addition to her books for the young Bolden has written several books for adults. She lives in New York.

BIBLIOGRAPHY

Mama, I Want to Sing. With Vy Higginsen. Scholastic, 1992.

Rites of Passage: Stories About Growing Up by Black Writers From Around the World. (Editor) Hyperion, 1994.

Just Family. Cobblehill, 1996.

Through Loona's Door: A Tammy and Owen Adventure. With Carter G. Woodson. Illustrated by Luther Knox. The Corporation for Cultural Literacy, 1997.

And Not Afraid to Dare: The Stories of Ten African-American Women. Scholastic, 1998.

33 Things Every Girl Should Know: Stories, Songs, Poems, and Smart Talk by 33 Extraordinary Women (Editor). Crown, 1998.

Rock of Ages: A Tribute to the Black Church. Illustrated by R. Gregory Christie. Knopf, 2001.

Tell All the Children Our Story: Memories & Mementos of Being Young and Black in America. Abrams, 2002.

33 Things Every Girl Should Know About Women's History (Editor). Crown, 2002.

American Patriots: The Story of Blacks in the Military from the Revolution to Desert Storm. Young Readers' edition. With Gail Buckley. Crown, 2003.

Portraits of African American Heroes. Illustrated by Ansel Pitcairn. Dutton, 2003.

Wake Up Our Souls: A Celebration of Black American Artists. Abrams, 2004.

The Champ: The Story of Muhammad Ali. Illustrated by R. Gregory Christie. Knopf, 2004.

Maritcha: A Nineteenth-Century American Girl. Abrams, 2005.

Bond, Higgins (Barbara)

(1951–)

ILLUSTRATOR

E-mail: bhigginsbond@netscape.net

Web site: www.higginsbond.com

A native of Little Rock, Arkansas, Bond is the second of five children. She attended Phillips University in Enid, Oklahoma, and transferred to Memphis College of Arts in Tennessee, where she earned a bachelor of fine arts degree in advertising design. She has worked as a freelance illustrator designing books, magazine posters, and similar projects for such clients as the publisher Houghton Mifflin, RCA, NBC Television, *Essence* magazine, *Black Enterprise* magazine, Avon Books, and numerous advertising firms. Over a twenty-year career, she has designed collectors' plates and commercial posters, too.

Bond has also gained national exposure through her designs of three commemorative stamps for the United States Postal Service's Black Heritage Series of W.E.B. Du Bois, educator and author; inventor Jan Matzeliger, and chemist Percy L. Julian. At the unveiling in 1992, in Atlanta, Georgia, she received a standing ovation, and she considers this accomplishment one of her most gratifying projects. In 1979, she was awarded the CEBA Award of Merit for her work in *Black Enterprise* magazine.

Her poster designs for Anheuser-Busch's Great Rulers of Africa Series, including pictures of a king of Mali (Mansa Kankan Mussi) and Queen Nefertiti of Egypt, were featured in the company's television commercial for *Roots: The Second Generation*. While Bond has painted other Black historical figures, she does not consider herself principally a Black artist. Rather, she sees herself simply as an illustrator trying to work as much as possible, preferring to paint nature scenes.

Bond was illustrator of four stamps for the United States Postal Administration on Endangered Species issued in February, 2001.

She is guest lecturer at numerous colleges, universities, and schools and a member of the National Society of Illustrators—New York, New York.

Her husband died in 1996 and now she lives alone in Nashville, Tennessee.

BIBLIOGRAPHY

1999 Facts About Blacks. By Raymond M. Cohn. Beckham House, 1986.

Ancient Rome. By Daniel Cohen. Doubleday, 1992.

When I Was Little. By Toyomi Igus. Just Us Books, 1992.

Time for Sleep. By Claire Chapelle. Macmillan/McGraw-Hill, 1993.

Young Martin's Promise. By Walter Dean Myers. Steck-Vaughn, 1993.

Susie King Taylor: Destined to Be Free. By Denise M. Jordon. Just Us Books, 1994.

Thurgood Marshall: Supreme Court Justice. By Garnet Nelson Jackson. Modern Curriculum, 1994.

Tom Morrison: Author. By Garnet Nelson Jackson. Modern Curriculum, 1995.

Handshake in Space. By Sheri Tan. Smithsonian Institution and the Trudy Corporation, 1998.

Son of La Selva: A Story of a Costa Rican Rain Forest. By Joan Banks. The Nature Corporation and the Trudy Corporation, 1998.

Do Whales Have Belly Buttons? By Melvin and Gilda Berger. Scholastic, 1998.

Why Do Volcanoes Blow their Tops? By Melvin and Gilda Berger. Scholastic, 1999.

Do Tornadoes Really Twist? By Melvin and Gilda Berger. Scholastic, 2000.

Do Penguins get Frostbite? By Melvin and Gilda Berger. Scholastic, 2000.

Hey, Daddy! Animal Fathers and their Babies. By Mary Batten. Peachtree Publishers, 2002.

Trails Above the Tree Line. By Audrey Fraggalosh. Soundprints Division of the Trudy Corporation, 2002.

Where Did the Butterfly Get Its Name? By Melvin and Gilda Berger. Scholastic, 2002.

Jesus Is Born. Adapted by Suzette Haden Elgin. American Bible Society, 2002.

Jesus Prays to His Father. Adapted by Suzette Hadin Elgin. American Bible Society, 2002.

The Seven Seas, Exploring the World Oceans. By Linda Viera. Walker & Company, 2003.

Groundhog at Evergreen Road. By Susan Korman. The Trudy Corporation and the Smithsonian Institution, 2003.

Then I Think of God. By Martha Whitmore Hickman. Albert Whitman & Company, 2003.

Who Has a Belly Button? By Mary Batten. Peachtree Publishers, 2004.

Pen Pals. By Michael Rose Ramirez. Mondo Publishing, 2004.

The Christmas Pea Coat. By Richard H. Schneider. Ideals Children's Books, 2004.

I am Sacajawea, I am York. By Claire Rudolf Murphy. Walker & Company, 2004.

Boné III, Thomas H.

(1970–)

ILLUSTRATOR

E-mail: paperandpencils@mindspring.com

Web site: www.paperandpencils.com

"For every story told, each and every one of us will try to visualize that story in our own minds. We'll try to picture each character, each setting and allow that story to take our imaginations to interesting places. I've always enjoyed creating cartoons, creating funny illustrations to stories, hoping to make others smile and to help take their imaginations to those interesting places. A book can be such a wonderful, inspirational and educational escape. If my illustrations can help to make a person smile, spark an imagination or inspire a child as I was inspired, then believe me, that's a reward in itself."

Born in Brooklyn, New York, and raised in Long Island, Boné knew before the age of five that he wanted to pursue a career as an animated cartoonist. Inspired by the cartooning greats of Disney, Warner Brothers, and Tex Avery cartoons, he pursued his career by receiving an education in cartoons from various art studies during his high school years and eventually furthering his studies at Pratt Institute in Brooklyn, New York, School of Visual Arts and New York University in New York City.

Boné's career began in 1994 as a cartoonist for a line of children's watches. From there he went on to produce animation and cartoons for television, feature film, Web, book illustrations, print, greeting cards, and product and packaging designs. He has held titles within the industry such as illustrator, cartoonist, senior animator, director, producer, and educator. He also enjoys teaching a successful digital animation class entitled "Flash for Animators" as a college professor at Pratt Institute in Brooklyn, New York.

Boné began producing book illustrations through Blue Marlin Publications and has through them produced illustrations for four book titles including a title in progress *Mrs. Belle Goes to Camp.* You can find him attending various book signings at bookstores, creating cartoons for children, and also giving presentations at schools demonstrating the art of creating book illustrations and animation.

BIBLIOGRAPHY

Why Can't I Spray Today? By Francine Poppo Rich. Blue Marlin Publications, 1999. *PeeWee Pipes and the Wing Thing.* By Francine Poppo Rich. Blue Marlin Publications, 2000.

The Teacher Who Would Not Retire. By Letty and Shiela Sustrin. Blue Marlin Publications, 2002.

Mama, Can Armadillos Swim? By Francine Poppo Rich. Blue Marlin Publications, 2004.

Boyd, Aaron

(1971–)

ILLUSTRATOR

E-mail: aaronboydarts@gmail.com

"I have known since the age of five that I wanted to be an artist. However, it was at the age of six that I knew I wanted to illustrate children's books after falling in love with The Funny Little Woman (illustrated by Blair Lent) and Strega Nona (illustrated by Tomie DePaola). I checked each of these books out from the school library every Friday for a year just to look at the pictures."

Upon graduating from high school, Boyd was accepted at MIAD (the Milwaukee Institute of Art and Design), where he received a BFA in Illustration (1989–1993). During college he began freelancing at local magazines, building up his portfolio and developing his style. Soon after graduating Boyd began freelance work for The Cricket Magazine Group, which he still does. Doing work for CMG eventually led to a meeting with Lee and Low Books where he illustrated his first book, *Juicy Peach*. Boyd has illustrated over ten books. His favorite themes focus on multicultural subjects as well as animals. He hopes to promote more books in the genre of classic fairy tales and fantasy but with a cast of characters from all over the world. He believes this can be very positive in showing children our similarities, whichever culture we are from. In between projects Boyd is developing several stories of his own in this genre.

Boyd resides in Milwaukee (Wisconsin), the city of his birth, where he works out of his studio at home.

BIBLIOGRAPHY

Juicy Peach. By Mary Dixon. Lee and Low, 2000.
Babu's Song. By Stephanie Stuve-Bodeen. Lee and Low, 2002.

Janna and the Kings. By Patricia Smith. Lee and Low, 2003.

I Can't Take a Bath. By Irene Smalls. Scholastic/Color Bridge, 2004.

The Low Down Bad Day Blues. By Derrik D. Barnes. Scholastic/Color Bridge, 2004.

Black Cat Creeping. Sterling, 2004.

Pigs in Love. By Teddy Slater. Sterling, 2005.

Ned Redd World Traveler. Kindermusik, Int., 2005.

Family Picnic. By Gaylia Taylor. Lee and Low, 2005.

Daddy Goes to Work. By Jabari Asim. Little Brown, 2006.

Boyd, Candy (Dawson)

(1946–)

AUTHOR

"I never wanted to be a writer of anything, except love letters to boyfriends or notes to friends. I loved to run my mouth. I spent more time writing, 'Marguerite Dawson will pay attention in class,' over and over again than learning. I daydreamed. I envisioned Black knights on black horses sweeping me up in their arms and taking me to paradise. I heard myself singing like the Divine Sarah Vaughn in a tight, pink, long satin dress in a crowded jazz club. Light-skinned, skinny, near-sighted, strange Black child that I was—I dreamed. Out of that tumultuous world came the stuff of stories."

Boyd was born in Chicago, Illinois. In the 1960s she worked with Dr. Martin Luther King, Jr. as a field staff worker for the Southern Christian Leadership Conference.

She earned her bachelor's degree at Northeastern and Illinois State universities, her master's degree at the University of California, Berkeley, in 1978, and her doctorate in education at Berkeley in 1982. Among her awards is an honorable mention for *Circle of Gold* given by the Coretta Scott King Award Committee in 1985.

She is a professor in the School of Education at Saint Mary's College in Moraga, California. Boyd was honored in 1981 as the first tenured African American professor and received the college's first Professor of the Year award in 1991. Boyd is on the Author Team of Pearson Scott Foresman Elementary Reading and Social Studies Programs.

She lives in San Pablo, California.

BIBLIOGRAPHY

Circle of Gold. Illustrated by Charles Lilly. Scholastic, 1984.

Forever Friends (formerly *Breadsticks and Blessing Places*). Illustrated by Jerry Pinkney. Macmillan, 1985. Puffin, 1986.

Charlie Pippin. Illustrated by Cornelius Van Wright. Macmillan, 1987. Viking, 1988.

Chevrolet Saturdays. Illustrated by Todd Doney. Macmillan, 1993.

Fall Secrets. Illustrated by Jim Carroll. Puffin, 1994.

Daddy, Daddy, Be There. Illustrated by Floyd Cooper. Philomel, 1995.

A Different Beat. Illustrated by Dominick Finnelle. Puffin, 1996.

Breinburg, Petronella

(1937–)

AUTHOR

Breinburg was born in Paramaribo, Suriname, South America. In 1965, she received a diploma in English from the City of London College. She attended Avery Mill Teachers College from 1969 to 1972 and Goldsmith College in London from 1972 to 1974. In Paramaribo, she taught school but was also a factory worker, a postal clerk, and a nurses' aide. She worked as a volunteer for the Red Cross and the Girls' Life Brigade in Suriname, lectured in creative writing, and was an outdoor storyteller in London. For about two years, starting in 1972, she taught English part time.

Her memberships include the Royal Society of Health, the Greenwich Playwright Circle, and the Poetry Circle. In 1962, she received an award from the Royal Society of Health and in 1972 was given an Honorary Place Award from the Suriname Linguistic Bureau for her book *The Legend of Suriname*. Her picture book *My Brother Sean*, illustrated by Errol Lloyd, was a runner-up for the Library Association of London Kate Greenaway Medal in 1974.

BIBLIOGRAPHY

My Brother Sean. Illustrated by Errol Lloyd. Bodley Head, 1973.

Shawn Goes to School. Illustrated by Errol Lloyd. HarperCollins, 1974.

Tiger, Tinker and Me. Macmillan, 1974.

Doctor Shawn [formerly *Doctor Sean*. Bodley Head, 1973]. Illustrated by Errol Lloyd. HarperCollins, 1975.

Shawn's Red Bike. Illustrated by Errol Lloyd. Crowell, 1976.

Tiger, Paleface and Me. Macmillan, 1976.

Sally-Ann in the Snow. Bodley Head, 1977, Random House, 1989.

Sally-Ann's Skateboard. Bodley Head, 1979.

Brooks, Gwendolyn

(1917–2000)

AUTHOR/POET

Pulitzer Prize-winner Gwendolyn Brooks was born in Topeka, Kansas, and began writing verses at the age of seven. Her inspiration came from poets James Weldon Johnson and Langston Hughes, whom she met in Chicago, Illinois, where she spent all of her childhood. Her first poem, "Eventide," was published in *American Childhood*, a magazine for young people, when she was only thirteen years old. She started her own neighborhood newspaper and, by age seventeen, she was a regular contributor to the *Chicago Defender*, where more than seventy-five of her poems and other writings appeared in its "Lights and Shadows" column.

In 1943 and 1944, Brooks won first prize for poetry from the Mid-West Writers' Conference and again in August 1945 for her book of verse, *A Street in Bronzeville*. She won the Pulitzer Prize in 1950, the first Black to be so honored, for her second book, *Annie Allen*, and was named poet laureate of Illinois in 1968. She has lectured widely and taught at several colleges.

The poet became the twenty-ninth appointment as consultant in poetry to the Library of Congress in 1985. She was a member of the American Academy and Institute of Arts and Letters. She was presented the Lincoln Laureate Award in Springfield, Illinois, in 1997 and the Gwendolyn Brooks Park was dedicated to her in her birthplace city, Topeka, Kansas. She celebrated her eightieth birthday in Chicago, Illinois, where the city council approved a resolution to recognize the day. The occasion was called "Eighty Gifts," a reading tribute for each of her years. Mayor Richard M. Daley announced that the entire city of Chicago would celebrate the week of June 1 through June 7, 1997. Eighty poets and writers came together at the Harold Washington Library for a five hour public reading of Brooks' work

Brooks was married to the author of *Windy Place*, Henry Blakely, who died in1996. She had two children, a son and a daughter.

In 1996 Brooks was honored at the Smithsonian Institute where she was recognized as their "Living Portrait" and in April and May of that year, the Netherlands created an exhibit featuring her works at the Stedelijk Museum in Amsterdam.

She was presented with the Lincoln Laureate Award, the highest award that the state of Illinois presents, by Governor Jim Edgar, in 1992.

Brooks died in 2000 at her home in Chicago. She was eighty-three years old.

BIBLIOGRAPHY

Bronzeville Boys and Girls. Illustrated by Ronni Solbert. HarperCollins, 1967.

Family Pictures. Broadside, 1970.

Aloneness. Broadside, 1971.

Report from Part One: An Autobiography. Broadside, 1972.

The Tiger Who Wore White Gloves. Illustrated by Timothy Jones. Third World, 1974.

Beckonings. Broadside, 1975.

Very Young Poets. Third World, 1991.

Winnie. Third World, 1991.

Brown, Margery Wheeler

(1912–)

AUTHOR/ILLUSTRATOR

Brown was born in Durham, North Carolina, the third and youngest child. While she was still an infant, the family moved to Atlanta, Georgia, where she received her education. After graduating from Spelman College in 1932, she continued art studies at Ohio State University. Upon completion of her studies, she became an art instructor from 1943 to 1946 at Spelman College and later in the public schools of Durham, North Carolina, Atlanta, Georgia, and Newark, New Jersey, where she taught for twenty-six years, retiring in 1974.

Growing up in a family where heavy emphasis was placed on reading, Brown always had a great interest in books. As an inner-city teacher, she directed her interest in writing to subjects about and for inner-city children. For most of her books, she has been her own illustrator.

In 1936, she married Richard Earle Brown, now deceased, and they had one daughter, Janice.

Brown lives in East Orange, New Jersey.

BIBLIOGRAPHY

Old Crackfoot. By Gordon Allred. Astor-Honor, 1965.
Dori the Mallard. By Gordon Allred. Astor-Honor, 1968.
That Ruby. Reilly & Lee, 1969.
Animals Made by Me. Putnam, 1970.
I'm Glad I'm Me—Steve. By Elberta H. Stone. Putnam, 1971.
The Second Stone. Putnam, 1976.
Yesterday I Climbed A Mountain. Putnam, 1976
No Jon, No Jon, No! Houghton, 1981.

Afro-Bets: Book of Colors. Illustrated by Culverson Blair. Just Us Books, 1991.

Afro-Bets: Book of Shapes. Illustrated by Culverson Blair. Just Us Books, 1991.

Baby Jesus, Like My Brother. Illustrated by George Ford. Just Us Books, 1995.

Bryan, Ashley

(1923–)

AUTHOR/ILLUSTRATOR

"I cannot remember a time when I have not been drawing and painting. In elementary school, I began to make books. My first books, made in kindergarten, were illustrated ABC and counting books. At that time, the entire book production was in my hands. I was author, illustrator, binder, and distributor. These one-of-a-kind 'limited editions' drew rave reviews from family and friends and were given as gifts on all occasions. That feeling, for the handmade book, is at the heart of my bookmaking today, even though my original is now printed in the thousands. I grew up in New York City, in the Bronx, the second of six children. My parents sent all of the children to the free Works Progress Administration (WPA) art and music classes. We all drew and painted and learned to play an instrument."

After high school graduation, Bryan attended the Cooper Union art school. There he began a project illustrating African tales. He knew of the profound influence of African art on Western art and decided to use the abundant African art resources in New York City museums and libraries for this project.

Walk Together Children: Black American Spirituals was an American Library Association Notable Book in 1974, as was *Beat the Story-Drum, Pum Pum* in 1980. The latter also won the 1981 Coretta Scott King Award for the illustrations. Bryan has received Coretta Scott King Book Awards Honors for his writings and illustrations for *I'm Going to Sing: Black American Spirituals* in 1983, *Lion and the Ostrich Chicks* and *Other African Folk Tales* in 1987, *What a Morning! The Christmas Story in Black Spirituals* in 1988 and *All Night, All Day: A Child's First Book of African-American Spirituals* in 1992. In 1993, he was the first recipient of the Lee Bennett Hopkins Poetry Award, and he was chosen as the 1990 Arbuthnot Lecturer. At the Twenty-Seventh Annual Children's Book Festival in 1994, Bryan was awarded the University of Southern Mississippi Medallion, presented annually for outstanding contributions in the field of children's literature. He holds honorary doctorates from the Massachusetts College of Art, awarded in 1989, and Framingham State College, awarded in 1995.

Alvin Singleton composed a work from Bryan's collection of poems in *Sing to the Sun: Poems and Pictures* to be performed with chamber orchestra and with children's voices, with narration by Bryan. The piece was commissioned by a consortium of five major music festivals for the 1995–1996 season.

Bryan won a 1998 Coretta Scott King Honor Book Illustrator Award for *Ashley Bryan's ABC of African American Poetry.*

In August of 2004, Bryan attended the International Board on Books for Young People's Conference (IBBY) in Cape Town, South Africa. While there, he brought books and supplies to very poor schools in a Township of Port Elizabeth, South Africa and to schools in Kenya.

He spoke before a large audience of children and adults for the Black, White and Read all over lecture series in 2006 at the Carnegie Library of Pittsburgh Lecture Hall in Pittsburgh, Pennsylvania sponsored in part by the Pennsylvania Council on the Arts.

He continues to lecture extensively and is a frequently requested speaker.

Bryan lives on a small island off the coast of Maine.

BIBLIOGRAPHY

Christmas Gif': An Anthology of Christmas Poems, Songs and Stories. Compiled by Charlemae Rollins and Augusta Baker. Follet, 1963; Morrow, 1993.

Moon, for What Do You Wait? Poems by Sir Rabindranath Tagore. Edited by Richard Lewis. Atheneum, 1967.

The Ox of the Wonderful Horns and Other African Folktales. Atheneum, 1971.

Walk Together Children: Black American Spirituals. Volume One. Atheneum, 1974.

The Adventures of Aku. Atheneum, 1976.

The Dancing Granny. Atheneum, 1977.

I Greet the Dawn: Poems by Paul Laurence Dunbar. Atheneum, 1978.

Jethro and the Jumbie. By Susan Cooper. Atheneum, 1979.

Jim Flying High. By Mari Evans. Doubleday, 1979.

Beat the Story-Drum, Pum-Pum. Atheneum, 1980.

I'm Going to Sing: Black American Spirituals. Volume Two. Atheneum, 1983.

The Cat's Purr. Atheneum, 1985.

Lion and the Ostrich Chicks and Other African Folk Tales. Atheneum, 1986.

What a Morning! The Christmas Story in Black Spirituals. Selected and edited by John Langstaff. McElderry, 1987.

Sh-ko and His Eight Wicked Brothers. Illustrations by Fumio Yoshimura. Atheneum, 1988.

Turtle Knows Your Name. Atheneum, 1989.

All Night, All Day: A Child's First Book of African-American Spirituals. Atheneum, 1991.

Climbing Jacob's Ladder: Heroes of the Bible in African American Spirituals. Selected and edited by John Langstaff. McElderry, 1991.

Sing to the Sun: Poems and Pictures. HarperCollins, 1992.

Story of Lightning and Thunder. Atheneum, 1993.

The Story of the Three Kingdoms. By Walter Dean Myers. HarperCollins, 1995.

What a Wonderful World. By George David Weiss and Bob Thiele. Atheneum, 1995.

The Sun Is So Quiet. By Nikki Giovanni. Holt, 1996.

Ashley Bryan's ABC of African American Poetry. Atheneum, 1997.

Ashley Bryan's African Tales, Uh-huh. Atheneum, 1998.

Carol of the Brown King. By Langston Hughes. Atheneum, 1998.

The House with No Door, African Riddles. By Brian Swann. Browndeer Press, 1998.

Why Leopard Has Spots. By Won-Loy Paye and Margaret Uppert. Fulcrum, 1998.

Aneesa Lee and the Weaver's Gift. By Nikki Grimes. Lothrop, Lee and Shepard, 1999.

The Night Has Ears, African Proverbs. Atheneum, 1999.

How God Fix Jonah. By Lorenz Graham. Boyds Mills Press, 2000.

Salting the Ocean. By Shihab Nye. Greenwillow, 2000.

Beautiful Blackbird. Atheneum, 2003.

A Nest Full of Stars. By James Berry. Greenwillow, 2004.

Bryant, Michael

(1963–)

ILLUSTRATOR

Web site: www.michaelbryantart.com

"I don't think of myself as illustrating only African American books. I like to illustrate books that have positive images."

Bryant was born in Newark, New Jersey, an unexpected twin. Drawing became his way of expressing himself. His mother was his greatest influence. Because of the encouragement of his family, after attending Clifford Scott High School, Bryant studied art and earned a bachelor's degree from Kean College in New Jersey and decided to pursue an art career. While in college, Bryant freelanced as a designer and layout artist. After college, he became an art director and illustrator for *Inview* magazine, a television guide.

Bryant had a lot of small jobs and was taking his portfolio out and was hearing "no." He was doing some romance painting and some magazine covers with just a couple of projects.

In 1991, he won a Multicultural Mirror Competition, a fellowship given at the University of Wisconsin. In 1992, he signed a contract for his first picture book, *Our People*, and another soon followed for his second book, *Bein' with You This Way*. Both books have received widespread recognition and various awards, including the Jane Addams Peace Award, *Parenting* Magazine's Reading Magic Award, the Parents Choice Award, and the Teacher's Choice Award. A review in the trade magazine *Publishers Weekly* describes Bryant as an "impressive accomplished artist."

Although he has studied the work of the masters, Bryant says his style has been mostly influenced by the American artists Norman Rockwell, Winslow Homer, and John Singer Sargent.

Bryant and his wife, Gina, live in Newark, New Jersey, with their two daughters.

BIBLIOGRAPHY

Madame C. J. Walker: Self-Made Millionaire. By Patricia and Fredrick McKissack. Enslow, 1992.

Sojourner Truth: A Voice for Freedom. By Patricia and Fredrick McKissack. Enslow, 1992.

A World of Holidays. By Louisa Campbell. Silver Moon Press, 1993.

Family Celebrations. By Diane Patrick. Silver Moon Press, 1993.

Bein' with You This Way. By W. Nikola-Lisa. Lee & Low, 1994.

Buffalo Soldiers: The Story of Emanual Stance. Reflections of a Black Cowboy Series. By Robert H. Miller. Silver Burdett, 1994.

Good-Bye Hello. By Barbara S. Hazen. Atheneum, 1994.

Our People. By Angela Shelf Medearis. Atheneum, 1994.

The Story of Nat Love. By Robert H. Miller. Silver Burdett, 1994.

A Missing Portrait on Sugar Hill. By Diane Patrick. Silver Moon, 1995.

Skin Deep and Other Teenage Reflections. By Angela Shelf Medearis. Macmillan, 1995.

Treemonisha. By Angela Shelf Medearis. Holt, 1995.

Come Sunday. By Nikki Grimes. Eerdmanns, 1996.

I Love Saturdays and Domingos. By Alma F. Ada. Atheneum, 1996.

Booker T. Washington: A Leader and Educator. By Patricia and Fredrick McKissack. Enslow, 1996.

Ziggy and the Black Dinosaurs: Lost in the Tunnel of Time. By Sharon M. Draper. Just Us Books, 1996.

The Mean Hyena: A Folktale from Malawi. By Judy Sierra. Lodestar Books, 1997.

Buchanan, Yvonne E.

(1956–)

ILLUSTRATOR

E-mail: ybuchanan@aol.com

Web site: www.yvonnebuchanan.com

Buchanan was born in New York City, the oldest of four children. As a child of the 1960s, she grew up in front of the television and consequently developed her drawing skills by copying Bugs Bunny, Speed Racer, and other cartoons.

Her interest in animation was heightened when she attended the New York High School of Art and Design. At Parsons School of Design, majoring in illustration, she experimented with various styles until she found her best expressions with line and watercolor. After graduation in 1977, she pursued a freelance career, working for many companies including the *New York Times*, the *Washington Post*, and the *Wall Street Journal*.

In 1992, she illustrated the video of *Follow the Drinking Gourd*, the story of the Underground Railroad, which won, among others, a Showtime Award and the Chicago Children's Festival Gold Award in 1993, and it was published as a children's book in 1996. Her work has been exhibited at the Studio Museum in Harlem, the Cinque Gallery, the Art Directors Club, the University of Denver, Syracuse University, and the Society of Illustrators in 1993.

Buchanan is a professor in the Department of Art at Syracuse University and lives in Syracuse, New York.

BIBLIOGRAPHY

Juneteenth Jamboree. By Carole Boston Weatherford. Lee & Low, 1995.
Tingo, Tango, Mango Tree. By Marcia K. Vaughan. Silver Burdett, 1995.

Follow the Drinking Gourd. By Bernadine Connelly. Simon & Schuster, 1996.
Fly, Bessie, Fly. By Lynn Joseph. Simon & Schuster, 1998.
God Inside of Me. By Della Reese. Jump at the Sun/Hyperion, 1999.

Burns, Khephra (Keith)

(1950–)

AUTHOR

The author was born Keith Karlyle Burns in Los Angeles, California. Khephra is an acquired nickname, which he uses professionally. He attended schools in Compton and Watts with never a thought of one day becoming a writer. He enrolled at the University of California, Santa Barbara, and graduated in 1972 with a bachelor's degree in

English. Over the next five years, Burns danced, painted, lectured part-time at Santa Barbara City College, drove a cab, moved to Oakland, California, played jazz, and sold insurance.

In 1978, Burns moved to New York City and sold his first work, *Marie Laveau*, a treatment for a screenplay, to Belafonte Enterprises. He was the writer and producer for a two-part series show, *Black Men in Dance*. Burns was also a writer on *Images and Realities, Part II: The African American Family; Images and Realities, Part III: The African American Woman,* and *Images and Realities, Part IV: African American Children.* He was also the senior writer for *Triple Threat*, a Black Entertainment Television (BET) music game show in 1992.

Burns is married to Susan L. Taylor, editor-in-chief of *Essence* magazine. He has written articles for numerous publications, including *Essence, Swing Journal* (Japan), *Omni,* and *Art and Auction.* Former editor of the *Boule Journal,* a quarterly publication of the Sigma Pi Phi fraternity, he now is on their board. He has written album liner notes for such noted jazz artists as Nancy Wilson, Miles Davis (his Grammy Award-winning album, *Aura*), Arthur Blythe, Kirk Whalum, and others. Burns was the writer for William Miles' award-winning film documentaries *Black Champions* and *Black*

Stars in Orbit; the latter he translated into a children's book. He and his wife, Susan Taylor, co-authored *The Spiritual Wisdom that has Shaped Our Lives*, published by Doubleday in 1999.

He is a member of the Writers Guild of America, The Author's Guild, and 100 Black Men. He is the 1981 recipient of the (CETA) Communications Excellence to Black Audiences award for his recruitment poster entitled "What Do You Do When Tough Ain't Enough?"

Since 1992, Burns has written the Essence awards show, which airs once a year as a two-hour prime-time television special. He lives in New York City.

BIBLIOGRAPHY

Black Stars in Orbit: The Story of NASA's African American Astronauts. With William Miles. Harcourt, 1995.

Mansa Musa: The Lion of Mali. Illustrated by Leo and Diane Dillon. Harcourt, 2001.

Burrowes, Adjoa J.

(1957–)

AUTHOR/ILLUSTRATOR

E-mail: Adjoa4art@aol.com

Web site: www.adjoaburrowes.com

"I live in color. I am inspired by the beauty and color of the natural world. As an illustrator, I want my art to celebrate the simple joy and wonder of childhood. My palette is very bright and lively. I hope the art will bring children into my books, and encourage even the most reluctant reader to enjoy the words. When I write, I often choose topics that challenge a child to find hope in difficult situations.

"My father worked with his hands, building houses in the south. My mother made clothes for my sister and myself when we were children, without using a pattern. From them, I learned the quiet discipline it takes to create something from practically nothing."

Adjoa J. Burrowes—children's book illustrator, author, and graphic artist, received her BFA degree from Howard University's College of Fine Arts. She has designed for a wide range of clients throughout the United States, from food manufacturer Campbell Soup to Mattel Toy company.

Burrowes began illustrating picture books in 1994 while freelancing for an educational publisher in California. Since then she has illustrated seventeen picture books for clients, including Lee & Low Books, McGraw Hill, Steck Vaughn, and Creative Teaching Press. She has also illustrated puzzles, posters, and greeting cards using her signature cut-paper collage technique.

She enjoys the physical nature of art making. Her formal training was as a printmaker—creating etchings, lithographs, and silkscreens. Now she paints her papers with watercolor, acrylic and dyes, paying special attention to color and texture. "The process of cutting out tiny shapes from paper and pasting them into my compositions becomes tedious work, but very fulfilling."

Grandma's Purple Flowers (which she both wrote and illustrated) was an American Booksellers Association (ABA) Kids Pick of the List winner; a Bank Street College Kids Book of the Year Selection; and a first-place winner of the 2001 Paterson Prize for Books for Young People.

Burrowes presents art and writing workshops nationally. She belongs to many art and writers groups, including the Washington Children's Book Guild and currently lives in the Washington, D.C., metropolitan area with her three children.

BIBLIOGRAPHY

What's the Weather Like Today? By Rozanne Williams. Creative Teaching Press, 1994.

It Started As a Seed. By Dr. Alden Kelly. Creative Teaching Press, 1994.

Rain. By Rozanne Williams. Creative Teaching Press, 1994.

Under the Sky. By Rozanne Williams. Creative Teaching Press, 1994.

The Four Seasons. By Rozanne Williams. Creative Teaching Press, 1994.

Turtle Lake. By Joseph Bruchal. Metropolitan Teaching Co., 1995.

The Seed Song. By Rozanne Williams. Creative Teaching Press, 1995.

The World in a Supermarket. By Rozanne Williams. Creative Teaching Press, 1996.

My Steps. By Sally Derby. Lee and Low Books, 1996.

Houses. By Marcia Fries. Creative Teaching Press, 1996.

America: My Land, Your Land, Our Land (contributing illustrator). By W. Nikola-Lisa. Lee and Low Books, 1997.

Crawl Caterpillar Crawl. By Katherine Mead. Steck-Vaughn, 1999.

Everybody Wears Braids. Bee Bop Books/Lee and Low Books, 2000.

Grandma's Purple Flowers. Lee and Low Books, 2000.

Go Go Gumbo. Bee Bop Books/Lee and Low Books, 2003.

Destiny's Gift. By Natasha Tarpley. Lee and Low Books, 2004.

Carter, Dorothy

(1918–)

AUTHOR

"African-American children enjoy stories that portray and reveal their child-hood feelings about wanting to be loved and cared for, their fears and insecuri-ties, their wishes, struggles and triumphs within their familiar communities lived in by people resembling the real people they know; Moms, Dads, Aunts and Uncles, School Teachers and Sunday School Teachers and Storekeepers and other people who live in their worlds and matter to them. They also enjoy the comic and the ridiculous, showing animals behaving like unruly children.

"Through voices that resonate and evoke vividly the plight of the story characters, young readers and listeners can begin to identify and respect their unique identities as well as those universal childhoods growing up dilem-mas and challenges awaiting all children. For example: Learning to read and becoming socially and morally competent and responsible."

In 1967 Carter joined the Graduate Faculty of Bank Street College of Education in New York City. There she taught courses in Children's Literature and Language Development. She has a doctor-ate from Columbia University Teachers College, a masters degree from the University of Wisconsin and a Bachelor's from Spelman College in Atlanta, Georgia. She began writing for children in 1998 following her retirement from Bank Street College. Her childhood and early adolescence were lived in a small town in Central Florida which is now the fountainhead of her writings about Children. Cur-rently, she serves as Chair of The Bank Street College Writers Lab, a part of the Publications/Media/Communications Division of the College. The author enjoys sharing her stories with teachers, par-ents, and children.

Carter lives in New York.

BIBLIOGRAPHY

Br'er Rabbit Meets His Match. Illustrated by Kirsti Frigell. SRA MacMillan/ McGraw-Hill, 1995.

Bye, Mis' Lela. Illustrated by Harvey Stevenson. Frances Foster Book – Farrar, Straus & Giroux, 1998.

Whilhe'mina Miles. Illustrated by Harvey Stevenson. Frances Foster Book – Farrar, Straus & Giroux, 1999.

Grandma's General Store: The Ark. Illustrated by Thomas B. Allen. Frances Foster Book – Farrar, Straus & Giroux, 2005.

Carter, Gail Gordon

(1953–)

ILLUSTRATOR

"I believe it is important to show the various shades of Black people in my work, both figuratively and literally. As a people, we come from many different backgrounds, mixes of races and cultures. I would love for young readers to see fictional characters whom they resemble living in and dealing with the multicultural world of today. Or, expose them to Black American subcultures, something real to which they may be able to relate and even experience."

Carter was born and grew up in Los Angeles, California. She earned a bachelor of arts degree in psychology from Pitzer College in Claremont, California, and then attended the School of Social Welfare at the University of California, Los Angeles, where she obtained a master of social welfare degree.

She began her career in social work, focusing on outpatient psychiatric and adoptions work. Her pursuit of art as a career began in late 1990 after her marriage and relocation to Portland, Oregon. Illustrating picture books is her first really enjoyable work. She is a member of both the national and local chapters of the Society of Children's Book Writers and Illustrators.

Her first book, *Mac and Marie and the Train Toss Surprise*, was praised in *Horn Book* for its "exquisite" illustrations. It also was the most highly recommended book on *Smithsonian* magazine's Christmas list for 1993 and has appeared in national textbooks (third-grade readers) for 1996–1997. Her second book, *May'naise Sandwiches and Sunshine Tea*, made the list of Notable Trade Books compiled by the joint committees of the National Council of Social Studies and Children's Book Council. Both books received good reviews from *School Library Journal. The Glass Bottle Tree* was included on The Bank Street College list of Children's books for the year 1996.

Carter's artwork has been exhibited in several Portland-based galleries, and her artistic interpretation of Martin Luther King's renowned "I Have a Dream" speech hangs in the City Hall of Corvallis, Oregon. She has also painted a 6 × 6 foot panel for a traveling multicultural mural addressing five hundred years of the Columbus legacy.

She and her husband have one daughter and live in Portland, Oregon.

BIBLIOGRAPHY

Mac and Marie and the Train Toss Surprise. By Elizabeth Fitzgerald Howard. Four Winds, 1993.

May'naise Sandwiches and Sunshine Tea . By Sandra Belton. Four Winds, 1994.

The Glass Bottle Tree. By Evelyn Coleman. Orchard, 1995.

Dear Creator: A Week of Poems for Young People and Their Teachers. By Lucille Clifton. Doubleday (Garden City, NY), 1997.

Celestin, Marie A.

(1971–)

AUTHOR

E-mail: mrcelest5@aol.com

"The twentieth century has produced a whole new wave of peer pressure, rejection, and lack of self worth for our Black children. There are things occurring now that were unheard of when I was a child. While national attention is being given to the many adverse events involving our Black children, very little attention is given to those who choose to excel in the midst of their environments. This is why I enjoy writing books for our children. In order to encourage children to read, I invite the reader into a world that is colorful and understandable. Most of all, I want it to be a world that they can identify with and learn from."

Born in 1971 in Sacramento, California, Celestin always knew that she wanted to share a positive message with children. So she designed a plan and put her plan into motion. She began by attending California State University, Sacramento, where she received a Bachelor of Arts degree in English. After leaving the corporate world, Celestin has dedicated her time to creating books for Black children that will empower them to be confident in who they are.

In 2003 she published her first book, *The Unaccepted Child*. The book was featured in local newspapers, a series of special events, recognized on KOVR 13 news, and featured in *Drum Voices Revue* (2005; a book dedicated to A Confluence of Literary, Cultural & Visual Arts). Her next book, *The Adventures of Victoria: The Art of Forgiveness*, illustrated by the legendary Morrie Turner, will be released March 2006. *The Adventures of Victoria* will be a series of seven books.

Because of her dedication to Black children and her determination to see them succeed, she has donated many copies of her book to foster care agencies, receiving homes, and various other organizations so that her message can reach children from all walks of life.

Celestin is a mother of three children and resides in Elk Grove, California.

BIBLIOGRAPHY

The Unaccepted Child. New Century Press, 2003.

Charles, Faustin O(lorun)

(1944–)

AUTHOR

Charles was born in Trinidad, in the Caribbean, the second of two children. As a child, he loved listening to stories told by his grandparents and reading books of folk tales. His maternal grandmother was his main influence in becoming a storyteller. At school, he began composing stories, and he published his first piece at the age of twenty-one in a national newspaper in Trinidad.

In 1962, he moved to England to pursue a literary career and began to publish poems in magazines and newspapers. From 1973 to 1977, Charles worked as a visiting speaker for the Commonwealth Institute in London, visiting schools and talking about the Caribbean and telling stories. From 1977 to 1980, he attended the University of Kent at Canterbury. He graduated with a bachelor of arts degree with honors.

His work has appeared in anthologies for children such as *Can You Hear? Can I Buy a Slice of Sky?, A Caribbean Dozen: Poems from Caribbean Poet,* by John Agard and Grace Nichols, and *Scary Stories;* and he has written a children's operetta that was staged by a primary school in London. He is a member of the Children's Writers and Illustrators Group of the Society of Authors in England and he does freelance storytelling all over that country.

He is married, with two daughters, and lives in London.

BIBLIOGRAPHY

Tales from the West Indies. W. H. Allen, 1985.
Under the Storyteller's Spell. Edited by Faustin O. Charles. Viking, 1989.
The Kiskadee Queen. Edited by Faustin O. Charles. Blackie, 1991.
Uncle Charlie's Crick Crack Tales. Karia, 1994.

Chocolate, Debbi

Deborah Mique Newton Chocolate

(1954–)

AUTHOR

E-mail: DAR60187@aol.com

"I grew up in Chicago, the youngest of five children. My grandparents were musicians and dancers in the theater. By the time I was seven, when I wasn't reading, painting, or drawing, I was busy re-creating my mother's childhood memories of the theater in my own stories. When I turned nine, my mother bought me an eight-millimeter film projector. On Saturday afternoons in late autumn and early winter, when the weather was too cold for my friends and I to play outside, I'd set up the folding chairs in my basement, pop popcorn, and sell tickets to my 'movie theater' to all the kids in the neighborhood. Later I turned to music and became quite an accomplished trumpet player.

"I still get my ideas from movies, paintings, music, and the theater. My childhood friends, the children I meet, and my own two little boys often provide the foundation for an interesting character. As a children's book author, my purpose is always the same: I write to entertain and to share my vision of life's hope, its beauty, and its promise."

Chocolate was born in Chicago, Illinois. She is a graduate of Spelman College in Atlanta, Georgia, where she received her bachelor's degree in political science and journalism in 1976. She was awarded a fellowship in creative writing from Brown University in Providence, Rhode Island, where in 1978 she earned a master of arts degree in creative writing and English. In 1990 and 1991, she received grants from the city of Chicago Council on the Arts to complete two picture books.

A former editor of books for children, Chocolate is a member of the Children's Reading Roundtable, the Children's Literature

Assembly, the Society of Children's Book Authors and Illustrators and The Midland Society of Writers.

In 1992, *My First Kwanzaa Book* was cited as a Book of the Month Club selection and an American Booksellers Association Pick of the List. In 1993, *Talk, Talk: An Ashanti Legend* won the Parents Choice Award. In 1994, *Imani in the Belly* was selected as an American Booksellers Association Pick of the List, and, in 1995, *On the Day I Was Born* was cited as a Book of the Month Club selection.

The author is married to Robert Chocolate and lives in Wheaton, Illinois, with their two sons, Bobby and Allen Whitney.

BIBLIOGRAPHY

Kwanzaa. Illustrated by Melodye Rosales. Children's Press, 1990.
My First Kwanzaa Book. Illustrated by Cal Massey. Scholastic, 1992.
NEATE: To the Rescue. Just Us Books, 1992.
Spider and the Sky God. Illustrated by Dave Albers. Troll, 1993.
Talk, Talk: An Ashanti Legend. Illustrated by Dave Albers. Troll, 1993.
Elizabeth's Wish. Illustrated by Melodye Rosales. Just Us Books, 1994.
Imani in the Belly. Illustrated by Alex Boies. BridgeWater, 1994.
On the Day I Was Born. Illustrated by Melodye Rosales. Scholastic, 1995.
The Best Kwanzaa Ever. Scholastic, 1996.
Kente Colors! Illustrated by John Ward. Walker, 1996.
The Piano Man. Illustrated by Eric Yalesquez. Walker, 1998.
Pigs Can Fly! Cricket Books, 2004.
El Barrio. Henry Holt, 2005.

Christie, R. Gregory

(1971–)

ILLUSTRATOR

A native of Plainfield, New Jersey, Christie is the youngest of three children. He showed an interest in the arts at an early age and began to paint at the age of thirteen. Honing his skills at the School of Visual Arts in New York City, he simultaneously began working at the Solomon R. Guggenheim Museum. Upon graduating in May, 1989 with a bachelor of fine arts degree, Christie traveled to Europe to discover other styles of art and cultures. This exposure led him to develop a new direction in his illustration, illustration with a fine-art edge.

Christie has illustrated for several companies, including Avon, MCA, Warner Brothers, various other record companies, and publications. He received a 1997 Coretta Scott King Illustrator Honor Award and the 1997 Firecracker Award for *The Palm of My Heart: Poetry by African American Children*. He is represented by Arts Council, New York City.

Christie lives in the Fort Greene section of Brooklyn, New York.

BIBLIOGRAPHY

The Palm of My Heart: Poetry by African American Children. By Davida Adedjouma. Lee & Low, 1996.

Richard Wright and the Library Card. By William Miller. Lee & Low, 2001.

Love to Langston. By Tony Medina. Lee & Low, 2002.

Only Passing Through: The Story of Sojourner Truth. By Anne F. Rockwell. Knopf, 2002.

Stars in the Darkness. By Barbara M. Joosse. Chronicle Press, 2002.

DeShawn Days. By Tony Medina. Group West, 2003.

Flower Girl. By Kathy Furgang. Penguin, 2003.

Letters to Santa: From Kids Who Never Got a Response. By Tony Medina. Just Us Books, 2003.

Richard Wright Y El Carne De Biblioteca. By William Miller. Lee & Low, 2003.

Rock of Ages: A Tribute to the Black Church. By Tonya Bolden. Knopf, 2003.

Ruler of the Courtyard. By Rukhsana Kahn. Viking, 2003.

Yesterday I Had the Blues. By Jeron Ashford Frame. Ten Speed Press, 2003.

Hot City. By Barbara M. Joosse. Putnam, 2004.

The Champ!: The Story of Muhammad Ali. By Tonya Bolden. Random House, 2004.

The Sun's Daughter: A Story Based on an Iroquois Legend. By Pat Sherman. Forthcoming, Houghton Mifflin, 2005.

Jazz Baby. By Lisa Wheeler. Harcourt, 2006.

Clay, Wil

(1938–)

ILLUSTRATOR

E-mail: wilclay@usa.com

Web site: www.wilclay.com

Clay was born in Bessemer, Alabama, and started his commercial art career at Macomber Vocational High School in Toledo, Ohio. Greatly encouraged by well-known Toledo artist Ernest Spring to pursue an art career, Clay received further training at the Vesper George School of Art in Boston, Massachusetts, 1959–1960.

He moved to Houston, Texas, where he set up a graphic-design firm, remaining there until about 1975. By 1989, he was back in Toledo, where he works and teaches in his studio located at Common Space.

His collaboration with Constancia Gaffeney-Brown resulted in his winning the international competition sponsored by the Arts Commission of Greater Toledo to honor Dr. Martin Luther King, Jr. His sculpture *Radiance*, a six-foot bronze-and-stainless-steel work of King, features modeled heads of King on a polished steel sphere. The work was dedicated in downtown Toledo in September, 1989.

In 1990, he visited Cameroon for six months. While in Africa, he worked with the Bamileke people and the Fulani, studying their art in beadwork, painting, woodworking, and the like in relation to their folkways and tribal lifestyles.

The illustrations for his first children's book, *Tailypo*, were inspired by childhood memories of visits to his two grandmothers, both of whom lived in rural Alabama. He won a 1993 Coretta Scott King Honor Book Award for *Little Eight John* by Jan Wahl.

He enjoys visiting schools, libraries, professional organizations and clubs to share "the wonderful world of creating books and storytelling."

Clay's art can be found in private collections not only in the United States but also in Canada, Sierra Leone, and Cameroon.

Clay is the father of two sons and four daughters. He lives in Toledo, Ohio.

BIBLIOGRAPHY

213 Valentines. By Barbara Cohen. Holt, 1991.

Tailypo. By Jan Wahl. Holt, 1991.

Little Eight John. By Jan Wahl. Lodestar, 1992.

The Real McCoy: The Life of an African American Inventor. By Wendy Towle. Scholastic, 1993.

Themba. By Margaret Sacks. Lodestar, 1992. Puffin, 1994.

The House in the Sky. By Robert D. San Souci. Dial, 1996.

I Am Rosa Parks. By Jim Haskins. Dial, 1997.

I Have a Dream. By Martin L. King, Jr. Scholastic, 1997.

Auntee Edna. By Ethel Footman Smothers. Eerdman's Books, 2001.

Cline-Ransome, Lesa

(1965–)

AUTHOR

E-mail: lclineransome@aol.com

"One of the greatest gifts we can give our children is the gift of stories. As the youngest of three children, I was my mother's constant companion. On our daily errands she shared her stories of family, childhood, daily experiences or her favorite books. Listening to my mother's stories taught me the power of language, dialogue, suspense and humor⊠tools I now use when creating my own stories. Though the books I write are not the stories of my own life, they are the stories of others, captured on pages to cherish and to share."

Born in Malden, Massachusetts, Cline-Ransome studied merchandising and fashion management at Pratt Institute in Brooklyn, New York. After earning a Bachelor of Fine Arts degree in 1987, she worked as a fashion copywriter for Lord & Taylor and R.H. Macy in New York City.

Cline-Ransome developed an interest in the field of education and began working first as a substitute teacher in the New York City school system. Later she became a teacher for the Living for the Young Family through Education (LYFE) program, designed to offer on-site infant and toddler childcare for teenaged parents returning to high school to complete their education. While working for the program, she earned a Master of Arts degree in Early Childhood and Elementary Education from New York University.

Cline-Ransome resigned from her teaching position and began writing for children when she was expecting her first child. She has written *Satchel Paige* (Simon & Schuster), a biography of the Negro League pitcher, *Quilt Alphabet* (Holiday House), a collection of alphabet poems, and the companion book *Quilt Counting* (North South Books).

Her most recent biography is of the African American world champion cyclist *Major Taylor* for Atheneum Books for Young Readers. *Pélé* was released by Atheneum Books in 2006. All books are in collaboration with her husband, children's book illustrator James Ransome.

The mother of four young children, Jaime, Maya, Malcolm, and Leila, she lives with her family in Rhinebeck, New York.

BIBLIOGRAPHY

Satchel Paige. Illustrated by James Ransome. Simon & Schuster, 2000.

Quilt Alphabet. Illustrated by James Ransome. Holiday House, 2001.

Quilt Counting. Illustrated by James Ransome. Seastar Books, 2002.

Major Taylor, Champion Cyclist. Illustrated by James Ransome. Simon & Schuster, 2004.

Pélé. Illustrated by James Ransome. Random House, 2006.

Helen Keller. Illustrated by James Ransome. HarperCollins, 2006.

Coleman, Evelyn

(1948–)

AUTHOR

Web site: www.evelyncoleman.com

"A child's mind is the most receptive to new ideas and thus more vulnerable to harm. When I write I pay attention to the subliminal messages that might be couched in words in order to make sure I do no harm to children. Too often people write for children without considering what the words will "feel" like in a classroom setting or a group. It is important to make sure you under-stand what your words mean, the subtle implications and the possible impact if handled by an insensitive adult. It is true that 'sticks and stones can break your bones' but it isn't true that 'words can't hurt you.' I am also vigilant when it comes to research, even when writing 'fiction' for children. If grapes can't be smelled through a window in North Carolina in a particular month, then I take the reference out. As writers we must remember that our work should have power, the power to force children to think, to ponder the world they live in and to be directed to what is positive and good. Children need to be critical thinkers in order to thrive in our world. Let's give them the tools they need. I also do not write stories that question the humanity of minority children. My premise is always that we are all one people. However, because I am aware that in the past minorities are usually relegated to the 'bad guy,' the 'helper,' or the 'maid,' I don't put my minority characters in those situations. In most of my stories, minority characters are the heroes. In addition, I work hard to respect elders and their wisdom in my stories. No writing that I do is more important than what I write for children, because in the end, writers can, do and will change the world through children."

Coleman, born July 3, 1948, in Burlington, North Carolina, believes that her children's writing education began when she was still a child making up stories for her younger brother. She credits her mother, father and close-knit relatives for allowing her the freedom to use her imagination and her teachers in an all Black school for nurturing her zeal for learning.

Coleman admits that even though she wasn't writing professionally, her love for writing never diminished. In fact, she forced her colleagues, while working as a psychotherapist at Mental Health centers, to listen to her stories. Finally the day came when she could no longer avoid writing. After winning a North Carolina writing fellowship, Coleman proceeded to pursue her "writing" education by attending classes, workshops, seminars and reading every writing book ever published.

After successfully writing for adults in magazines, newspapers, and the short story market, Coleman decided maybe she had enough writing under her belt to pursue her life-long dream—writing for children. She read over five hundred children's books and literally typed in one hundred of them to teach herself the rhythm of a picture book. In addition, she joined the Society of Children's Book Writers and Illustrators and attended their workshops.

Among the many honors she has received, she was selected for inclusion in the Ninth Book of Junior Authors and Illustrators published by The H. W. Wilson Company (New York) in 2004 and also honored by The National Teachers of English, Latino & Black Caucus. She was the first African American to win the North Carolina Arts Council's $5,000 fiction fellowship in 1987. *White Socks Only* was produced as a live-action film by Academy Award winner, Barbara Bryant for Phoenix Films, Inc. in 1999. The Feature Film won the Bronze Award at Worldfest Film Festival in Houston, Texas.

Coleman lives in Atlanta, Georgia with her husband, her dog, and feels fortunate to have her daughters and granddaughter nearby so they can visit a whole bunch.

BIBLIOGRAPHY

The Foot Warmer and Her Crow. Illustrated by Daniel Minter. Simon & Schuster, 1994.

The Glass Bottle Tree. Illustrated by Gail Gordon Carter. Orchard/Scholastic, 1995.

White Socks Only. Illustrated by Tyrone Geter. Albert Whitman, 1996.

To Be a Drum. Illustrated by Aminah Brenda Lynn Robinson. Albert Whitman, 1998.

The Riches of Oseola McCarty. Illustrated by Daniel Minter. Albert Whitman, 1998.

Born in Sin. Atheneum, 2001.

Mystery of the Dark Tower. Pleasant Company, 2000.

Circle of Fire. Pleasant Company, 2002.

Cooper, Afua

(1957–)

AUTHOR

Cooper is Jamaican born of African descent. As a young child, Cooper liked reading poetry and historical fiction and decided to write both when she grew up. *The Red Caterpillar on College Street* is her first book of children's poetry and has been widely acclaimed. The *Canadian Book Review Annual* said in 1989 that is it "a refreshing change from the almost adult-oriented and lavish picture books of more affluent publishers." Cooper is completing *Waiting for the Moon*, a collection of short stories, and a series of children's stories entitled *Fatima's Nightgown*.

Her poems have been published in anthologies in Britain, the United States, Canada, and the Caribbean. She also recorded her poetry on the album *Womantalk* (Heartbeat Records) in 1984.

Cooper has been writer in-residence at two Ontario school boards and is a regular participant in the League of Canadian Poets' Poetry in the Schools series. She enjoys writing and performing her poetry to children and is a well-known figure on the Canadian children's poetry scene.

In addition to the literary works, Cooper is pursuing a doctorate in African-Canadian history at the University of Toronto, where she teaches a course in Canadian Black history. She serves on a number of juries for the Toronto, Ontario Arts and the Canada Council. She is publishing poetry and working on an adult manuscript.

Cooper is married and has a son and two daughters. She lives in Toronto.

BIBLIOGRAPHY

The Red Caterpillar on College Street. Illustrated by Stephanie Martin. Sister Vision, 1989.

Cooper, II, Floyd Donald

(1956–)

ILLUSTRATOR

Cooper states that he hopes his work will "produce books about blacks for white kids. One of the more satisfying rewards for my work comes when I get the opportunity to do a book about the black experience to broaden and enlighten someone who may not be aware ... I feel children are at the front line in improving society."

Cooper was born in Tulsa, Oklahoma. A graduate of Tulsa Central High School, he earned a bachelor of fine arts from the University of Oklahoma at Norman. Children's book illustration initially was a way to complement his work in advertising. While at the university, he studied under Mark English and after graduation worked with a greeting card company in Missouri.

After moving to the eastern part of the country, he discovered the diversity and creativity he sought in children's book illustration in 1984. His first book, *Grandpa's Face*, was an American Library Association Notable Book. He has received recognition from the Society of Illustrators and exhibited at "The One Show."

Cooper has illustrated innumerable books for children and young adults. In addition to stories which highlight the Black experience, he has also illustrated picture books and poetry books for young readers as well as biographies.

He has explored the African American experience both on the individual level and on the larger historical scene.

Cooper has received many awards and honors, notably several Coretta Scott King awards, notable book selections, American Library Association (ALA), and Parents' Choice Awards, among others.

Cooper states that he hopes his illustrations will help children to become aware.

Cooper currently resides in East Orange, New Jersey. He has one son.

BIBLIOGRAPHY

The Story of Jackie Robinson, Bravest Man in Baseball. By Margaret Davidson. Dell (New York, NY), 1988.

Grandpa's Face. By Eloise Greenfield. Philomel, 1988.

Chita's Christmas Tree. By Elizabeth Fitzgerald Howard. Bradbury Press, 1989.

Laura Charlotte. By Kathryn Osebold Galbraith. Philomel, 1990.

Martin Luther King Jr. and His Birthday. By Jacqueline Woodson. Silver-Burdett, 1990.

When Africa Was Home. By Karen Lynn Williams. Orchard Books, 1991.

Petey. By Deborah Eaton. Silver Burdett, 1992.

Imani's Gift at Kwanzaa. By Denise Burden-Patmon. Modern Curriculum Press, 1992.

The Girl Who Loved Caterpillars: A Twelfth-Century Tale from Japan. By Jean Merrill. Philomel, 1992.

Be Good to Eddie Lee. By Virginia M. Fleming. Philomel, 1993.

Brown Honey in Broomwheat Tea: Poems. By Joyce Carol Thomas. HarperCollins, 1993.

Pass It On: African-American Poetry for Children. By Wade Hudson, selector. Scholastic, 1993.

From Miss Ida's Porch. By Sandra Belton. Four Winds Press, 1993.

Coyote Walks on Two Legs: A Book of Navajo Myths and Legends. By Gerald Hausman, reteller. Philomel, 1993.

Meet Danitra Brown. By Nikki Grimes. Lothrop, 1994.

Happy Birthday, Dr. King. By Kathryn D. Jones. Modern Curriculum Press, 1994.

Daddy, Daddy, Be There. By Candy Dawson Boyd. Philomel, 1995.

Gingerbread Days: Poems. By Joyce Carol Thomas. HarperCollins, 1995.

Papa Tells Chita a Story. By Elizabeth Fitzgerald Howard. Simon & Schuster, 1995.

How Sweet the Sound: African-American Songs for Children. By Wade and Cheryl Hudson, selectors. Scholastic, 1995.

King Sejong's Secret. By Carol J. Farley. Lothrop, 1995.

Jaguarundi. By Virginia Hamilton. Blue Sky Press, 1995.

Pulling the Lion's Tale. By Jane Kurtz. Simon & Schuster, 1995.

Satchmo's Blues. By Alan Schroeder. Doubleday, 1996.

One April Morning: Children Remember the Oklahoma City Bombing. By Nancy Lamb. Lothrop, 1996.

Si Won's Victory. By Bill Martin and Michael Sampson. Celebration Press, 1996.

Ma Dear's Aprons. By Patricia C. McKissack. Atheneum, 1997.

Miz Berlin Walks. By Jane Yolen. Philomel, 1997.

Be Good to Eddie Lee. By Virginia Fleming. Paper Star Book, 1997.

Faraway Drums. By Virginia L. Kroll. Little Brown, 1998.

I Have Heard of a Land. By Joyce Carol Thomas. HarperCollins, 1998.

Sea Girl and the Dragon King: A Chinese Folktale. By Ziporah Hildebrandt, reteller. Atheneum, 1998.

African Beginnings. By James Haskins and Kathleen Benson. Lothrop, 1998.

Shake Rag: From the Life of Elvis Presley. By Amy Littlesugar. Philomel, 1998.

Tree of Hope. By Amy Littlesugar. Philomel, 1999.

Reflections of a Black Cowboy, Second edition, Volume 1: *Cowboys*, 1999, volume 2: *The Buffalo Soldiers*, 1999, volume 3: *Pioneers*, 1999, volume 4: *Mountain Men*, 1999. By Robert H. Miller. Silver Burdett, 1999.

Caddie, The Golf Dog. By Michael Sampson. Tommy Nelson, 1999.

On Mardi Gras Day. By Fatima Shaik. Dial, 1999.

Granddaddy's Street Songs. By Monalisa DeGross. Jump at the Sun/Hyperion, 1999.

Bound for America: The Forced Migration of Africans to the New World. By James Haskins and Kathleen Benson. Lothrop, 1999.

A Child Is Born. By Margaret Wise Brown. Jump at the Sun/Hyperion, 2000.

Sweet, Sweet Memory. By Jacqueline Woodson. Jump at the Sun/Hyperion, 2000.

City Scenes. By Bill Martin, Jr. and Michael Sampson. Learning Matters Africa, 2000.

Freedom School, Yes! By Amy Littlesugar. Philomel, 2001.

Tree of Hope. By Amy Littlesugar. Penguin, 2001.

The Blacker the Berry: Poems. By Joyce Carol Thomas. HarperCollins, 2002.

Danitra Brown Leaves Town. By Nikki Grimes. HarperCollins, 2002.

Mississippi Morning. By Ruth Vander Zee. Eerdmans Books, 2003.

Jump! From the Life of Michael Jordan. Penguin Group, 2004.

Crews, Donald

(1938–)

AUTHOR/ILLUSTRATOR

Crews was born in Newark, New Jersey, and attended Arts High School, where admission for music and art training is by competitive examination. He also attended Cooper Union in New York City. Crews served two years of military service in Germany, where he married Ann Jones, a fellow student from Cooper Union.

Freight Train and *Truck* were Caldecott Honor Books in 1979 and 1981, respectively. *Freight Train* was also an American Library Association Notable Book and a Junior Literary Guild choice, along with *Truck* and *Carousel*. In 1979, the American Institute of Graphic Arts Children's Book Show exhibited *Rain* and *Freight Train*. *Flying* was listed as one of the *New York Times* best illustrated books. The artist's work has also appeared in *Graphis* magazine.

Crews lives in upstate New York. He and his wife have two adult daughters, Nina and Amy.

BIBLIOGRAPHY

We Read: A to Z. Harper, 1967.

Ten Black Dots. Scribner, 1968.

Freight Train. Greenwillow, 1978.

Rain. By Robert Kalan. Greenwillow, 1978.

Blue Sea. By Robert Kalan. Greenwillow, 1979.

The Talking Stone. Edited by Dorothy de Wit. Greenwillow, 1979.

Truck. Greenwillow, 1980.

Light. Greenwillow, 1981.

Carousel. Greenwillow, 1982.

Harbor. Greenwillow, 1982.

Parade. Greenwillow, 1983.

School Bus. Greenwillow, 1984.

Bicycle Race. Greenwillow, 1985.

Flying. Greenwillow, 1986.

Eclipse: Darkness in Daytime. By Franklyn M. Branley. HarperCollins, 1988.

How Many Snails? A Counting Book. By Paul Giganti, Jr. Greenwillow, 1990.

Bigmama's. Greenwillow, 1991.

Shortcut. Greenwillow, 1992.

When This Box Is Full. By Patricia Lillie. Greenwillow, 1993.

Sail Away. Greenwillow, 1995.

Tomorrow's Alphabet. By George Shannon. Greenwillow, 1996.

More Than One. By Miriam Schlein. Greenwillow, 1996.

Cloudy Day/Sunny Day. GreenLight (Harcourt), 1999.

Inside Freight Train. HarperFestival, 2001.

Colors and Shapes. By Loretta Krupinski. Milwaukee Public Library, 2002.

Crews, Nina

(1963–)

AUTHOR/ILLUSTRATOR

E-mail: letters@ninacrews.com

Web site: ninacrews.com

"Children's books offer an ideal opportunity to create narrative with words and pictures. This is one of this genre's greatest pleasures. To drink in a story lushly illustrated is a wonderful experience. The reader 'reads' two texts, one written and one drawn, painted, collaged or photographed. I chose photography and collage to tell my stories. Photography allows for a wealth of details to be shown about people and places. When children read these books they see people, places and things which are familiar or known to them. The photographs ground the stories while the collages allow for fantasy to be a part of the tale. All of my subjects are family, friends and friends of friends. The interaction between us always adds something to the project; their performances often generate new ideas."

Crews was born in Frankfurt, Germany. She graduated from Yale University with a BA in Art and also participated in the Whitney Independent Study program for studio artists. While living in New York City, she pursued fine art photography and editorial work for magazines while also working in commercial animation production. Daughter of children's book authors Donald Crews and Ann Jonas, Nina's first book, *One Hot Summer Day*, was published in 1995. *Snowball*, 1997, was chosen as one of Bank Street College Best Books of the Year in 1998 and Chicago Public Library's Best of the Best for 1997. *You Are Here*, 1998, was chosen as one of Chicago Public Library's Best of the Best for 1998. *When Will Sarah Come*, 1999, by Elizabeth Fitzgerald Howard was a CCBC Choices 2000—

Charlotte Zolotow Highly Commended book. *The Neighborhood Mother Goose*, 2004, was selected as an ALA Notable Book for 2004, *Kirkus*, and *School Library Journals* Best Books of 2004 lists, The New York Public Library's 100 Books for Reading and Sharing list, Capitol Choices Noteworthy Books for Children.

Crews lives in Brooklyn, New York.

BIBLIOGRAPHY

One Hot Summer Day. Greenwillow, 1995.

I'll Catch the Moon. Greenwillow, 1996.

Snowball. Greenwillow, 1997.

You Are Here. Greenwillow, 1998.

A High Low Near Far Loud Quiet Story. Greenwillow, 1999.

When Will Sarah Come? By Elizabeth Fitzgerald Howard. Greenwillow, 1999.

We the People. By Bobbi Katz. Greenwillow, 2000.

A Ghost Story. Greenwillow, 2001.

The Neighborhood Mother Goose. Greenwillow, 2004.

Below. Greenwillow, 2006.

Crichlow, Ernest

(1914–2005)

ILLUSTRATOR

Crichlow was born in New York City and remembered loving to draw since grade-school days when he drew from models suggested by his teacher. He was the second of nine children born to immigrants from Barbados, and the immigrant experience was often a subject in his art. After his graduation from Haaren High School (now defunct) in New York City, some of his art teachers arranged for his scholarship at the Commercial Illustration School of Art and raised money for his art supplies. Crichlow first exhibited in 1938 and 1939 in the artist-organized Harlem Community Center Organization. In 1960 he had his first one man show at the ACA Gallery in New York City.

His collaboration with Lorraine and Jerrold Beim on *Two Is a Team*, an easy book about the interracial friendship of two little boys, was the beginning of a successful career in children's-book illustration, generally on Black themes. His artwork has been exhibited in many art shows. He had taught at Shaw University, the State University of New York at New Paltz, the City College of New York, and the Brooklyn Museum Art School.

In 1969, with Norman Lewis and Romare Bearden, he founded the Cinque Gallery in New York City for beginning Black artists, and codirected a group of Black artists at Saratoga, New York, under the aegis of the State Education Department of Arts and Humanities. Crichlow was also a member of the Black Academy of Arts and Letters. He received the first-ever medallion for lifetime achievement during the opening of the University of Pittsburgh's second annual "Images" Black Artist exhibition in 1987.

In 1990, Crichlow held a one-man show at the Cinque Gallery, at which actor Morgan Freeman bought three of his paintings. Crichlow taught art classes for thirty years in Trump Village, a middle-class development community in Brooklyn, New York.

Chrichlow's work is in numerous private and public collections all over the world. The list includes the Brooklyn Museum, the Hewitt Collection, and the private collections of Morgan Freeman and Lena Horne.

BIBLIOGRAPHY

Two Is a Team. By Lorraine and Jerrold Beim. Harcourt, 1945.

Freedom Train: The Story of Harriet Tubman. By Dorothy Sterling. Doubleday, 1954.

Corrie and the Yankee. By Mimi Cooper Levi. Viking, 1959.

Mary Jane. By Dorothy Sterling. Doubleday, 1959.

William. By Anne Welsh Guy. Dial, `95`.

Forever Free. By Dorothy Sterling. Doubleday, 1961.

Galumph. By Brenda Lansdown. Houghton, 1963.

Lift Every Voice. By Dorothy Sterling and Benjamin Quarles. Doubleday, 1964.

Lincoln's Birthday. By Clyde R. Bulla. HarperCollins, 1965.

Street Dog. By Richard E. Drdek. Singer, 1967.

African Folk Tales. Edited by Jessie Alford Nunn. Funk & Wagnalls, 1969.

The Magic Mirrors. By Judith Berry Griffin. Putnam, 1971.

Cummings, Pat

1950–)

AUTHOR/ILLUSTRATOR

Cummings was born in Chicago, Illinois. As part of an army family, she spent her childhood in many places in and out of the United States. She received her bachelor's degree from Pratt Institute in 1974 and became a freelance illustrator.

Cummings won Coretta Scott King Honor Book Awards for her illustrations in 1983, 1987, and 1989; her illustrations for *My Mama Needs Me* won the 1984 Coretta Scott King Award; and *Talking With Artists* won the 1992 Boston Globe-Horn Book Award for nonfiction. She also received the Communications Excellence to Black Audiences Award for an illustration advertising Con Edison and an honorable mention in 1978 for a poster for the United Nations Committee on Apartheid.

Cummings is a professor in the Illustrations Department at Parsons School of Design in New York City. She is a member of the Graphic Artists Guild, the Society of Children's Book Writers and Illustrators, the Authors Guild, and the Writers Guild of America.

Cummings is married to Chuku Lee. They live in Brooklyn, New York.

BIBLIOGRAPHY

Good News. By Eloise Greenfield. Coward, 1977.
Beyond Dreamtime. By Trudie MacDougall. Coward, 1978.
The Secret of the Royal Mounds. By Cynthia Jameson. Coward, 1980.
Just Us Women. By Jeannette Caines. Harper, 1982.
My Mama Needs Me. By Mildred Pitts Walter. Lothrop, 1983.
Fred's First Day. By Cathy Warren. Lothrop, 1984.
Jimmy Lee Did It. Lothrop, 1985.
Chilly Stomach. By Jeannette Caines. Harper, 1986.

C.L.O.U.D.S. Lothrop, 1986.

Springtime Bears. By Cathy Warren. Lothrop, 1986.

I Need a Lunch Box. By Jeannette Caines. Harper, 1988.

Mariah Loves Rock. By Mildred Pitts Walker. Bradbury, 1988.

Storm in the Night. By Mary Stolz. Harper, 1988.

Willie's Not the Hugging Kind. By Joyce Durham Barrett. Harper, 1989.

Mariah Keeps Cool. By Mildred Pitts Walter. Bradbury, 1990.

Two and Too Much. By Mildred Pitts Walter. Bradbury, 1990.

Clean Your Room, Harvey Moon! Bradbury, 1991.

Go Fish. By Mary Stolz. HarperCollins, 1991.

Petey Moroni's Camp Runamok Diary. Bradbury, 1992.

Talking with Artists. Bradbury, 1992.

Carousel. Bradbury, 1994.

C Is for City. By Nikki Grimes. Lothrop, 1995.

Talking with Artists: Volume Two. Simon & Schuster, 1995.

My Aunt Came Back. HarperCollins, 1997.

Pickin' Peas. By Margaret Read. HarperCollins, 1998.

Lulu's Birthday. By Elizabeth Fitzgerald Howard. Greenwillow, 1999.

Ananse & the Lizard. Henry Holt, 2003.

Squashed in the Middle. By Elizabeth Winthrop. Henry Holt, 2005.

Curry, Barbara K.

AUTHOR

E-mail: SLR986@aol.com

Curry was born and educated during the early part of her life in southeastern Pennsylvania. She is the third of four girls who grew up with her parents Ralph and Carolyn in a small turn of the century town home in what would have been described at the time as a colored neighborhood. She attended Catholic primary and secondary schools and attended Franklin and Marshall College. She later received degrees from the University of Wisconsin and Harvard University. In addition to her doctorate she has a LCSW and ACSW. She is currently a professor in the College of Human Services, Education, and Public Policy at the University of Delaware.

Curry's work has focused on identity development; consequently, her children's book *Sweet Words So Brave* was a creative combination of her clinical and academic interests. It is her only children's book to date.

BIBLIOGRAPHY

Sweet Words So Brave: The Story of African American Literature (co-author James Michael Brodie). Illustrated by Jerry Butler. Zino Press, 1996.

Curtis, Christopher Paul

(1953–)

AUTHOR

Web site: www.Christopherpaulcurtis.com

"To me the highest accolade comes when a young reader tells me, 'I really liked your book.' The young seem to be able to say 'really' with a clarity, a faith, and an honesty that we as adults have long forgotten. That is why I write."

Curtis was born in Flint, Michigan. After high school, he worked on the assembly line of Flint's historic Fisher Body Plant #1 for thirteen years. His job of hanging car doors left him with an aversion to getting in and out of large automobiles—particularly big Buicks.

His greatest influences were from his family and his wife, Kaysandra in particular.

Curtis believes he is genetically predestined to entertain. He has won numerous awards for his essays and short stories, including a 1996 Newbery Honor Book Award and a 1996 Coretta Scott King Honor Book Award for *The Watsons Go to Birmingham-1963*, which is being translated into seven languages.

BIBLIOGRAPHY
The Watsons Go to Birmingham-1963. Random House, 1995.
Bud, Not Buddy. Random House, 1999.
Bucking the Sarge. (Wendy Lamb Books) Random House, 2004.
My Chickee's Funny Monkey. (Wendy Lamb Books) Random House, 2005.

Davis, Ossie

(1918– 2005)

AUTHOR

An actor, playwright, director, and activist, Davis was born in Cog-dell, Georgia, and performed on stage, screen, and television. He and his actress wife, Ruby Dee, appeared on Howard University's WBBM-TV's *In Other Words ... Ossie and Ruby*, and cohosted the *Ossie Davis and Ruby Dee Story Hour* on radio from 1974 to 1978 and the Public Broadcasting System (PBS) television series *With Ossie and Ruby* in 1981.

Davis preferred to be known foremost as a writer. His role as chairman of the board of the Institute of New Cinema Artists, which specialized in training young film and television production talent, is perhaps his proudest contribution to the industry.

Through their company, Emmalyn Enterprises, he and his wife, Ruby Dee, produced, with PBS, some of their best work: *Martin Luther King: The Dream and the Drum*; *A Walk Through the 20th Century* with Bill Moyers; and the critically acclaimed series *With Ossie and Ruby*. Together they have received a number of honors, including the Frederick Douglass Award from the New York Urban League for their work in the play *Boseman and Lena*; the Drama Desk Award in 1974; and the Martin Luther King, Jr., Award from Operation PUSH in 1977. Davis' film performances were in the movie *The Client*, the film production of John Grisham's bestselling novel and in the movie *Grumpy Old Men* with Jack Lemmon and Walter Matthau. Originally a stage actor and writer, he wrote the screen play for and directed the film *Cotton Comes to Harlem* in 1970 and appeared in a number of movies including Spike Lee's *Do the Right Thing* in 1989, *Jungle Fever* in 1991, and *Get On the Bus* filmed in 1996, and did the voice narration in the movie *Malcolm X*.

His *Escape to Freedom: A Play About Young Frederick Douglass* won the1979 Coretta Scott King Award.

In 2003, the Chicago Public Library adapted *A Raisin in the Sun* for its "One Book, One Chicago" project. For the culminating citywide event, the library invited Ruby Dee and Davis to come to town to be interviewed about their lives and their performances in the Broadway production of the play.

In his theatrical life, Davis wrote the play *Purlie Victorious* and starred in it with his wife. It has been performed nationally. When performed in 2005 at the Kelly-Strayhorn Theatre in Pittsburgh, Pennsylvania, it was introduced by Ruby Dee.

BIBLIOGRAPHY

Escape to Freedom: A Play About Young Frederick Douglass. Viking, 1978.
Langston: A Play. Delacorte, 1982.
Just Like Martin. Simon & Schuster, 1992.

Dee, Ruby

Ruby Ann Wallace

(1923–)

AUTHOR

Dee was born Ruby Ann Wallace in Cleveland, Ohio, and was married to the late actor-playwright Ossie Davis, who has written plays for children as well as adults.

She is primarily known as an actress but has also published books. Dee wrote poetry before venturing into the children's book world, and she has said her purpose in writing is to "create exciting and challenging reading for children—to inform the senses and entertain."

Among her treasured experiences are working with her husband and their son Guy Davis in the storytelling, folklore, and music review *Two Hahs and a Homeboy.* Compiled by Dee, the program draws on her own works, along with the original writings of her husband and son, and of the late anthropologist/folklorist Zora Neale Hurston.

Dee received her bachelor of arts degree from Hunter College in New York City and in the 1950s attended actors' workshops at Fairfield University, Iona College, and Virginia State College. She has been active as an actress in films, an actress and writer in the American Negro Theater, and the cohost with her husband of the radio program *Ossie Davis and Ruby Dee Story Hour* from 1974 to 1978 and of the Public Broadcasting System's series *With Ossie and Ruby* in 1981.

She won an Emmy from the Academy of Television Arts and Sciences for a single performance in 1964 in *Express Stop from Lenox Avenue.* With Davis, she received the Frederick Douglass Award from the New York Urban League for their work in the play *Boseman and Lena;* the Martin Luther King, Jr. Award from Operation PUSH in 1977; and the Drama Desk Award in 1974. She is enrolled in the Hunter College Hall of Fame and received the college's President's Medal. She was inducted into the Theater Hall of Fame in 1988 and into the National Association for the Advancement of Colored People (NAACP) Image Award Hall of Fame in 1989.

Some of her favorite roles have been Lutiebelle in *Purlie Victorious* (stage and film), written by her husband Ossie Davis; Lena in Athol Fugard's *Bossman and Lena*, for which she received an Obie; Julia in Alice Childress' *Wedding Band* for the New York Shakespeare Festival (a Drama Desk Award); on television as Mary Tyrone in Eugene O'Neill's *Long Day's Journey into Night* (an ACE award); Ruth in Lorraine Hansberry's *A Raisin in the Sun*; Cordelia in *King Lear*; Kate in *The Taming of the Shrew* at the American Shakespeare Festival in Connecticut; and Cassandra in *Agamemnon* for the Greek Ypsilanti Theater in Michigan.

Dee has also appeared in the following: James Baldwin's *Go Tell It On The Mountain*; *Uptight*, a Jules Dasson film; and *Take It From The Top* (a musical which she authored); as Estelle on the CBS network pilot, *Middle Ages*; in the Walt Disney Release of *The Ernest Green Story*. With her husband, Ossie Davis, Dee has appeared in Spike Lee's *Do The Right Thing* and *Jungle Fever*; *Cop And A Half* with Burt Reynolds; *Just Cause* with Laurence Fishburne and Sean Connery; as "Mother Abigail" in the acclaimed TV miniseries, *The Stand*, by Stephen King; in *Tuesday Morning Ride*, an adaptation of an Arna Bomtemps classic with Bill Cobb; *Mr. & Mrs. Loving*; and *The James Mink Story*, with Louis Gossett. Dee and her husband, Ossie Davis, have also hosted the African Heritage Movie Network Series of Black film classics for several seasons.

In 1998, Dee was inducted into the Theater Hall of Fame and in 1989, into the NAACP Image Award Hall of Fame. She was also awarded an Emmy for her role in *Decoration Day*, a Hallmark Hall of Fame presentation.

Dee is also a writer. *My One Good Nerve* is a compilation of some of her short stories, humor and poetry. Dee is presently working on the second volume of this book. She appeared in 2005 at the Kelly Strayhorn Theatre in Pittsburgh, Pennsylvania, performing excerpts from the book.

Dee and her husband had three grown children.

BIBLIOGRAPHY

Glowchild and Other Poems. Edited by Ruby Dee. Third World Press, 1972.

Two Ways to Count to Ten. Illustrated by Susan Meddaugh. Holt, 1988.

Tower to Heaven. Illustrated by Jennifer Bent. Holt, 1991.

My One Good Nerve. John Wiley & Son, 1998.

Diakité, Baba Wagué

(1961–)

AUTHOR/ILLUSTRATOR

E-mail: ronnawague@juno.com

"The greatest influences in my life have come from traditional stories told by my mother and my grandmother. As children, we loved to listen to these stories. Stories are much more than just entertainment. I have always asserted that storytelling is a true way of learning. They give us encouragement and good morals. They teach us life skills, and educate us about our environment and the relationship between Man and Nature. They are basic to education in Africa.

"As one proverb says, 'Words must go from old mouths to new ears.' Storytelling is a gift to me from my elders and I simply want to pass this gift on to all children."

Diakité was born in Bamako, Mali, West Africa. His mother gave him her father's name of "Wagué," which means "A Man of Trust." He spent his early childhood with his grandmother in the village of Kassaro for his first education. There, he tended his uncles' sheep and helped in his grandmother's rice and peanut fields. His free time was spent with friends in the bush; catching lizards and protecting fields from monkeys.

Later Diakité moved to Bamako to be with his mother and to get formal schooling. He maintains his best education came from stories that were told him by his grandmother and mother about animals and the First People.

He grew up drawing, first for his own pleasure, then for schoolwork, and finally for part-time jobs. He first learned claywork, however, after meeting American artist Ronna Neuenschwander, and moving to Portland, Oregon in the United States in 1985. There he began using clay as his canvas.

His first solo exhibition was in 1988, and since then he has been shown in group and solo shows throughout the United States. His work has received critical acclaim in the Portland area publications as well as international magazines such as *Ceramics Monthly*, *African Arts*, and *AFRIQUE/Etats Unis*. He has taught in the Oregon public school systems through the Art-in-Education program since 1989. He has traveled throughout the United States for author visits and workshops, including Washington State University, the Holter Museum of Art in Montana, the Los Angeles County Museum of Art, and the Smithsonian African Art Museum. He has been commissioned to create poster designs for a number of city-wide art festivals, and was honored to be chosen to create the artworks for recipients of the 1990 Governor's Arts Awards in Oregon. In 2001, Diakité created an 84 foot long mural and other artworks for Disney's Animal Kingdom Lodge in Orlando, Florida. Diakité is represented by Pulliam/Deffenbaugh Gallery of Portland, Oregon and Pacini Lubell Gallery in Seattle, Washington.

Scholastic Press published Wagué's first children's book, *The Hunterman and the Crocodile*, in 1997. It received a Coretta Scott King Honor Book Award. He has illustrated two children's books entitled *The Pot of Wisdom* and *Jamari's Drum* for Groundwood Books in 2001 and 2004 respectively. His most recent project was to illustrate a book written by his daughter, Penda Diakité, entitled *I Lost My Tooth in Africa*.

Diakité and his wife, artist Ronna Neuenschwander, have collaborated artistically on a number of projects, including an animated film, an award-winning documentary film of their lives, and a number of public art projects. They continue to return to Mali with their two daughters every other year for extended stays.

Diakité is in the process of building a cultural center (the Toguna Cultural Center) in Bamako, Mali to enable artists from other countries to live, meet, study, and collaborate with artists of Mali.

He lives in Portland, Oregon.

BIBLIOGRAPHY

The Hunterman and the Crocodile. Scholastic Press, 1997.
The Hatseller and the Monkeys. Scholastic Press, 1999.

The Pot of Wisdom: Ananse Stories. By Adwoa Badoe. Groundwood Books, 2001.

The Magic Gourd. Scholastic Press, 2003.

Jamari's Drum. By Eboni Bynum and Roland Jackson. Groundwood Books, 2004.

I Lost My Tooth in Africa. By Penda Diakité. Scholastic Press, 2006.

Dillon, Leo and Diane Dillon

(1933–)

ILLUSTRATORS

Leo Dillon:."I'm constantly surprised at how our work is melding more and more as the years go by. In the beginning it was a conceived plan for us to work in a particular style which we both could master. So, in reality, we were both working for 'someone else' in their style. Forty years ago there were techniques neither of us would attempt and somewhere along the line, one picked it up and the other followed, and back and forth."

Diane Dillon: "We never specialized. At the very beginning we had trouble with that. Art directors kept telling us we had too many styles in our portfolio and that they needed to know a specific style. We even split our portfolio up into three portfolios just so we could simplify. We thought that would be more acceptable with so many styles. Despite our refusal to specialize with technique or style, it's interesting that even when we thought we were doing things that people would never recognize, people would say, 'Oh, did you do such and such? It looks like your work'."

Born in Brooklyn, New York, Dillon attended the Parsons School of Design and the School of Visual Arts, both in New York City. He and his wife, Diane, work as a team, and all of the books listed below are illustrated by both of them. They met at Parsons, married shortly after graduating, and have illustrated book jackets, magazines, posters, and children's books. They received doctorates of Fine Arts in 1991 from the Parsons School of Design.

The Dillons began a freelancing career in 1958 and have done work for a variety of prestigious clients such as *Ladies Home Journal*, *Saturday Evening Post*, Bantam Books, Time/Life Books, *the*

Washington Post, Balantine Books, RCA Victor, Revlon Company, John F. Kennedy Center, and a variety of publishing houses.

Their books have won many honors and awards, including their Caldecott-winning books Why Mosquitoes Buzz in People's Ears and Ashanti to Zulu: African Traditions and Coretta Scott King Honor Books Aida, and The People Could Fly: American Black Folktales.

They have taught Materials and Techniques from 1969 to 1977 at the School of Visual Arts and also have been asked to speak at many engagements, including appearances at Cooper Union, the Illustrators Workshop, Princeton University of Utah, the University of Washington, Simmons College, Boston Public Library, Donnell Library and the Cleveland Public Library, among many others.

Leo and Diane Dillon have one son, Lee, and live in Brooklyn, New York.

BIBLIOGRAPHY

Hakon of Rogen's Saga. By Eric Christian Haugaard. Houghton Mifflin, 1964.

A Slave's Tale. By Eric Christian Haugaard. Houghton, Mifflin, 1965.

Claymore and Kilt. By Sorche Nic Leodhas. Holt, Rinehart, Winston, 1967.

Shamrock and Spear. By Francis Meredith Pilkington. Holt, Rinehart, Winston, 1968.

The Rider and His Horse. By Eric Christian Haugaard. Houghton Mifflin, 1968.

The Ring in the Prairie: A Shawnee Legend. By John Bierhorst. Dial, 1970.

The Untold Tale. By Eric Christian Haugaard. Houghton Mifflin, 1971.

The Search. By Murray/Thomas. Scholastic, 1971.

Honey, I Love. By Eloise Greenfield. Viking, 1972.

Behind the Back of the Mountain: Black Folktales from Southern Africa. By Verna Aardema. Dial, 1973.

Whirlwind is a Ghost Dancing. By Nataila Maree Belting. Dutton, 1974.

Songs and Stories from Uganda. By William Moses Serwadda. World Music Press, 1974.

The Third Gift. By Jan Carew. Little Brown, 1974.

Burning Star. By Eth Clifford. Houghton Mifflin, 1974.

The Hundred Penny Box. By Sharon Bell Mathis. Viking, 1975.

Song of the Boat. By Lorenz Graham. Crowell, 1975.

Why Mosquitoes Buzz in People's Ears. By Verna Aardema. Dial, 1976.

Ashanti to Zulu: African Traditions. By Margaret Musgrove. Dial, 1977.

Who's in Rabbit's House? By Verna Aardema. Dial, 1977.

Children of the Sun. By Jan Carew. Little Brown, 1980.

Two Pair of Shoes. By P.L. Travers, et al. Viking, 1980.

Listen Children: An Anthology of Black Literature. Edited by Dorothy S. Strickland. Bantam, 1982.

Brother to the Wind. By Mildred Pitts Walter. Lothrop, 1985.

The People Could Fly. By Virginia Hamilton. Knopf, 1985.

All in a Day. By Mitsumasa Anno. Hamish Hamilton (London), 1986.

The Porcelain Cat. By Michael Patrick Hearn. Little Brown, 1987.

Sing a Song of Popcorn. By B. deRegniers, et al. Scholastic, 1988.

The Color Wizard. By Barbara Brenner. Bantam Little Rooster, 1989.

Moses' Ark. By Bach/Exum. Delacourte, 1989.

The Tale of Mandarin Ducks. By Katherine Paterson. Lodestar, 1990.

Aida. By Leontyne Price. Harcourt Brace Jovanovich, 1990.

Miriam's Well. By Bach/Exum. Delacourte, 1991.

The Race of the Golden Apples. By Claire Martin. Dial, 1991.

Pish, Posh, Said Hieronymus Bosch. By Nancy Willard. Harcourt Brace Jovanovich, 1991.

Many Thousand Gone. By Virginia Hamilton. Knopf, 1992.

Northern Lullaby. By Nancy White Carlstrom. Putnam, 1992.

Switch on the Night. By Ray Bradbury. Knopf, 1992.

The Sorcerer's Apprentice. By Amy Willard. Scholastic/Blue Sky Press, 1993.

It's Kwanzaa Time. By Linda Goss, et al. Putnam, 1993.

What Am I? By N. N. Charles. Scholastic/Blue Sky Press, 1994.

Her Stories: African American Folktales, Fairy Tales and True Tales. By Virginia Hamilton. Scholastic/Blue Sky Press, 1995.

The Girl Who Dreamed Only Geese. By Howard Norman. Harcourt Brace, 1997.

To Everything There is a Season. By Leo & Diane Dillon. Scholastic/Blue Sky Press, 1997.

Wind Child. By Shirley Rousseau Murphy, et al. HarperCollins, 1999.

Switch on the Night (Reissued) By Ray Bradbury. Knopf, 2000.

The Girl Who Spun Gold. By Virginia Hamilton. Scholastic/Blue Sky Press, 2000.

20,000 Leagues Under the Sea. By Jules Verne. HarperCollins, 2000.

Mansa Musa. By Khephra Burns. Harcourt, 2001.

Two Little Trains. By Margaret Wise Brown. HarperCollins, 2001.

Rap A Tap Tap. By Leo and Diane Dillon. Scholastic/Blue Sky, 2002.

One Winter's Night. By John Herman, et al. Philomel, 2003.

Between Heaven and Earth. By Howard Norman. Harcourt, 2004.

Where Have You Been? By Margaret Wise Brown. HarperCollins, 2004.

Earth Mother. By Ellen Jackson, et al. Walker, 2005.

The People Could Fly: American Black Folktales. By Virginia Hamilton. Knopf, 2005.

Draper, Sharon M(ills)

(1952–)

AUTHOR

Web site: www.sharondraper.com

Draper was born in Cleveland, Ohio. She has spent twenty-five years teaching junior high school students how to appreciate the beauty of literature and how to communicate their ideas effectively. As a challenge from one of her students, she entered and won first prize in the 1991 *Ebony* magazine literary contest, for which she was awarded $5,000 and the publication of her short story, "One Small Torch."

Draper is a professional educator as well as an accomplished writer. She has been honored as the National Teacher of the Year, is a three-time winner of the Coretta Scott King Literary Award, and is a *New York Times* bestselling author. She was selected as Ohio's Outstanding High School Language Arts Educator, Ohio Teacher of the Year, and was chosen as a NCNW Excellence in Teaching Award winner. She received the Excellence in Education Award, is a Milken Family Foundation National educator Award winner, and was the Duncanson Artist-in-Residence for the Taft Museum. She is a YWCA Career Woman of Achievement, and is the recipient of the Dean's Award from Howard University School of Education, the Pepperdine University Distinguished Alumnus Award, the Marva Collins Education excellence Award, and the Governor's Educational Leadership Award. Last year she was named Ohio Pioneer in Education by the Ohio State Department of Education.

After becoming one of the first teachers in the nation to achieve National Board Certification in English/Language Arts, she was elected to the Board of Directors of the National Board for Professional Teaching Standards. She is currently on the Board of the National Commission on Teaching and America's Future. Her award-winning essay on education, "The Touch of a Teacher," was published by the National Governor's Association in What Governors Need to Know about Education.

Actively involved in encouraging and motivating all teachers and their students as well, she has worked all over the United States, as well as in Russia, Ghana, Togo, Kenya, Ethiopia, Bermuda, and Guam, spreading the word about the power of accomplished teaching and excellence in education.

Tears of a Tiger has received numerous awards, including the American Library Association/Coretta Scott King Genesis Award for an outstanding new book, and was also honored as an ALA Best Book for Young Adults. It has been recognized as one of the best of the year by the Children's Book Council, the New York City Library, Bank Street College, and the National Council for Social Studies. It was also named as Best of the Best by VOYA and the American Library Association as one of the top 100 books for young adults. *Forged by Fire*, the sequel to *Tears of a Tiger*, is the 1997 Coretta Scott King Award winner, as well as the winner of the ALA Best Book Award and the Parent's Choice Award. *Darkness Before Dawn*, the third book in the trilogy, is an ALA Top Ten Quick Pick, and has received the Children's Choice Award from the International Reading Association. *Romiette and Julio* is also listed as an ALA Best Book and has been selected by the International Reading Association as a 2000 Notable Book for a Global Society, and by the New York Public Library in their 2000 Books for the Teen Age. *Darkness Before Dawn* was named an IRA Young Adult Choice for 2003, and received the Buckeye Book Award for 2005. *Double Dutch* was honored as a Notable Social Studies Trade Book for Young People by the Children's Book Council as well as one of the top ten sports books for young adults for 2003 by the ALA, and Best of the Best for 2004. *The Battle of Jericho* is the 2004 Coretta Scott King Honor Book, one of the New York Public Library's Book for the Teen Age, and is one of the 2005 Young Adult Choice Books named by the International Reading Association. *We Beat the Street* is listed on the *New York Times* Bestseller List.

Draper spent more than thirty years teaching junior high and high school students how to appreciate the beauty of literature and how to communicate their ideas effectively. Each year her students received their own rewards in donning the class-designed "I Survived the Draper Paper" tee shirt commemorating the legendary research project that all her seniors had to complete to graduate.

She is an active member of the National Council of Teachers of English, the International Reading Association, Top Ladies of Distinction, and Links, Incorporated. Draper travels extensively and has been a guest on television and radio programs throughout the country, discussing issues of literature, reading, and education. She is an accomplished public speaker who addresses educational and literary groups of all ages, both nationally and internationally, with entertaining readings of her poetry and novels, as well as enlightening instructional presentations. She lives in Cincinnati, Ohio, with her husband and a golden retriever named Honey.

BIBLIOGRAPHY

Tears of a Tiger. Simon & Schuster, 1994.

Ziggy and the Black Dinosaurs. Illustrated by Jams Ransome. Just Us Books, 1994.

Ziggy and the Black Dinosaurs: Los in the Tunnel of Time. Illustrated by Michael Bryant. Just Us Books, 1996.

Forged by Fire. Simon & Schuster, 1997.

Ziggy and the Black Dinosaurs: Shadows of Caesar's Creek. Illustrated by James Ransome. Just Us Books, 1997.

Romiette and Julio. Illustrated by Adam Lowenbein. Simon & Schuster, 1999.

Darkness Before Dawn. Simon & Schuster, 2001.

Double Dutch. Simon & Schuster, 2002.

The Battle of Jericho. Simon & Schuster, 2003.

We Beat the Street. Dutton, 2005.

Copper Sun. Simon & Schuster, 2006.

Ziggy and the Black Dinosaurs: The Space Mission Mystery. Illustrated by Jesse Joshua Watson. Aladdin Books, 2006.

Dunbar, Paul Laurence

(1872–1906)

POET

Web site: www.dunbarsite.org

"Little brown baby wif' spa'klin' eyes,
Who's pappy's darlin' an who is pappy's chile? ..."

Although he preferred writing in standard English, Paul Laurence Dunbar was best known for his poetry in dialect. He was born in Dayton, Ohio on June 27, 1872. His widowed mother, an ex-slave, married Joshua Dunbar, who died when Paul was twelve years old. His mother could read and write and encouraged young Paul with his writing. He attended Dayton public schools. At Central High School, he had great success with his peers and teachers. He was a member of the school's literary society and wrote for the school paper, editing the paper in his senior year. He wrote his first poem at age six and gave his first public recital at age nine. Dunbar's first published work came in a newspaper put out by his high school friends, Wilbur and Orville Wright, who owned a printing plant. The Wright brothers later invested in the *Dayton Tattler*, a newspaper aimed at the Black community and edited by Dunbar. He kept a lifelong friendship with the Wrights and was also closely associated with Frederick Douglass and Booker T. Washington.

Dunbar worked as an elevator operator and a courthouse messenger and, while working at the Chicago World's Fair in 1893, he met Frederick Douglass, the commissioner of the Haitian exhibit, who hired him as a clerical assistant.

With the help of many White friends and the "Introduction" written by the leading literary critic William Dean Howells to his third collection of poems, *Lyrics of Lowly Life*, Dunbar achieved wide recognition. Tuskegee University's song was among his many works. In spite of his personal evaluation of his work, his dialect poetry is considered his best.

The poet married schoolteacher Alice Ruth Moore in 1898; the marriage ended in separation in 1902.

Dunbar contracted tuberculosis when he was almost thirty. He tried various cures, alcohol being one of them, and he became addicted.

The Dunbar House at 219 North Summit Street in Dayton, Ohio, which the poet shared with his mother in his last days, has been maintained as a state memorial by the Ohio Historical Society.

He was the first African American poet to garner national critical acclaim.

BIBLIOGRAPHY

Complete Poems of Paul Laurence Dunbar. With an introduction to *Lyrics of Lowly Life* by W.D. Howells. Dodd, 1914.

Little Brown Baby. Illustrated by E. Berry. Edited by Bertha Rogers. Dod, 1940.

Oak and Ivy. Reprint Services Corporation, 1985.

Lyrics of Lowly Life (Paperback). Beaufort Books, 1992.

The Collected Poetry of Paul Laurence Dunbar. Editor: Joanne M. Braxton. (Paperback) University of Virginia Press, 1993.

Howdy Honey Howdy (Paperback). Ams Press. Reprint Edition, 1997.

Jump Back Honey. Hyperion, 1999.

In His Own Voice: Dramatic and Other Uncollected Works (Paperback). Ohio University Press, 2002.

The Sport of the Gods: And Other Essential Writings (Paperback). Modern Library Classics, 2005.

The Heart of Happy Hollow (Paperback). Ayer Company Publishing, 1904, 2005.

The Negro Problem (Classics in Black Studies) (Paperback) Indy Publishing Company, 2005.

Duncan, Alice Faye

(1967–)

AUTHOR

Duncan, an only child, was born and reared and still lives in the city of Memphis, Tennessee. Visiting museums and watching movies are her favorite pastimes. Music, art, and books provide her with the inspiration to write. While in the tenth grade, Duncan discovered playwright Lorraine Hansberry's memoirs and short stories by author Toni Cade Bambara. She was so taken with Bambara's characters and Hansberry's passion for life that she tried her hand at creating tales. Her poetry, essays, and plays won several local and state student contests.

Duncan attended the University of Memphis and with encouragement and instruction from several of her professors, she began writing profile stories and record reviews for a music magazine called the *Memphis Star.*

In 1992, Duncan enrolled in a children's literature class to help her with her new job as a children's librarian. This new world of literature captured her attention and she soon wrote a children's book, *Willie Jerome*, a tribute to kids who know to follow their own dreams. Duncan serves as a school librarian and motivational "entertainer" for youth and adults.

Duncan lives in Memphis, Tennessee.

BIBLIOGRAPHY

The National Civil Rights Museum Celebrates Everyday People. BridgeWater, 1994.

Willie Jerome. Illustrated by Tyrone Geter. Macmillan, 1995.

Miss Viola & Uncle Ed Lee. Illustrated by Monica Stewart. Simon & Schuster, 1998.

Christmas Soup. By Alice Faye Duncan and Phyllis Dooley. Illustrated by Jan Spivey Gilchrist. Zonder Kidz, 2005.

Ellis, Veronica F.

(1950–)

AUTHOR

E-mail: vfellis@msn.com

"I always stress that teachers include multicultural children's books in the literature they present to students. American society is a mosaic of different cultures. Children must learn to understand the differences in people. The knowledge they gain from reading quality multicultural literature will ensure that understanding."

Ellis is a native of Liberia, West Africa. She received a bachelor of arts degree in English from Boston University in 1972 and a master's degree in education from Northeastern University in 1974. She has taught African culture and English from junior high school to the college level. For ten years, she was a reading-textbook editor with the Houghton Mifflin publishing company in Boston, Massachusetts.

She has taught writing at Boston University and multicultural children's literature at Wheelock College, also in Boston. She was a consultant/instructor for the Children's Literature In-Service Program from 1990 to 1992, sponsored by the University of Massachusetts Davis Foundation and the Foundation for Children's Books in Massachusetts. She is adjunct professor teaching communication writing courses at the College of Communication, Boston University. Ellis has written several theme books to accompany the Macmillan Reading Series and the Houghton Mifflin Readers.

Ellis is a board member of the Massachusetts Youth Teenage Unemployment Reduction Network (MY TURN), Inc. In 1990, she was recognized as a Distinguished Role Model in Brockton, Massachusetts, where she lives with her husband and two children.

BIBLIOGRAPHY

Afro-Bets First Book About Africa. Illustrated by George Ford. Just Us Books, 1990.

Book of Black Heroes: Great Women in the Struggle. Volume 2. With Toyomi Igus and Valerie Wilson Wesley. Just Us Books, 1991.

Land of the Four Winds. Illustrated by Sylvia Walker. Just Us Books, 1993.

Wynton Marsalis.. Raintree Steck-Vaughn, 1997.

Elster, Jean Alicia

(1953–)

AUTHOR

"I try to address themes common to the urban experience in ways that are entertaining as well as educational for both child and parent."

Educated at the University of Michigan where she received a bachelor of arts degree in English and at the University of Detroit School of Law where she received her juris doctor degree, Elster is the author of the children's book series "Joe Joe in the City," published by Judson Press. The first volume in that series, *Just Call Me Joe Joe*, was released in October 2001 and is in its second printing. She was awarded the 2002 Governors' Emerging Artist Award by ArtServe Michigan in recognition of the series, *I'll Do the Right Thing* and was awarded the 2004 Atlanta Daily World Atlanta Choice Award in the category of children's books.

A professional writer, Elster has edited several other books including *The Death Penalty* and *The Outbreak of the Civil War* (Greenhaven Press, an imprint of the Gale Group, Inc., 2004 and 2003, respectively) and *Building Up Zion's Walls: Ministry for Empowering the African American Family* (Judson Press, 1999). In addition, her essays have appeared in national publications including *Ms., World Vision, Black Child*, and *Christian Science Sentinel* magazines. She also collaborated in the preparation of the manuscript for *Dear Mrs. Parks: A Dialog with Today's Youth*, by Rosa Parks (Lee and Low, 1996), which was honored with four awards including the *NAACP Image Award* and the *Teachers' Choice Award*.

In 2001, 2003, and 2005, in recognition of outstanding work, Elster was awarded residencies at the internationally acclaimed Ragdale Foundation in Lake Forest, Illinois. With these awards, she became one of a select group of artists-in-residence chosen annually by the foundation from across the United States and many other countries.

Elster lives in Detroit, Michigan, with her husband and two teenage children.

BIBLIOGRAPHY

Just Call Me Joe Joe. Judson Press, 2001.
I Have a Dream Too! Judson Press, 2002.
I'll Fly My Own Plane. Judson Press, 2002.
I'll Do the Right Thing. Judson Press, 2003.

Emecheta, Buchi

(Florence Onye)
(1944–)

AUTHOR

The author was born in Lagos, Nigeria. Emecheta displayed advanced intellectual ability at an early age and attended Methodist Girls' High School from age ten. After winning a scholarship to study in England, she followed her husband, by an arranged marriage, to London, and they later separated. Emecheta was left to support their five children. She eventually earned an honor's degree in sociology from London University. Her persistence in writing and submitting manuscripts resulted in the publication of a number of her articles in the *New Statesman*.

In 1978, the year she was recognized as the best Black British writer, Emecheta won the Jock Campbell New Statesman Award for Literature. In 1983, she was cited among the best young British writers. Since 1979, she has been a member of the Home Secretary's Advisory Council, and in 1982–1983 she served in the Arts Council of Great Britain.

Emecheta lives in Crouch End, London, England, where she works as a sociologist and a writer of historical novels.

BIBLIOGRAPHY
Titch the Cat. Illustrated by Thomas Joseph. Allison & Bushy, 1979.
Nowhere to Play. Illustrated by Peter Archer. Schocken, 1980.
The Moonlight's Bride. Braziller, 1983.
The Wrestling Match. Braziller, 1983.

English, Karen

(1947–)

AUTHOR

"A child who becomes a lover of books is blessed with a gift that money can't buy. I've always felt most excited about my students who were passionate about reading. I knew they would see more in life, understand more and experience the comfort and expanding perspective that books can give. It is up to us, as parents, teachers, and all adults who have some influence in a child's life to support and encourage the love of reading and books. Very early, about the time children learn to write, I became a writer. My mother called my ever expanding collection of stories The Miss Flouncy Stories. When I was in the sixth grade, I wrote a hundred page novel, written on both sides of loose leaf notebook paper. It was about a little girl who had to leave the city and move to the country. There were two things I found challenging in this first major writing endeavor. I had never been to the country, so I found description of scenery very difficult, to say the least. Further, I could not imagine my main character black. In my heart I made her black—or colored, as was the term in those days, but I gave her long blond hair and blue eyes. I felt vindicated because in the spring of my fifth grade a new student had entered the fourth grade at 42nd Street School. A Negro girl by the name of Linda Shannonh. Lo and behold, she had long blond hair and green eyes."

English was born in Vallejo, California in 1947. She grew up in Los Angeles, California with her mother, step-father, brother and sister. She received her BA in Psychology from California State University at Los Angeles as well as a teaching credential. Until recently, she taught second grade.

English has always been a lover of books. She can still remember the first book she got her hands on. It was one of those cheap Golden Books sold in the supermarket. She can still remember the colors and a unique fruity smell in the binding. Books became her friend. The only problem was, during that time there were no children's books that had Black characters, thus no Black characters with which to relate. English grew up relating to Ellen Tebbits, the main character of her favorite author, Beverly Cleary. She related to Caddie Woodlawn and Janey in *The Moffats* and Flossie Bobbsey in *The Bobbsey Twins.*

English continued writing, but not seriously, throughout teens and during college. But it wasn't until her youngest child was in high school that she attempted to take writing seriously and submit a children's book manuscript to a publisher. As her children were growing up, she'd had the opportunity to get into children's literature. This produced a passion in her that often kept her in the children's department of libraries or bookstores for hours. Many rejections later, she sold her first book, *Neeny Coming, Neeny Going*, to Bridgewater Books.

English feels blessed to be a writer. For her it makes life so much more interesting because she sees a story in almost everything.

English has won the Coretta Scott King Honor Award for *Francie*, a BABRA Award for *Francie*, the Parent Choice for *Francie*, and a Judy Lopez Award for *Francie*. She also won the Jane Addams Award for *Hot Day on Abbott Avenue*. She has membership in the Authors Guild, the Society of Children's Book Writers and Illustrators, the International Black Writers and Illustrators and the Muslim Writers and Islamic Writers Alliance.

She is the mother of four grown children and grandmother of one. She currently lives with her husband in Los Angeles.

BIBLIOGRAPHY

Big Wind Coming. Illustrated by Cedric Lucas. Albert Whitman & Company, 1996.

Neeny Coming, Neeny Going. Illustrated by Synthia Saint-James. Bridgewater, 1996.

Just Right Stew. Illustrated by Anna Rich. Boyds Mills Press, 1998.

Nadia's Hands. Illustrated by Anna Rich. Boyds Mills Press, 1999.

Francie. Farrar, Straus & Giroux, 1999.

Speak English for Us, Marisoi. Illustrated by Enrique O. Sanchez. Albert Whitman & Company, 2000.

Strawberry Moon. Farrar, Straus & Giroux, 2001.

Speak to Me and I Will Listen Between the Lines. Illustrated by Amy Bates. Farrar, Straus and Giroux, 2004.

Hot Day on Abbott Avenue. Illustrated by Javaka Steptoe. Clarion, 2005.

The Baby on the Way. Illustrated by Sean Qualls. Farrar, Straus & Giroux, 2005.

Epanya, Christian A(rthur Kingue)

(1956–)

ILLUSTRATOR

Epanya was born in Bonadoumbe-Douala, Cameroon, the second of six children. His family placed a strong value on reading, and his love of books influenced his desire to become an illustrator.

Epanya graduated from the Lycee du Manengouba at Nkongsamba with a baccalaureat Serie D in 1977, and in 1978 he attended the Universite de Yaounde, where he studied chemistry and biology. He traveled to France, where he attended the Ecole Emile Cohl art school from 1990 to 1992 and graduated with distinction. That same year, his work was selected at the Montreuil Children's Book Fair, and in 1993 his illustrations were selected at the Bologna Children's Book Fair, where he received the UNICEF (United Nations Children's Fund) Illustrator of the Year Award.

His artwork was exhibited at the Ninth District Library of Lyon, France, the Social Center and the Cultural Center of Venissieux, a suburb of Lyon, in 1994. In December 1994, UNICEF issued a greeting card with his illustration titled *The Sorcerer's Dance*.

Epanya is the father of two daughters and lives in Lyon, France, where he works as a freelance illustrator.

BIBLIOGRAPHY

Ganekwane and the Green Dragon. By Cortia Fourie. Whitman, 1994.
Why the Chameleon Never Hurries. By Christina Kessler. Boyds Mills, 1995.
Konte Chameleon Fine, Fine, Fine! By Christina Kessler. Boyds Mills, 1997.

Eskridge, Anne Elizabeth

(1949–)

AUTHOR

E-mail: annesk@ameritech.net

The author, born and reared in Chicago, Illinois, believes that writing has always been an integral part of her life. Observing the way teenagers behaved, talked, and thought provided her with many hours of material for stories. Growing up, she wanted to write stories about Black youth that reflected their personalities and, at the same time, to add a mystical/magical quality to her stories. Eskridge began taking writing seriously as a professional option when she started teaching writing for mass media at a vocational school in Detroit, Michigan. She has won numerous writing grants and has participated in a variety of writing workshops. A documentary *Black Communities After the Civil War: Echoes Across the Prairie* was produced by Films for the Humanities and Sciences in 1998.

One of Eskridge's works, *Brother Future*, was produced as a Wonderworks Family movie that aired in 1991 on the Public Broadcasting System (PBS). The movie's director won the Directors Guild of America Award, and the work won Eskridge the Communications Excellence to Black Audiences Award of Distinction from the World Institute of Black Communicators.

The Sanctuary, a children's book, was written during Eskridge's teaching experience and received excellent reviews in *Publisher's Weekly* and *School Library Journal*.

Eskridge lives in Detroit, Michigan.

BIBLIOGRAPHY

The Sanctuary. Cobblehill, 1994.
Slave Uprisings and Runaways: Fighting for Freedom and the Underground Railroad. Enslow Publishers Inc., 2004.

Evans, Freddi Williams

(1957–)

AUTHOR

E-mail: freddiwevans@aol.com

"Growing up among extended family members in my rural hometown of Madison, Mississippi enabled me to visit older relatives almost daily. Those visits were filled with stories of how their lives used to be. My writing grew out of a desire to share my family's history as well as the untold and 'undertold' stories of other African Americans."

Evans received a bachelor's degree in piano performance and psychology from Tougaloo College, Tougaloos, Mississippi, and a master's degree in Creative Arts Therapy with an emphasis in Music from Hahnemann University, Philadelphia, Pennsylvania. While at Tougaloo, she participated in a West African study-travel that enabled her to study the traditional music of Ghana. She returned to the continent twice as a Teacher Abroad Fulbright Scholar—to Zimbabwe in 1995 and to South Africa in 2000. Tours in several European countries and participation in the Japan Fulbright Memorial Teacher Fund Program are also included among her international experiences.

As an artist, therapist, educator, and administrator, Evans has worked with children of all ages and exceptionalities in public and private institutions. As a writer, she has edited two books, her articles have appeared in local newspapers, and her poems are published in several anthologies. She works full-time as an artist facilitator for a public school district.

Her first book for children, *A Bus of Our Own*, received several recognitions including: 2002 Notable Social Studies Trade Book for Young Children; 2002 Oppenheim Toy Portfolio Platinum Book

Award; 2002 Best Children's Books—Bank Street College of Education, New York; 2003 Young Hoosier Book Award Nominee—Association of Indiana Media Educators; 2003 Living the Dream Book Award—Manhattan Country School & P.S. 198, New York; and a 2004 Mississippi Library Association Juvenile Book Award.

Evans, a divorcee, has two children and resides in New Orleans.

BIBLIOGRAPHY

A Bus of Our Own. Albert Whitman & Company, 2001.

The Battle of New Orleans: The Drummer's Story. Pelican Publishing Company, 2005.

Evans, Shane

E-mail: sevans26@aol.com

Web site: www.shaneevans.com

Evans is an artist and illustrator who travels around the world sharing experiences, stories, and the gift of art and creative expression. Through his journeys in Africa, South America, Asia, Europe, the Caribbean, and the United States, Evans has assembled a unique slide presentation of international beauty that demonstrates artistic influences from around the world and communicates the wonders of humanity. His presentations are specifically tailored to each audience and combine storytelling, slide presentations and art workshops for people of all ages, cultures, ethnic groups, and backgrounds. Evans firmly believes in the education and creative development of all people. His presentations provide a stimulating and refreshing atmosphere in which to work.

Evans has shown his work in West Africa, Paris and the United States. He has done illustration, graphic design, and Web design and projects for many companies, working for *Rolling Stone* magazine, Hollywood Records and Hallmark Cards, Inc. He has illustrated numerous children's books which have been featured on *The Oprah Winfrey Show*, *The Today Show*, *NBA Inside Stuff*, *Reading Rainbow*, *Late Night with David Letterman*, and an animated short on the Disney Channel (*Shanna Show*). Evans was honored by First Lady Laura Bush at the 2002 National Book Festival and has received much acclaim within the children's literary field. His awards include The Boston Globe-Horn Book Award and the Orbis Pictus Award for Outstanding Nonfiction for Children.

BIBLIOGRAPHY

Shaq and the Beanstalk and Other Very Tall Tales. By Shaquille O'Neal. Hyperion/Jump at the Sun, 1999.

Osceola. Memories of a Sharecropper's Daughter. By Alan Govenor. Hyperion/Jump at the Sun, 2000.

Take It to the Hoop Magic Johnson. By Quiney Troupe. Hyperion/Jump at the Sun, 2000.

Down the Winding Road. By Angela Johnson. D.K. Publishing, 2000.

Feelings, Tom

(1933–2003)

ILLUSTRATOR

"When I am asked what kind of work I do, my answer is that I am a storyteller in picture form, who tries to reflect and interpret the lives and experiences of the people who gave me life. When I am asked who I am, I say I am an African who was born in America. Both answers connect me specifically with my past and present; therefore, I bring to my art a quality which is rooted in the culture of Africa and expanded by the experience of being Black in America."

Feelings was born and reared in Brooklyn, New York. He received a three-year scholarship to the Cartoonists and Illustrators School after high school. After serving in the United States Air Force (1953–1959), he attended New York's School of Visual Arts. His comic strip, *Tommy Traveler in the World of Negro History*, was a feature of Harlem's newspaper *New York Age*.

In 1964, he worked in Ghana for the Ghana Government Publishing Company. He returned to the United States two years later and began working on children's books on African and African American subjects. In his work for the Guyana government (1971–1974), he served as a consultant for the Guyanese Children's Book Division and taught Guyanese illustrators.

He illustrated *Moja Means One: Swahili Counting Book* and *Jambo Means Hello: Swahili Alphabet Book*, Caldecott Honor Books written by his former wife, Muriel. His illustrations have won the Coretta Scott King Award three times—in 1979 for *Something on My Mind*, by Nikki Grimes; in 1994 for *Soul Looks Back in Wonder*; and in 1996 for *The Middle Passage: White Ships, Black Cargo*—and honorable mention in 1982 for *Daydreamers* by Eloise Greenfield. Feelings was awarded a National Endowment for the Arts fellowship in 1982. He illustrated more than twenty books and, in addition to the above awards, also received the School of Visual Arts Outstanding Achievement Award and at least eight certificates of merit from the Society of Illustrators.

His paintings are in the private collections of many notable African Americans, including Maya Angelou, Roberta Flack, the late Alex Haley, and Cicely Tyson. In 1990, he was named artist-in-residence at the University of South Carolina, Columbia.

Feelings received an honorary degree of Doctor of Fine Arts from the School of Visual Arts in New York City in 1996 and the following year received an honorary doctorate of Humane Letters from John Jay College of Criminal Justice in New York City.

He retired from teaching at the University of South Carolina where he taught for five years to do freelance book illustrations full time. He spent twenty years researching and writing *The Middle Passage*, an epic depiction of the African slave trade.

Feelings died in 2003 in Mexico at the age of seventy.

BIBLIOGRAPHY

Bola and the Oba's Drummers. By Letta Schatz. McGraw-Hill, 1967.

Song of the Empty Bottles. By Osmond Molarsky. H.Z. Walck, 1968.

To Be A Slave. By Julius Lester. Dial, 1968.

The Tuesday Elephant. By Nancy Garfield. Crowell, 1968.

When the Stones Were Soft: East African Fireside Tales. By Eleanor Butler Heady. Funk & Wagnalls, 1968.

 Black Folktales. By Julius Lester. R.W. Baron, 1969.

Tales of Temba: Traditional African Stories. Edited by Kathleen Arnott. H.Z. Walck, 1969.

Zamani Goes to Market. By Muriel Feelings. Seabury, 1970. Houghton, 1979.

Moja Means One: Swahili Counting Book. By Muriel Feelings. Dial, 1971, 1976.

Black Pilgrimage. Lothrop, 1972.

Jambo Means Hello: Swahili Alphabet Book. By Muriel Feelings. Dial, 1974. Reprint, 1985.

Something on My Mind. By Nikki Grimes. Dial, 1978.

Daydreamers. By Eloise Greenfield. Dial, 1981.

Now Sheba Sings the Song. By Maya Angelou. Dial, 1987.

Tommy Traveler in the World of Black History. Black Butterfly, 1991.

Soul Looks Back in Wonder. Edited by Phyllis Fogelman. Dial, 1993.

The Middle Passage: White Ships, Black Cargo. Dial, 1995.

I Saw Your Face. By Kwame Dawes. Dial, 2005.

Ferguson, Amos

(1920–)

ILLUSTRATOR

Ferguson, who prefers to be called Mr. Amos Ferguson, was born in Exuma, the Bahamas. He was one of fourteen children, and his preacher father, who was also a carpenter, inspired his Bible reading. Ferguson left home as a teenager and moved to Nassau, where he polished furniture, learned to paint houses, and then decided to work as a house painter.

The subject matter of his paintings reflects his Bahamian background and origin. His paintings are rich with the colors depicting the flora and fauna of the Bahamas, and many display his deep religious bent and interest in Bible readings.

His exhibition at the Wadsworth Atheneum in Hartford, Connecticut, in 1985 traveled around the United States for two years. The Connecticut Public Television documentary on this island artist received an Emmy nomination. Ferguson's religious convictions are evident in his artwork, some of which is displayed at the Pompey Museum's permanent exhibition in the Bahamas.

He won a Coretta Scott King Honor Book Award in 1989 for his illustration of *Under the Sunday Tree*. During a brief 1978 visit, New Yorker Sukie Miller bought one of his paintings, the first in a series which led to the 1985 Wadsworth Atheneum exhibition "Paint By Mr. Amos Ferguson." He is now well represented in significant collections worldwide.

Ferguson was honored in 2005 in the Bahamas by having the name of the street on which he has lived for years (Exuma Street) changed to Amos Ferguson Street.

His work was part of the National Black Fine Arts Show to be displayed in Soho, New York, in 2005. He is one of fourteen

Bahamian artists whose work was represented at the well-respected exhibition.

He is married and lives in Nassau, Bahamas.

BIBLIOGRAPHY

Under the Sunday Tree. By Eloise Greenfield. Harper, 1988.

Forché, Carolyn A.

AUTHOR

E-mail: carolynsquill@aol.com

Forché is a native Chicagoan, now residing in Houston, Texas. She has enjoyed an exciting career that spans a number of disciplines including social worker, journalist, presidential public affairs director and speechwriter, grant writer, and at present, her writing and editorial consulting service.

She received her education from St. John's Liberal Arts College in Annapolis, Maryland, and at Governor's State University in Chicago, Illinois. She initiated one of the first Black Adoption Agencies in Chicago, Homes Limited, under the auspices of the Woodlawn Community Development Corporation. This agency encouraged Black families to legally adopt the children they were rearing as unofficial parents, and promoted the adoption of Black children statewide. It received much positive media attention. She became the first woman and the first African American to be appointed U.S. Health & Human Services Director of Public Affairs and Freedom of Information Act for the six-state Midwest Region under the administration of President Jimmy Carter.

Her first book, *Colors Come From God ... Just Like Me*! is a best seller, with 25,000 copies sold and growing. It is a book encouraging children of all cultures to celebrate the beauty of their various skin colors, by celebrating all things God made with colors. This book received glowing reviews from publications across the country. Her current book is written to bring healing to children who have been sexually abused. She has received cover endorsements from national leaders, both religious and secular, for the content of this inspiring book on a very difficult subject for children. Like her *Colors* book, it is also Biblically inspired.

She is presently teaching writers how to get their books published through a series of writing workshops, and is editing a number of books that are being written by her students and other authors. She is also a frequent guest speaker at national writers' conferences.

BIBLIOGRAPHY

The Story of a Man Named Job. Self published, 1995.

Colors Come From God ... Just Like Me! Illustrated by Charles Cox. Abingdon Press, 1996.

That's Not Nice What You Did to Me. Illustrated by Elvin Breau. My Bestseller Publishing, 2005.

Ford, Bernette (Goldsen)

(1950–)

AUTHOR

Born in New York City, Ford recalls that she was a "dreamy child" with her head always buried in a book. She grew up on Long Island, the child of an interracial couple. Both parents were deeply involved in the civil rights movement; her mother, an African American, and her father, a child of Russian/Polish immigrants, instilled in her and her brother and sister a strong sense of identity and Black pride. She credits her cousin, the playwright, director, and actor Douglas Turner Ward—founder of the Negro Ensemble Company in the mid-1960s—with inspiring her to pursue a career in publishing. She remembers how proud she was in junior high school when he elected to display her review of one of the NEC's earliest productions on the theater's bulletin board for months.

After graduating from Connecticut College in 1972, Ford joined Random House as an editorial assistant in the children's division. It was during her seven-year tenure there that she became dedicated to her mass-market publishing philosophy—"to offer a large audience of very young children the best quality books at the lowest possible prices."

In 1979, Ford moved to Western Publishing Company/Golden Books as senior editor of Golden Press. The next step in Ford's career brought her in 1983 to Grosset & Dunlap, which had recently been acquired by G.P. Putnam's—that house's first venture into the juvenile mass-market arena. As editor-in-chief and later vp/associate publisher, she spent six years developing a reputation for publishing quality mass-market books, pop-ups, and novelty books. One of only a handful of African American children's book editors, she was the first to be named a vice president at a mainstream house.

Ford, who was vice president and editorial director of Cartwheel Books for the Very Young at Scholastic Inc., joined that company in 1989 to start up a mass-market imprint designed especially for preschoolers. The imprint grew to produce more than one hundred books a year, for an age range spanning babies to beginning readers. In summer 2001, Ford stepped down as editorial director, eventually leaving Scholastic in May 2002 to start her own company, College-Bridge Books, LLC, an independent packager of children's books, with an emphasis on multicultural books. Her first major project was a series of twenty-four African American easy-readers, the Just for You Books, created for Scholastic. A long-time children's book publishing professional, Bernette Ford still has a hard time thinking of herself as an author, although her new career path allows her more time to write.

Ford and her husband, illustrator George Ford, live in a one hundred-year-old house in Brooklyn, New York, and have one daughter who lives and works in the San Francisco Bay area.

BIBLIOGRAPHY

Bright Eyes, Brown Skin. By Bernette G. Ford and Cheryl Willis Hudson. Illustrated by George Ford. Just Us Books, 1990.

The Hunter Who Was King and Other African Tales (Retold). Illustrated by George Ford. Hyperion, 1994.

Hurry Up! A "Just for You!" Book. Illustrated by Jennifer Kindert. Scholastic. (A "Just for You" Book), 2003.

Don't Hit Me! A "Just for You!" Book. Illustrated by Gary Grier. Scholastic. (A "Just for You" Book), 2004.

First Snow. Illustrated by Sebastien Braun. Holiday House, Fall 2005.

Ford, George Jr.

(1926–)

ILLUSTRATOR

"For me—an illustrator whose subject is the portrayal of black life and black children—it's important to use the text as a beginning, an opportunity to arouse in myself and express to my readers those human qualities that have helped us to survive this long—those qualities that are positive, full of energy and life force and enthusiasm. I hope these things come out automatically in the work, and inspire and uplift the young people who read the books ...."

George was born in Brooklyn, New York, the first child of Viola and George Ford, Sr., immigrants from Barbados in the West Indies. His father was a carpenter, as well as a bishop in the African Orthodox Church, and his mother worked as a domestic. George spent part of his early childhood in Barbados. His vivid memories include those of his maternal grandmother, Louisa Pilgrim, who drew amazing portraits of friends and family on slate with chalk. He credits her with inspiring him to become an artist, and his sister Marguerita, a children's librarian, with encouraging him to illustrate children's books. The artist grew up in Bedford-Stuyvesant and studied in New York City at the Cooper Union, Pratt Institute, the Art Student's League, the School of Visual Arts, and was graduated from the College of the City of New York with a BS in Education. His drawings and paintings appeared in *Harper's* magazine and the Brooklyn Museum, including the 1971 exhibition, "Black Artists in Graphic Communications." Ford was art director at Eden Advertising in New York City and design director of *Black Theater* magazine, published by The New Lafayette Theater. He is married to children's book editor Bernette G. Ford, and they have one daughter, Olivia, who lives and works in the San Francisco Bay area. They live in a one hundred-year-old house in Brooklyn, New York.

A veteran artist who has a wealth of experience in publishing, Ford has illustrated more than thirty books for children and has received numerous awards and honors for his work, including the first Coretta Scott King Award for Illustration in 1974 (presented annually by the American Library Association to books of outstanding and inspirational value to African American children) for the biography *Ray Charles*, written by Sharon Bell Mathis, as well as the Jane Addams Peace Award for *Paul Robeson*, written by Eloise Greenfield.

The artist has said of his work: "The object of the drawing is not just to elicit admiration for one's technique, or admiration of any kind. Experimentation with techniques is valuable in the execution of a work, and in tapping one's intuition, one's own creativity. But technique is not my primary aim. As an illustrator whose subject is the portrayal of black life and black children, I feel the content and the emotion in the work are far more important than stylistic innovation or anything of that sort. I strive to touch my readers at an emotional level, and thereby change their lives."

BIBLIOGRAPHY

Walk On. By Mel Williamson and George Ford, Jr. Third Press, 1972.

Ray Charles. By Sharon Bell Mathis. HarperCollins, 1973.

Ego Tripping and Other Poems for Young People. By Nikki Giovanni. Lawrence Hill, 1974.

Paul Robeson. By Eloise Greenfield. HarperCollins, 1975.

Far Eastern Beginnings. By Olivia Vlahos. Viking, 1976.

The Best Time of Day. By Valerie Flournoy. Random House, 1978.

Baby's First Picture Book. Random House, 1979.

Darlene. By Eloise Greenfield. Methuen, 1980.

Afro-Bets First Book About Africa. By Veronica Freeman Ellis. Just Us Books, 1989.

Bright Eyes, Brown Skin. By Cheryl Willis Hudson and Bernette G. Ford. Just Us Books, 1990.

Jamal's Busy Day. By Wade Hudson. Just Us Books, 1991.

Good Morning, Baby. By Cheryl Willis Hudson. Scholastic/Just Us Books, 1992.

Good Night, Baby. By Cheryl Willis Hudson. Scholastic/Just Us Books, 1992.

Willie's Wonderful Pet. By Mel Cebulash. Hello Reader/Scholastic, 1993.

The Hunter Who Was King and Other African Tales. Retold by Bernette G. Ford. Hyperion, 1994.

Animal Sounds for Baby. By Cheryl Willis Hudson. Scholastic/Just Us Books, 1995.

Let's Count, Baby. By Cheryl Willis Hudson. Scholastic/Just Us Books, 1995.

The Story of Ruby Bridges. By Robert Coles. Scholastic Press, 1995.

Baby Jesus, Like My Brother. By Margery Wheeler Brown. Just Us Books, 1995.

Wild, Wild Hair. By Nikki Grimes. Hello Reader/Scholastic, 1996.

Hanging Out With Mom. By Sonia Black. Hello Reader/Scholastic, 2000.

Martin Luther King: Man of Peace. By Garnet Jackson. Hello Reader/Scholastic, 2001.

Franklin, Harold L(eroy)

Chikuyo Alimayo

(1934–)

AUTHOR/ILLUSTRATOR/FILMMAKER

E-mail: HaroldLFranklin@aol.com

Franklin was born in Mobile, Alabama, an only child. His childhood creative expression began with art, for which he won numerous awards. Upon graduating from high school, he was awarded a full scholarship to the Philadelphia College of Art, where he was graduated with honors. He also served in the United States Army, assigned to special services. His award-winning design of Fort Eustis's newspaper masthead was used for many years after he left the Army. He has chosen the African name of Chikuyo Alimayo but publishes under the name of Harold L. Franklin.

Franklin is a graphic design specialist for the city of Philadelphia. In addition to his full-time position, he has done freelance artwork for many local and national publications, including the *Philadelphia Inquirer* and the *New York Times* newspapers and *Business Week* magazine.

He illustrated the award-winning children's book *Boss Cat*, written by Kristin Hunter Lattany, and has also written, illustrated, and published three books of his own. *Once Around the Track* was developed into a motion picture, which he filmed, directed, and edited and for which he composed the music score. It has been broadcast on several Public Broadcasting System (PBS) stations.

Franklin lives in Philadelphia.

BIBLIOGRAPHY

Which Way to Go. EKO, 1969.

Boss Cat. By Kristin Hunter. Scribner, 1971.

A Garden on Cement. EKO, 1973.

Once Around the Track. EKO, 1974.

A Trip Back to Elmwood. EKO, 1991.

Freeman-Hines, Laura

(1959–)

ILLUSTRATOR

Web site: www.lfreemanart.com

*"The importance of showing children from diverse ethnicities in my illustra-
tions simply as a matter of fact, whether pertaining to the story or not, seems
self-evident to me. In A Wild Cowboy and its successor A Brave Spaceboy ,I
created an interracial family at the center of the story. It's something I can
relate to. Although the FAMILIES race is never mentioned or alluded to by the
author, it just seemed to fit perfectly. So many cowboys were African American, and Chinese Americans played an important part in the expansion of our
country.*

*I am fortunate in that I've known since I was five that I wanted to illustrate
children's books. Although I did get sidetracked for a few years I managed to
eventually get back on track."*

Laura was born and still lives in New York City with her husband
and their two children. She received her BFA from the School of
Visual Arts in 1981 and began her career as a conceptual illustrator
for various editorial clients, some of which include: the *New York
Times Book Review*, the *National Law Journal*, and *New York*
magazine. There was a long stint as a computer artist for Polo/Ralph
Lauren, where she picked up the skills to make the seamless transi-
tion from traditional media to using the computer programs Painter
and PhotoShop for her illustrations.

BIBLIOGRAPHY

Babies, All You Need To Know. By Deborah Heligman. National Geographic
Children's Books, 2002.
Jazz Baby. By Carole Boston Weatherford. Lee & Low Books, 2002.

A Wild Cowboy. By Dana Kessimakis Smith. Hyperion/Jump at the Sun, 2004.

A Brave Spaceboy. By Dana Kessimakis Smith. Hyperion/Jump at the Sun, 2005.

Gilchrist, Jan Spivey

(1949–)

AUTHOR/ILLUSTRATOR

"As in over twenty years of fine art works having the same philosophy, I wish to always portray a positive and sensitive image for all children, especially the African American children."

Gilchrist was born in Chicago, Illinois. She obtained her bachelor of science degree in art education at Eastern Illinois University in 1973 and her master of arts degree in painting from the University of Northern Iowa in 1979. In 1990, she received the Coretta Scott King Award for her illustrations in *Nathaniel Talking* by Eloise Greenfield. Her illustrations for another Greenfield book, *Night on Neighborhood Street*, won her a Coretta Scott King Honor Book Award in 1992, as well as the Distinguished Alumni Award from Eastern Illinois University, also in 1992. *Life Ev'ry Voice and Sing* received a starred review in *Booklist*.

In 1985, Gilchrist received the first award given by the National Academic Artists association. Her artwork has won five Purchase Awards from the DuSable Museum of African American History in Chicago, Illinois. She is an honorary member of Alpha Kappa Alpha sorority and a member of Phi Delta Kappa.

Jan Spivey Gilchrist's career as a fine artist and illustrator has spanned over a quarter of a century. Her large paintings and pencil drawings have been exhibited extensively throughout the United States and in Canada. Her illustrations appeared for years in textbooks for adults and children.

Gilchrist's artwork is held in many collections, both public and private. Her exhibitions include The Poet: Portrait of Eloise Greenfield at the Anacostia Museum of the Smithsonian Museum, Washington, D.C., a one-person exhibition at the Art Institute of

Chicago, St. Louis Museum of Art, Museum of the National Center of African American Artists, Boston, Ward-Nasse Gallery, New York. Group exhibitions include the National Museum of Women's Artists, Washington, D.C., California Museum of African American Artists, Los Angeles, Del Bello Gallery, Toronto, Catherine Lorillard Wolfe National Exhibitions, New York.

Gilchrist was commissioned in February, 2004 to produce seven paintings for Oxygen Television to run as an African American History Month segment, entitled "Everybody's History." Her paintings were accompanied by words and music and ran throughout each day for the entire month.

Jan Spivey Gilchrist travels annually throughout the United States and Europe. Outstanding features and reviews of her work have appeared in the *New York Times, Boston Globe, Chicago Defender, Washington Post, Chicago Tribune, L.A. Times, U.S.A. Today, Chicago Sun-Times* (Kup's Column) and *Ebony* magazine, as well as television and radio.

She holds a PhD in English, an MFA in Writing, an MA in Painting, and a BS Degree in Art Education.

Gilchrist was inducted into the *International Hall of Fame for Writers of African Descent* in October of 2000. She was inducted into the *Society of Illustrators* in 2001. In 2004 the Park Forest Illinois Public Library named a room in her honor. In 1992 Eastern Illinois University bestowed on her its highest honor, that of Distinguished Alumni, for her contributions to children's literature. In 1990, she joined a long line of historical women as an Honorary Member of Alpha Kappa Alpha Sorority. The 1998 Chicago Black Book fair named Gilchrist Illustrator of the Year. She is a member of the Midland Authors and the Society of Children's Book Writers and Illustrators. She teaches Children's Literature at National Louis University.

Gilchrist is the mother of an adult daughter and a young son. Her husband, Dr. Kelvin Gilchrist, is both her literary agent and her strongest supporter. They live in Olympia Fields, Illinois.

BIBLIOGRAPHY

Children of Long Ago. By Lessie Jones Little. Philomel, 1988.

Nathaniel Talking. By Eloise Greenfield. Black Butterfly, 1989.

Big Friend, Little Friend. By Eloise Greenfield. Black Butterfly, 1991.

Everett Anderson's Christmas Coming. By Lucille Clifton. Holt, 1991.

First Pink Light. By Eloise Greenfield. Black Butterfly, 1991.

I Make Music. By Eloise Greenfield. Black Butterfly, 1991.

My Daddy and I. By Eloise Greenfield. Black Butterfly, 1991.

My Doll, Keshia. By Eloise Greenfield. Black Butterfly, 1991.

Night on Neighborhood Street. By Eloise Greenfield. Dial, 1991.

Red Dog, Blue Fly. By Sharon Bell Mathis. Viking, 1991.

Aaron and Gayla's Alphabet Book. By Eloise Greenfield. Black Butterfly, 1992.

Aaron and Gayla's Counting Book. By Eloise Greenfield. Black Butterfly, 1992.

Indigo and Moonlight Gold. Black Butterfly, 1992.

Lisa's Daddy and Daughter Day. By Eloise Greenfield. Black Butterfly, 1991, Sundance, 1993.

William and the Good Old Days. By Eloise Greenfield. HarperCollins, 1993.

Baby. By Monica Greenfield. HarperCollins, 1994.

On My Horse. By Eloise Greenfield. HarperCollins, 1994, 1995.

Sweet Baby Coming. By Eloise Greenfield. HarperCollins, 1994.

Honey, I Love. By Eloise Greenfield. HarperCollins, 1995.

Lift Ev'ry Voice and Sing. By James Weldon Johnson. Scholastic, 1995.

Recycling Dump. By Andrea Butler. Good Year Books, 1995.

Sharing Danny's Dad. By Angela Shelf Medearis. HarperCollins, 1995.

Mimi's Tutu. By Tynia Thomassie. Scholastic, 1996.

Waiting for Christmas. By Monica Greenfield. Scholastic, 1996.

For the Love of the Game: Michael Jordan and Me. By Eloise Greenfield. HarperCollins, 1997.

Kia Tanisha. By Eloise Greenfield. HarperCollins, 1997.

Kia Tanisha Drives Her Car. By Eloise Greenfield. HarperCollins, 1997.

Singing Down the Rain. By Joy Cowley. HarperCollins, 1997. Madelia. Dial, 1997.

When The Horses Ride By. By Eloise Greenfield. Lee & Low, 2006.

Graham, Lorenz (Bell)

(1902–1989)

AUTHOR

E-mail: grahambooks@aol.com

Web site: www.grahambooks.com

Graham was born in New Orleans, Louisiana, and educated at the University of California, Los Angeles. He graduated from Virginia Union University, and attended the New York School of Social Work, and New York University. He taught at Monrovia College, Liberia, from 1925 to 1929.

The religious influence of his minister father is reflected in Graham's early work. His own trip to Liberia to teach in a missionary school heightened his awareness of the African people and inspired him to attempt to dispel some of the stereotypes he had read in books. This experience showed him that mainstream ideas about Africa were stereotypical and that few books existed describing Africans realistically. His first book, *How God Fix Jonah*, was followed by other Bible stories for young readers using the African speech patterns he had heard. It was his sister, author Shirley Graham, the widow of W.E.B. DuBois, who alerted publishers to her brother's stories.

Later, Graham dealt more directly with race relations in the United States with *South Town, North Town, Whose Town?* And *Return to South Town*. This series relates the continuing saga of a family in a small Southern town and later in an urban setting in the North, where racial tensions were even greater after World War II and the Korean War and the disparities between the races were quite pronounced.

Graham won a Coretta Scott King Honor Book Award in 1971, the Thomas Alva Edison Foundation Citation in 1956, the Charles W. Follett Award in 1958, the Southern California Council of Literature for Children and Young People Award in 1968, and first prize from Book World in 1969.

In 1987, at the age of 85, he was one of two invited authors from the United States to speak at a Symposium on Literature for Children and Young Readers at the University of the Western Cape, South Africa From that experience, he began a novel, *Cape Town*, which he did not finish.

Although he wrote primarily for the young, as did his sister, his reviewers often insisted that his suspenseful, realistic books are also appropriate for adults. Most of Graham's manuscripts are at the University of Minnesota, Minneapolis, and others are in the North Carolina Central University Library in Durham. Through his books, Graham promoted understanding and acceptance of all people. His primary message was that "people are people." He believed that when this concept is embraced, great strides can be made toward establishing social and racial justice.

He was married to author Ruth Morris-Graham, and they had five children.

BIBLIOGRAPHY

Tales of Momolu. Illustrated by Letterio Calapai. Reynal & Hitchcock, 1947.

I, Momolu. Illustrated by John Biggers. Crowell, 1966.

Whose Town? Crowell, 1969.

A Road Down in the Sea. Crowell, 1971.

David He No Fear. Illustrated by Ann Grifalconi. Crowell, 1971.

God Wash the World and Start Again. Crowell, 1971.

John Brown's Raid. Scholastic, 1972.

Song of the Boat. Illustrated by Leo and Diane Dillon. Crowell, 1975.

John Brown: A Cry for Freedom. Crowell, 1980.

Every Man Heart Lay Down. Illustrated by *Colleen Browning*. Crowell, 1970. (Reissued Boyds Mills Press, 1993)

How God Fix Jonah. Illustrated by Letterio Calapai. Reynal & Hitchcock, 1946. (Reissued Boyds Mills Press, 2000)

North Town. Crowell, 1965. (Reissued Boyds Mills Press, 2003)

South Town. Follett, 1958. (Reissued Boyds Mills Press, 2003)

Return to South Town. Crowell, 1976. (Reissued Boyds Mills Press, 2003)

Graham, Ruth Morris

(1901–1996)

AUTHOR

E-mail: grahambooks@aol.com

Web site: www.webgiraffe.com

Born in Charleston, South Carolina, the author was active in Christian work most of her life. Graham was educated at Nyack Missionary College in New York and studied at Shelton College and Hampton Institute in Virginia. She became a teacher and lecturer at the Boydton Institute and Virginia Seminary in Virginia.

Graham traveled widely, visiting more than fifty countries, and in 1969–1970 she made a six-month trip around the world, visiting missions and schools to counsel students, workers, and officials.

In 1975, Graham was awarded the Martin Luther King, Jr. Award by the Pacific Southwest Region, Disciples of Christ Church; in 1987, she received the Los Angeles Mayor's Certificate of Appreciation for Outstanding Service as president of Los Angeles's oldest Black organization of women, the Phys Art Lit Mor Club. She was also profiled in 1978 in *The World Who's Who of Women.*

She was married to Lorenz Graham, noted author, world traveler, and missionary to West Africa, who died in 1989. They had five children (one predeceased her), fifteen grandchildren, and sixteen great grandchildren. *Notable Americans*, a volume of books by the American Biographical Institute, profiled Graham in 1997. She was interviewed and appeared in the film "W.E.B. DuBois: A Biography in Four Voices," produced for television in 1995 by the Public Broadcasting System.

She was the sister-in-law of author Shirley Graham (Mrs. W.E.B. DuBois). Graham died in Claremont, California in 1996.

BIBLIOGRAPHY

The Happy Sound. Illustrated by Hans Zander. Follet, 1970.

Penny Savings Bank: The Story of Maggie L. Walker. Houghton, 1976.

Big Sister. Illustrated by Julie Downing. Houghton, 1981.

Graham (DuBois), Shirley (Lola)

(1907–1977)

AUTHOR

E-mail: grahambooks@aol.com

Graham was born in 1907, the daughter of the Reverend David A. Graham, a Methodist minister and his wife, the former Etta Bell. The family traveled frequently from one of Dr. Graham's pastoral assignments to another, and as a child she spent stretches of her youth in New Orleans, Spokane, and Colorado Springs.

Professionally known as Shirley Graham, she was born in Indianapolis, Indiana. She studied music in Paris, obtained a French certificate from the Sorbonne, and earned her bachelor's and master's degrees from Oberlin College. She also studied at Yale University Drama School and received an honorary doctorate of letters from the University of Massachusetts in 1973.

Graham's many talents are reflected in the variety of positions she held in her career, including head of the Fine Arts Department of Tennessee State College, director of the Chicago Federal Theater, director of the YWCA, field secretary for the National Association for the Advancement of Colored People (NAACP), director of Ghana Television, founding editor of *Freedomways* magazine, and English editor in 1968 of the Afro-Asian Writers Bureau in Bejing, China.

She received many awards, including Rosenwald and Guggenheim fellowships from Yale University Drama School for historical research and in 1950 the Julian Messner Award for *There Was Once a Slave*. She also wrote five additional adult books.

In the latter years of her life, Graham usually was viewed in the shadow of her late husband, the Black writer, cofounder of the

National Association for the Advancement of Colored People and controversial civil rights crusader W.E.B. DuBois.

However, she won fame on her own, many years before, as a biographer, playwright, composer, and stage director. She was a long-time supporter of leftist causes and organizations.

She married twice and had two sons (one died in his twenties) from her first marriage. W.E.B. DuBois became her second husband in 1951. Her brother was author Lorenz Graham. She died in Beijing, China, on March 27, 1977. A biography, *DuBois: A Pictorial Biography*, was published posthumously in 1978 by Johnson Publishing Company.

BIBLIOGRAPHY

Dr. George Washington Carver, Scientist. Illustrated by Elton C. Fax. Messner, 1944.

Paul Robeson, Citizen of the World. Messner, 1971.

There Once Was A Slave: The Heroic Story of Frederick Douglass. Messner, 1947.

The Story of Phyllis Wheatley. Illustrated by Robert Burns. Messner, 1949.

Jean Baptiste Pointe de Sable, Founder of Chicago. Messner, 1953.

The Story of Pocahontas. Grosset & Dunlap, 1953. Messner, 1955.

Booker T. Washington: Educator of Hand, Head and Heart. Messner, 1955.

His Day Is Marching On: A Memoir of W.E.B. DuBois. Lippincott, 1971.

Gamal Abdel Nasser, Son of the Nile. Third Press, 1972.

Julius K. Nyerere: Teacher of Africa. Messner, 1975.

DuBois: A Pictorial Biography. By Shirley Graham DuBois. Johnson, 1978.

Green, Jonathan

(1955–)

ILLUSTRATOR

E-mail: jonathangreen@jonathangreenstudios.com

Web site: www.jonathangreenstudios.com

"I believe that there is not enough literature available for Black children in churches, schools and daycare centers. In particular, I believe there are not enough children's books that adequately represent ethnic diversity, offering varieties of viewpoints that help shape young people's identities. I believe that ethnically and culturally relevant children's books with which children can readily identify help to bolster education and encourage healthy development in all children."

Green was born in Gardens Corner, South Carolina and graduated from the School of the Art Institute of Chicago in 1982. He holds an honorary doctoral degree from the University of South Carolina. In his art Green draws upon his own intimate personal experiences, steeped in the traditions of family, community and life of South Carolina's Gullah country. Each of his paintings is a testament to the motivating power of place.

As a result of his tremendous and prolific talent, Green's work has been embraced by collectors and critics throughout the world. His paintings can be found in major museum collections in South Carolina including the McKissick Museum, the Gibbes Museum of Art, and the Greenville Museum of Art. Among his numerous awards, Green has received recognition for Outstanding Contributions to the Arts in 1991 and the Martin Luther King, Jr., Humanitarian Award for the Arts in 1993. In 2004, Jonathan Green was the featured poster artist for the Spoleto Festival USA in Charleston, South Carolina.

Green's art itself serves as a powerful artistic catalyst. His work has been used in promoting programs for healthcare, education and community awareness worldwide. He lives and works in his private studio located in Naples, Florida.

BIBLIOGRAPHY

Father and Son. By Denizé Lauture. Philomel, 1992.

Noah. By Patricia A. Gauch. Philomel, 1994.

Cosby. By Dennis Haseley. Harcourt, 1996.

Amadeus. By Delores Nevils. Sandlapper Publishing, 2004.

Greenfield, Eloise (Glynn Little)

(1929–)

AUTHOR

"The problems that existed in children's literature when my first book was published more than twenty years ago still face us today. Therefore, my major goals for my work have changed very little since that time. I want to depict African American people in the variety and complexity in which we appear in real life. I want to counteract the stereotypes with which we are bombarded daily by books, films, and television and provide a mirror in which African American children can find themselves and their families. I write with the hope that my work will inspire in readers a love for themselves, a love for language and literature, and a commitment to humane values."

Greenfield was born Eloise Glynn Little in Parmele, North Carolina, to Weston Wilbur Little, Sr., and Lessie Jones Little, who collaborated in later years with her in writing two children's books.

Greenfield grew up in Washington, D.C., where she had moved with her family at the age of four months. From 1949 to 1971, she held a number of secretarial and administrative-assistant positions in the District of Columbia and federal governments. She began writing when she was in her twenties and had her first publication, a poem in the *Hartford Times*, in 1962. Her first children's book was published in 1972.

Now the author of more than thirty books, Greenfield continues to live in Washington. Under the auspices of the D.C. Commission on the Arts and Humanities, she has taught creative writing to children. She has received more than forty awards and citations for her books, including the first Carter G. Woodson Award, in 1974, from the National Council for Social Studies for *Rosa Parks*, the 1978 Coretta Scott King Award for *African Dream*, and the 1990

Recognition of Merit Award from the George G. Stone Center for Children's Books for *Honey, I Love.* In 1993, she received the Ninth Annual Celebration of Black Writing Lifetime Achievement Award from Moonstone, Incorporated.

She received an award for Excellence in Poetry for Children in 1997 from the National Council of Teachers of English given for her body of works and the 1997 Humanist of the Year award given by the Washington, D.C., Humanities Council. She is a member of the African American Writers Guild and the Authors Guild.

Greenfield won the Parents' Choice Silver Honor Award in 2001 for her book *I Can Draw a Weeposaur and Other Dinosaurs* and in 2003 *How They Got Over: African Americans and the Call of the Sea* was selected to be on the list of Best Children's Book of the Year by the Children's Book Committee, Bank Street College of Education.

She has published (not counting reissues) more than forty books.

Recent awards for her body of work have included a 1998 Hope S. Dean Award from the Foundation for Children's Literature; the 1999 Induction into the National Literary Hall of Fame for Writers of African Descent, and the 2003 Hurston/Wright Foundation's North Star Award for Lifetime Achievement.

Greenfield, who was formerly married to Robert J. Greenfield, has a son, Steven, a daughter, Monica, who also writes children's books, and four grandchildren. Greenfield lives in Washington, D.C.

BIBLIOGRAPHY

Bubbles. Illustrated by Eric Marlow. Drum & Spear, 1972.

Rosa Parks. Illustrated by Eric Marlow. Crowell, 1973.

She Come Bringing Me That Little Baby Girl. Illustrated by John Steptoe. Lippincott, 1974.

Sister. Illustrated by Moneta Barnett. Crowell, 1974.

First Pink Light. Illustrated by Moneta Barnett. Crowell, 1975. Black Butterfly (Illustrated by Jan Spivey Gilchrist), 1991.

Me and Neesie. Illustrated by Moneta Barnett. Crowell, 1975.

Paul Robeson. Illustrated by George Ford. Crowell, 1975.

Africa Dream. Illustrated by Carole Byard. HarperColllins, 1977.

Good News. Illustrated by Pat Cummings. Coward, 1977.

Mary McLeod Bethune. Illustrated by Jerry Pinkney. Crowell, 1977.

Honey, I Love and Other Love Poems. Illustrated by Leo and Diane Dillon. Crowell, 1978. HarperCollins (Illustrated by Jan Spivey Gilchrist), 1995.

I Can Do It by Myself. With Lessie Jones Little. Illustrated by Carole Byard. Crowell, 1978.

Talk About a Family. Illustrated by James Calvin. Lippincott, 1978.

Childtimes: A Three-Generation Memoir. With Lessie Jones Little. Illustrated by Jerry Pinkney. Harper, 1979.

Darlene. Illustrated by George Ford. Methuen, 1980.

Grandmama's Joy. Illustrated by Carole Byard. Philomel, 1980.

Alesia. With Alesia Revis. Illustrated by George Ford. Philomel, 1981.

Daydreamers. Illustrated by Tom Feelings. Dial, 1981.

Grandpa's Face. Illustrated by Floyd Cooper. Philomel, 1988.

Under the Sunday Tree. Illustrated by Amos Ferguson. Harper, 1988.

Nathaniel Talking. Illustrated by Jan Spivey Gilchrist. Black Butterfly, 1989.

Big Friend, Little Friend. Illustrated by Jan Spivey Gilchrist. Black Butterfly, 1991.

I Make Music. Illustrated by Jan Spivey Gilchrist. Black Butterfly, 1991.

Lisa's Daddy and Daughter Day. Illustrated by Jan Spivey Gilchrist. Black Butterfly, 1991. Sundance, 1993.

My Daddy and I. Illustrated by Jan Spivey Gilchrist. Black Butterfly, 1991.

My Doll, Keshia. Illustrated by Jan Spivey Gilchrist. Black Butterfly, 1991.

Night on Neighborhood Street. Illustrated by Jan Spivey Gilchrist. Dial, 1991.

Aaron and Gayla's Alphabet Book. Illustrated by Jan Spivey Gilchrist. Black Butterfly, 1992.

Aaron and Gayla's Counting Book. Illustrated by Jan Spivey Gilchrist. Black Butterfly, 1992.

Koya DeLaney and the Good Girl Blues. Scholastic, 1992.

William and the Good Old Days. Illustrated by Jan Spivey Gilchrist. Harper-Collins, 1993.

On My Horse. Illustrated by Jan Spivey Gilchrist. HarperCollins, 1994, 1995.

Sweet Baby Coming. Illustrated by Jan Spivey Gilchrist. HarperCollins, 1994.

Rosa Parks (New edition). Illustrated by Gil Ashby. HarperCollins, 1995.

For the Love of the Game: Michael Jordan and Me. Illustrated by Jan Spivey Gilchrist. HarperCollins, 1997.

Kia Tanisha. Illustrated by Jan Spivey Gilchrist. HarperCollins, 1997.

Kia Tanisha Drives Her Car. Illustrated by Jan Spivey Gilchrist. HarperCollins, 1997.

Easter Parade. Illustrated by Jan Spivey Gilchrist. Hyperion, 1998.

Angels. Illustrated by Jan Spivey Gilchrist. HarperCollins, 1999.

I Can Draw a Weeposaur and Other Dinosaurs. Illustrated by Jan Spivey Gilchrist. Greenwillow, 2001.

Honey, I Love. Illustrated by Jan Spivey Gilchrist. HarperCollins, 2003.

How They Got Over: African Americans and the Call of the Sea. Illustrated by Jan Spivey Gilchrist. HarperCollins, 2003.

In the Land of Words: New and Selected Poems. Illustrated by Jan Spivey Gilchrist. HarperCollins, 2004.

When The Horses Ride By. Illustrated by Jan Spivey Gilchrist. Lee & Low, 2006.

Greenfield, Monica

(1958–)

AUTHOR

Greenfield was born in Washington, D.C. As a child, she wrote poetry and loved to read and draw. She also loves music and has sung all of her life and hopes one day to combine the two careers.

Greenfield worked for many years as a secretary at Howard University, the Children's Defense Fund, and other organizations. She is the mother of teenage daughter, Kamaria, and is herself the daughter of the prominent children's author Eloise Greenfield.

Both books, *Baby* and *Waiting for Christmas* were selected to be listed on The Pick of the Lists by American Bookseller.

She lives in Washington, D.C.

BIBLIOGRAPHY

Baby. Illustrated by Jan Spivey Gilchrist. HarperCollins, 1994.

Waiting for Christmas. Illustrated by Jan Spivey Gilchrist. Scholastic, 1996.

Grimes, Nikki

(1950–)

AUTHOR

E-mail: info@nikkigrimes.com

Web site: www.nikkigrimes.com

"Life can be tough sometimes, especially if you're young. I know. When I was growing up, I had lots of problems, but praying helped me through them all. So, if something serious is bothering you, and you don't have anybody to talk to, I'd be honored to join you in praying about it.

"Is prayer magic? No. Does prayer change things? Not always. But prayer does change you on the inside so that you can deal with your problems better. That can make all the difference in the world."

Grimes was born in Harlem, New York. She has worked at different times as a secretary, a library assistant, a literary consultant, a children's-book editor, a photographer, and a radio producer/host. Grimes majored in English and studied African languages at Livingston College and Rutgers University. She received a Ford Foundation grant in 1974 that enabled her to spend a year in Tanzania collecting folk tales and poetry. Journalism, photography, and poetry writing have kept her busy since 1975. Her poetry often appears in anthologies of modern American poetry.

Her book *Growin'* was named a Child Study Association's Best Book in 1977. *Something on My Mind* was selected in 1978 as an American Library Association Notable Book, a Library of Congress Children's Book, a Coretta Scott King Honor Book for its illustrations by Tom Feelings, a *Saturday Review* Best Book of the Season, and the *Philadelphia Inquirer* Best Book of the Year. *Malcolm X: A Force for Change* was a 1993 Image Award finalist, and *Meet Danitra Brown* was a Coretta Scott King Honor Book for illustration in 1995, an American Library Association Notable Book in the same year and received several starred reviews. *C Is for City* was included in the 1995 New York Public Library list of Children's Books—100 Titles for Reading and Sharing. *Come Sunday* was named as an American Library Association Notable Book in the category of poetry for all ages in 1996. *Jazmin's Notebook* won a total of eight honors and awards including a Coretta Scott King Honor in 1998. Eleven honors and awards were given to Grimes' book *My Man Blue*. Among them, the book won the Bank Street College Children's Book of the Year.

From 1999 to 2004, the seventeen books she published during that time span won a total of thirty-nine selections, awards and honors.

An accomplished and widely anthologized poet of both children's and adult verse, Grimes has conducted poetry readings and lectures at international schools in Russia, China, Sweden and Tanzania, while short-term mission projects have taken her to Haiti.

In her spare time, she likes to make wearable-art-garments, beaded jewelry, and handmade cards.

Grimes lives in Corona, California.

BIBLIOGRAPHY

Growin'. Illustrated by Charles Lilly. Dial, 1977.

Something on My Mind. Illustrated by Tom Feelings. Dial, 1978.

Malcolm X: A Force for Change. Fawcett, 1992.

From a Child's Heart. Illustrated by Brenda Joysmith. Just Us Books, 1993.

Meet Danitra Brown. Illustrated by Floyd Cooper. Lothrop, 1994.

Come Sunday. Illustrated by Michael Bryant. Eerdmanns, 1996.

Wild. Wild Hair. Illustrated by George Ford. Scholastic, 1996.

It's Raining Laughter. Illustrated by Myles C. Pinkney. Dial, 1997.

A Dime A Dozen. Illustrated by Angelo. Dial, 1998.

Jazmin's Notebook. Dial, 1998.

My Man Blue. Illustrated by Jerome Lagarrigue. Dial, 1999.

At Break of Day. Illustrated by Paul Morin. Eerdmans, 1999.

Aneesa Lee and the Weaver's Gift. Illustrated by Ashley Bryan. Lothrop/HarperCollins, 1999.

Is It Far to Zanzibar? Illustrated by Betsy Bowen. Lothrop/HarperCollins, 2000.

Shoe Magic. Illustrated by Terry Widener. Orchard, 2001.

A Pocketful of Poems. Illustrated by Javaka Steptoe. Clarion, 2001.

Stepping Out with Grandma Mac. Illustrated by Angelo. Orchard, 2001.

C is for City. Illustrated by Pat Cummings. Boyds Mills, 2002.

When Daddy Prays. Illustrated by Tim Ladwig. Eerdmans, 2002.

Danitra Brown Leaves Town. Illustrated by Floyd Cooper. HarperCollins, 2002.

Bronx Masquerade. Dial Books, 2002.

Under the Christmas Tree. Illustrated by Kadir Nelson. HarperCollins, 2002.

Talkin' About Bessie: The Story of Aviator Elizabeth Coleman. Illustrated by E.B. Lewis. Orchard, 2002.

A Day with Daddy. Illustrated by Nicole Tadgell. Scholastic, 2004.

Tai Chi Morning Snapshots of China. Illustrated by Ed Young. Cricket Books, 2004.

What is Goodbye? Illustrated by Raul Colón. Hyperion, 2004.

Guirma, Frederic

AUTHOR/ ILLUSTRATOR

Guirma was born in Ouagadougou, Upper Volta, in West Africa. He claims Naba Koumdoum "ue," the eighth emperor of the Mois people in the fourteenth century, as one of his ancestors. Guirma attended an elementary school taught by the Sisters of Our Lady of Africa and later the Seminary of Padre. He received his bachelor's degree in France and a master's degree from Loyola University in Los Angeles, California.

He has been secretary of the French Embassy in Ghana and served as vice consul in Kumesi, Ghana. When Upper Volta (which is now known as Burkina Faso) became an independent nation in 1960, he was its first ambassador to the United Nations and Washington, D.C. He has also been senior political affairs officer at United Nations headquarters in New York City.

In his spare time, Guirma writes and paints. His book *Princess of the Full Moon*, which he wrote and illustrated, is based on folklore of Upper Volta.

BIBLIOGRAPHY
Princess of the Full Moon. Macmillan, 1970.
Tales of Mogho: African Stories from Upper Volta. Macmillan, 1971.

Gunning, Monica

(1930–)

AUTHOR

E-mail: monicagunning@aol.com

"I was born in Jamaica in the West Indies in a poor village with few opportunities. The Bible was the only book in our humble home. I grew up reading all the bible stories and loved the poetic verses of the Psalms. I think my love of poetry started then. I loved to recite poetry as a child in elementary school."

Gunning emigrated from the sandy beaches of the Caribbean to the United States to work and study. She became a teacher with the Los Angeles Unified School system and became interested in writing after taking a course in Children's Literature at Mount St. Mary's College in Los Angeles. She was encouraged by the author, Leo Politi and also by Myra Cohn Livingston under whom she studied poetry at U.C.L.A.

Gunning was graduated in 1948 from Mannings High School in Jamaica and then graduated in 1957 from City University of New York with a BSC in Education, minor in Spanish.

She attended U.C.L.A. extension classes for teaching methods in early childhood education during 1965 to 1969.

Between 1969 and 1971 Gunning attended Mt. St. Mary's College in Southern California and received a Master's in Education.

Fluent in Spanish, Gunning had studied at the University of Guadalajara during their summer sessions.

Among her many awards and recognitions, she received an Outstanding Elementary Teachers of America Award in 1973; a Who's Who in American Women Award in 1976 and in 1983, an Outstanding Church School Teachers Award.

She belongs to the Society of Children's Bookwriters and Illustrators and has been President of the Beverly Hills Toastmasters for two years.

Gunning has been anthologized in many publications.

She is the mother of two grown sons, Michael and Mark Gunning, and grandmother of four, Elon, Mark, Emma and Matthew Gunning.

Gunning resides in Laguna Niguel, California.

BIBLIOGRAPHY

Not A Copper Penny In Me House — Poems from the Caribbean. Boyds Mills Press, 1993.

Under the Breadfruit Tree — More Poems from the Caribbean. Boyds Mills Press, 1998.

A Shelter in Our Car. Children's Book Press, 2004.

America, My New Home — Poems on Coming to America. Boyds Mills Press, 2004.

Hamilton, Virginia (Esther)

(1936–2002)

AUTHOR

Hamilton was born in southern Ohio, Yellow Springs, where her maternal ancestors settled after the Civil War. John Rowe Townsend, in *Written for Children*, describes Virginia Hamilton as "the most subtle and interesting of today's Black writers for children." Hamilton's books have always centered on Black heritage and more personally on her own family history. Her themes go beyond family experiences, weaving mysticism, fantasy, and realism.

Hamilton received many major literary awards and much recognition for her children's books. *M.C. Higgins, the Great* won the 1975 Newbery Medal, the National Book Award, and the 1974 Boston Globe-Horn Book Award. *The Planet of Junior Brown* and *Sweet Whispers, Brother Rush* were also Newbery Honor Books, as was *In the Beginning: Creation Stories from Around the World*. Hamilton won the Coretta Scott King Award in 1983, 1986, and 1996, the latter for *Her Stories: African American Folktales, Fairy Tales and True Tales*, and Boston Globe-Horn Books Awards in 1974, 1983, and 1988. The Virginia Hamilton Lectureship on Minority Experiences in Children's Literature at Kent State University in Ohio was established in her honor. Her novel *The House of Dies Drear* was produced for television by the Public Broadcasting System (PBS).

The author of more than thirty books, mostly novels but also nonfiction and picture books, she won every major children's book award, including the Newbery Medal, the National Book Award, and the Boston Globe-Horn Book Award. She was given Hans Christian Andersen and Laura Ingalls Wilder awards for the body of her work and a MacArthur Fellowship for the quality of her mind.

Hamilton died on February 19, 2002. She was one of America's most honored writers of children's literature. She created memorable stories and positive images for children of color for thirty-five years.

She was married to poet Arnold Adoff and they had two children; a son, Jaime Levi Adoff living in Manhattan, and a daughter, Leigh Adoff-Zeise who lives in Berlin, Germany.

BIBLIOGRAPHY

Zeely. Macmillan, 1967.

The House of Dies Drear. Collier, 1968.

The Time-Ago Tales of Jadhu. Macmillan, 1968.

The Planet of Junior Brown. Macmillan, 1971.

Time-Ago Lost: More Tales of Jahdu. Illustrated by Ray Prather. Macmillan, 1973.

M.C. Higgins, the Great. Macmillan, 1974.

Paul Robeson: The Life and Times of a Free Black Man. Harper, 1974.

The Writing of W.E.B. DuBois. Edited by Virginia Hamilton. Crowell, 1975.

Arilla Sun Down. Greenwillow, 1976.

Jahdu. Illustrated by Jerry Pinkney. Greenwillow, 1976, 1980.

Alabama. Norton, 1977.

Dustland. Greenwillow, 1980.

Sweet Whispers, Brother Rush. Philomel, 1982.

A Little Love. Philomel, 1984.

Junius Over Far. Harper, 1985.

The People Could Fly: American Black Folktales. Illustrated by Leo and Diane Dillon. Knopf, 1985.

The Magical Adventures of Pretty Pearl. Harper (1983) 1986.

The Mystery of Drear House. Greenwillow, 1987.

A White Romance. Philomel, 1987.

Anthony Burns: The Defeat and Triumph of a Fugitive Slave. Knopf, 1988.

In the Beginning: Creation Stories from Around the World. Illustrated by Barry Moser. Harcourt, 1988.

Willie Bea and the Time the Martians Landed. Aladdin, 1989.

The Bells of Christmas. Illustrated by Lambert Davis. Harcourt, 1989.

Cousins. Philomel, 1990.

The Dark Way: Stories from the Spirit World. Illustrated by Lambert Davis. Harcourt, 1990.

The All Jadhu Storybook. Illustrated by Barry Moser. Dial, 1991.

Drylongso. Illustrated by Jerry Pinkney. Harcourt, 1992.

Many Thousand Gone: African Americans from Slavery to Freedom. Illustrated by Leo and Diane Dillon. Knopf, 1992.

Zeely. Illustrated by Symeon Shimin. Aladdin, 1993.

Plain City. Scholastic, 1993.

Her Stories: African American Folktales, Fairy Tales and True Tales. Scholastic, 1995.

Jaguarundi. Illustrated by Floyd Cooper. Scholastic, 1995.

When Birds Could Talk and Bats Could Sing: The Adventures of Broh Sparrow, Sis Wren and their Friends. Illustrated by Barry Moser. Blue Sky, 1996.

A Ring of Tricksters. Illustrated by Barry Moser. Blue Sky, 1997.

A Collection of 3 Newbery Medal Winners. Also E.L. Konigsburg and Robert C. O'Brien. Simon & Schuster, 1997.

Justice and Her Brothers. (Harcourt Brace, 1978). Scholastic, 1998.

The Gathering. Scholastic (1981), 1998.

Bluish. Blue Sky Press, 1999.

The Girl Who Spun Gold. Illustrated by Leo and Diane Dillon. Blue Sky Press, 2000.

Time Pieces: The Book of Times. Scholastic, 2002.

Bruh Rabbit and the Tar Baby Girl. Illustrated by James Ransome. Blue Sky Press, 2003.

Wee Winnie Witch's Skinny. Illustrated by Barry Moser (contributor). Blue Sky Press, 2004.

Hansen, Joyce (Viola)

(1942–)

AUTHOR

E-mail: joycevhansen@aol.com

Web site: www.joycehansen.com

"Some writers have recurring or favorite themes—mine are the importance of family, belief in self, maintaining a sense of hope and a determination to overcome obstacles, and being responsible for oneself and other living things."

Hansen was born in New York City, attended Pace University, and received her master's degree from New York University in 1978. She worked as an administrative assistant at Pace University until 1995 and as a teacher of remedial reading and English for the New York City Board of Education.

Her novel *The Gift Giver* received the Spirit of Detroit Award and was also designated a Notable Children's Trade Book in the field of social studies in 1980. In 1986, *Yellow Bird and Me* received the Parents Choice Award. Hansen received a Coretta Scott King Honor Book Award for *Which Way Freedom?* in 1987 and for *The Captive* in 1995.

Her memberships include the Society of Children's Book Writers and Illustrators and the Harlem Writers Guild.

Hansen won the 1998 Coretta Scott King Honor Book Award for *I Thought My Soul Would Rise and Fly: The Diary of Patsy, a Freed Girl. Breaking Ground, Breaking Silence: The Story of New York's African Burial Ground*, won the Coretta Scott King Honor Book Award in 1999.

She is married to Matthew Nelson and lives in West Columbia, South Carolina.

BIBLIOGRAPHY

The Gift Giver. Clarion, 1980.

Home Boy. Clarion, 1982.

Which Way Freedom? Walker, 1986.

Yellow Bird and Me. Clarion, 1986.

Out from This Place. Walker, 1988.

Between Two Fires. Watts, 1993.

The Captive. Scholastic, 1994.

I Thought My Soul Would Rise and Fly: The Diary of Patsy, a Freed Girl. Scholastic, 1997.

Women of Hope. Scholastic, 1998.

Breaking Ground, Breaking Silence. Henry Holt, 1998.

The Heart Calls Home. Walker and Company, 1999.

Bury Me Not in a Land of Slaves: African Americans in the Time of Reconstruction. Franklin Watts, 2000.

One True Friend. Clarion Books, 2001.

Freedom Roads: Searching for the Underground Railroad. Cricket Books, 2003.

African Princess: The Amazing Lives of Africa's Royal Women. Hyperion, 2004.

Hanson, Regina

(1944–)

AUTHOR

Hanson was born and raised in Jamaica, West Indies. During her childhood years, television had not yet reached the island. The family cherished books for entertainment as well as for education. After high school, she worked as a trainee journalist at the *Daily Gleaner* in Kingston, Jamaica. The family migrated to the United States in 1963.

In 1967, Hanson graduated from Hunter College in New York City, Phi Beta Kappa, with a BA in English. She then returned to Jamaica to teach high school English. In 1970, she moved to Boulder, Colorado, where she served on the staff of the University of Colorado until 1992. Hanson's first children's story appeared in *Highlights* and was voted Best of the Issue by the magazine, which named her Author of the Month for February 1995.

The Tangerine Tree, Hanson's first picture book, was reviewed in *School Library Journal, Kirkus Reviews, Booklist* and *Publishers Weekly*, all in the year of publication. Hanson's realistic, cultural fiction has been described as "both topical and universal." Her second picture book, *The Face at the Window*, received a pointer review in *Kirkus Reviews* in 1997 and was the winner of the Americas Award for Children's Literature.

Other awards for her work include the Magazine Merit Honor Certificate for Fiction from the Society of Children's Book Writers and Illustrators, Top Hand Awards from the Colorado Authors' League, and the *Skipping Stones* Award for multicultural and ecological awareness in children's literature.

Hansen lives in Boulder, Colorado.

BIBLIOGRAPHY

The Tangerine Tree. Illustrated by Harvey Stevenson. Clarion, 1995.
The Face at the Window. Illustrated by Linda Saport. Clarion, 1997.
A Season for Mangoes. Illustrated by Eric Velasquez. Clarion, 2005.

Harrington, Janice

(1956–)

AUTHOR

"I have always loved stories: reading them, listening to them, imagining myself inside them. I believe that all children have gifts although they may lose them, or doubt them, or never recognize their value. Children who love stories, who imagine stories of their own, or who secretly harbor a dream of one day being a writer—are gifted. Those are the children I want to reach through my writing and storytelling. I want them to know that they also have stories and that they can tell them."

Harrington has a Bachelor of Science in Education from the University of Nebraska at Lincoln and her Master of Arts in Library Science from the University of Iowa. An experienced youth services professional, she has worked as a teacher, school librarian, and director of public library children's departments. She has also taught school library administration, young adult literature, and children's literature at Indiana State University, and storytelling at the University of Illinois at Urbana-Champaign. As a storyteller, she has performed at the National Storytelling Festival, Jonesboro, Tennessee, the Annual Festival of Black Storytelling, and many other venues.

A poet, her work has appeared in numerous journals, including *The Beloit Poetry Journal, Field, Harvard Review, Prairie Schooner,* and *Southern Review.* Harrington's first children's book, *Going North*, was awarded the Ezra Jack Keats Award for new authors.

Married, Harrington is currently the children's services coordinator for the Champaign Public Library and lives in Champaign, Illinois.

BIBLIOGRAPHY

Going North. Illustrated by Jerome Lagarrigue. Farrar, Straus, Giroux, 2004.
Chicken Chasing Queen of Lamar County. Farrar, Straus, Giroux, scheduled 2007.

Hart, Ayanna (Kai)

(1971–)

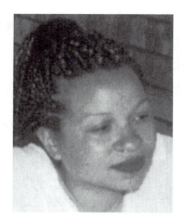

AUTHOR

E-mail: ayannahb@aol.com

Hart was born in Lansing, Michigan, the daughter of author Philip S. Hart and producer Tanya Hart, and mastered reading and writing at an early age. In 1990, the family relocated to Los Angeles, California.

Hart has worked in and around the television and film industry since she was a child. Over the years, she has worked with her parents on a variety of projects, including a video press release for the publication of a singing group New Kids on the Block's Harvey Comics comic book; a documentary film on the Atlantic slave trade; a documentary film on America's early Black aviators; several infomercials; and other independent film and television projects. In some of these projects, Hart also served as researcher and writer.

Hart has worked at Walt Disney Studios with her parents and other producers. She worked as a production coordinator at E! Entertainment Television in Los Angeles, California, on the NBC drama, *Profiler*, and in post-producing on such shows as *Friends* and *Dawson's Creek*.

She has long wanted to be a published author, and her 1995 book for young readers has allowed her to reach this goal.

Hart lives in Los Angeles, California with her husband Brendan and daughter Chloe.

BIBLIOGRAPHY

Africans in America. With Earl Spangler. Lerner, 1995.

Hart, Philip Shaw

(1944–)

AUTHOR

E-mail: hartpshaw@aol.com

Hart was born in Denver, Colorado, the middle child among three brothers. His mother was a schoolteacher, so reading and writing were priorities in his household.

Hart has been writing and publishing articles since high school. After graduating from East Denver High School, he went on to attend Colorado College for one year before transferring to the University of Colorado, Boulder, where he was a student and an athlete. He graduated cum laude in 1966.

Hart worked on his graduate degrees at Michigan State University, where he earned a master's degree in sociology in 1970 and a doctorate in sociology in 1974. He met his wife, Tanya, while in college, and they began many years of collaboration on television, film and radio projects. They relocated to Boston, Massachusetts, in 1971, and he joined the faculty of the College of Public and Community Service at the University of Massachusetts, Boston, in 1974. In 1990, the family moved to Los Angeles, California.

While listening to family stories as he was growing up in Denver, Hart became interested in early Black aviators. He helped put together an exhibit titled *Black Wings* for the Smithsonian Institute's National Air and Space Museum in 1982. In 1987, a documentary film he and his wife produced titled *Flyers in Search of a Dream* was broadcast on the Public Broadcasting System (PBS). Among those who saw this film was Reeve Lindbergh, youngest daughter of the famous aviator Charles Lindbergh, who contacted Hart and encouraged him to write these stories in the form of children's books.

Hart's first book under this arrangement, *Flying Free: America's First Black Aviators*, was published in 1992 and received many positive reviews. The book was recognized that same year as a Notable Children's Trade Book in the field of social studies by the National Council for Social Studies and the Children's Book Council Joint Committee. Another book published in 1996 under this arrangement is *Up in the Air: The Story of Bessie Coleman.*

Hart has been developing the story of his great uncle J. Herman Banning and his mechanic, Thomas C. Allen, taken from one of the chapters in *Flying Free* into a motion picture titled *The Hallelujah Flight*. Hart's book on Bessie Coleman has been optioned for a television movie which Hart will coproduce. Hart is partnered with his wife Tanya in a television film, radio and internet production company in Hollywood. Hart took early retirement from the University of Massachusetts–Boston in June, 2002 where he was Professor of Sociology and Director of The William Monroe Trotter Institute for the Study of Black Culture.

Hart's daughter, Ayanna Kai Hart-Beebe, is also a children's-book writer. He lives in Los Angeles, California, and Martha's Vineyard off Cape Cod in Massachusetts.

BIBLIOGRAPHY

Flying Free: America's First Black Aviators. Lerner, 1992.
Up in the Air: The Story of Bessie Coleman. Carolrhoda, 1996.

Haskins, James (Jim)

(1941–2005)

AUTHOR

"My career as a writer began when I was teaching music and special-educa-tion classes in Harlem; my first book, Diary of a Harlem Schoolteacher, was a result of my experiences. So were my first books for young adults. It was the 1960s, and there were very few books on the events of that tumultuous decade written on my students' level. I believe that the same void in literature for Black children continues to this day; and to this day I continue to write such books. Another void I see in literature for Black children is biographies of undeservedly obscure Black people in history; every year, more biographies are published about Mary McLeod Bethune, George Washington Carver, and Booker T. Washington, but where are the biographies of Ella Baker and Bayard Rustin?

"I like to describe my method of writing books as having conversations with myself. I include what interests me, and hope that it also interests young readers. I have not changed the way I write very much over the years, except at the request of editors. My books tend to be shorter now, and I suspect that is a response to the TV and video age and shorter attention spans in all of us. Another trend in young-adult books is to simplify the writing, but I have resisted that trend, believing that young people are willing to stretch their minds to understand books written about people and events that interest them. More than the best TV film or video, books can both enable one to find a private world and open up new worlds."

Born in Demopolis, Alabama, Haskins received a bachelor's degree in psychology from Georgetown University and one in history from Alabama State University. In 1963, he earned a master's degree from the University of New Mexico and a certificate of work of the Stock Exchange after attending the New York Institute of Finance.

Professional memberships include the National Advisory Com-mittee, Statue of Liberty-Ellis Island Commission, the National

Book Critics Circle, the Authors Guild, 100 Black Men, and Phi Beta Kappa. *Social Studies* magazine has selected many of his books as Notable Children's Books, and the Child Study Association selected *Barbara Jordan* in 1979. The Coretta Scott King Award was presented to Haskins for *The Story of Stevie Wonder* in 1977, and his books won Coretta Scott King honor citations in 1978, 1980, 1984, and 1991. He received the *Washington Post* Children's Book Council Award for his body of work in nonfiction for young people in 1994 and, also in 1994, the Carter G. Woodson Award for *The March on Washington* at the National Council on the Social Studies Conference in Phoenix, Arizona. Haskin's book *Bayard Rustin: Behind the Scenes of the Civil Rights Movement* was selected as a 1998 Coretta Scott King Honor Book.

BIBLIOGRAPHY

Resistance: Profiles in Nonviolence. Doubleday, 1970.
The War and the Protest: Vietnam. Doubleday, 1970.
Revolutionaries: Agents of Change. Lippincott, 1971.
Profiles in Black Power. Doubleday, 1972.
Jokes from Black Folks. Doubleday, 1973.
Ralphe Bunche: A Most Reluctant Hero. Hawthorne, 1974.
Street Gangs: Yesterday and Today. Hasting House, 1974.
Witchcraft, Mysticism & Magic in the Black World. Hasting House, 1974.
Babe Ruth and Hank Aaron: The Home Run Kings. Lothrop, 1974.
Jobs in Business and Office. Lothrop, 1974.
The Consumer Movement. Watts, 1975.
The Picture Life of Malcolm X. Watts, 1975.
The Creoles of Color of New Orleans. Crowell, 1975.
Fighting Shirley Chisholm. Dial, 1975.
Dr. J: A Biography of Julius Erving. Doubleday, 1975.
Your Rights: Past and Present. Hawthorn, 1975.
The Story of Stevie Wonder. Lothrop, 1976.
A New Kind of Joy: The Story of the Special Olympics. Doubleday, 1976.
The Long Struggle: American Labor. Westminster, 1976.
Teenage Alcoholism. Hawthorn, 1976.
Pele: A Biography. Doubleday, 1976.
The Life and Death of Martin Luther King, Jr. Lothrop, 1977.
Barbara Jordan. Dial, 1977.
Who are the Handicapped. Doubleday, 1978.
Bob McAdoo, Superstar. Lothrop, 1978.
Real Estate Careers. Watts, 1978.

From Lew Alcindor to Kareem Abdul-Jabbar. Lothrop, 1978.

The Quiet Revolution: The Struggle for the Rights of Disabled Americans. With J. M. Stifle. Crowell, 1979.

Andrew Young: Man with a Mission. Lothrop, 1979.

Gambling: Who Really Wins? Watts, 1979.

George McGinnis: Basketball Superstar. Hasting House, 1979.

I'm Gonna Make You Love Me! The Story of Diana Ross. Dial, 1980.

The New Americans: Vietnamese Boat People. Enslow, 1980.

Werewolves. Watts, 1981.

The New Americans: Cuban Boat People. Enslow, 1982.

The Child Abuse Help Book. With Pat Connolly. Addison-Wesley, 1982.

Sugar Ray Leonard. Lothrop, 1982.

Katherine Dunham. Coward McCann, 1982.

The Guardian Angels. Enslow, 1982.

Black Theater in America. Crowell, 1982.

Donna Summer. With Jim Stifle. Atlantic Monthly, 1983.

Lena Horne. Coward McCann, 1983.

Space Challenger: The Story of Guion Bluford. With Kathleen Benson. Carolrhoda, 1984.

Double Dutch. With David Walker. Enslow, 1985.

About Michael Jackson. Enslow, 1985.

Breakdancing. Lerner, 1985.

Diana Ross: Star Supreme. Viking, 1985.

The Statue of Liberty: America's Proud Lady. Lerner, 1986.

Black Music in America: A History Through Its People. Harper and Row, 1987.

Count Your Way Through the Arab World/China/Japan/Russia. Carolrhoda, 1987.

Shirley Temple Black: Actress to Ambassador. Viking, 1988.

Winnie Mandela: Life Struggle. Putnam, 1988.

Corazon Aquino: Leaders of the Philippines. Enslow, 1988.

Bill Cosby: America's Most Famous Father. Walker, 1988.

The Sixties Reader. With Kathleen Benson. Viking, 1988.

India Under Indira and Rajiv Gandhi. Enslow, 1989.

Count Your Way Through Africa/Canada/Korea/Mexico. Carolrhoda, 1989.

Count Your Way Through Germany/Italy. Carolrhoda, 1990.

Black Dance in America. Harper & Row, 1990.

Count Your Way Through India/Israel. Carolrhoda, 1991.

Outward Dreams: Black Inventors and Their Inventions. Walker, 1991.

Religions. Lippincott, 1973. Reissued Hippocrene, 1991.

James Van Der Zee: The Picture Takin' Man. Dodd, Mead, 1979. Africa World Press, 1991.

The Day Martin Luther King, Jr. Was Shot. Scholastic, 1992.

Christopher Columbus. Admiral of the Ocean Sea. (Scholastic, 1991). French Canadian Edition. Scholastic, 1992.

One More River to Cross. Scholastic, 1992.

Sports Star: Magic Johnson. Enslow, 1992.

Adam Clayton Powell: Portrait of a Marching Black. Africa World Press, 1992.

Always Movin' On: The Life of Langston Hughes. Africa World Press, 1992.

Amazing Grace: The Story Behind the Song. Millbrook, 1992.

. Walker, 1992.

Colin Powell. Scholastic, 1992.

I am Somebody! A Biography of Jesse Jackson. Enslow, 1992.

Rosa Parks: My Story. With Rosa Parks. Dial, 1992.

Thurgood Marshall: A Life for Justice. Holt, 1992.

Get On Board: The Story of the Underground Railroad. Scholastic, 1992.

I Have a dream: The Life of Martin Luther King, Jr. Millbrook, 1992.

The March on Washington. HarperCollins, 1993.

The Headless Haunt and Other African-American Ghost Stories. HarperCollins, 1994.

The Scottsboro Boys. Holt, 1994.

Freedom Rides. Hyperion, 1994.

Black Eagles: African Americans in Aviation. Scholastic, 1995.

The Day They Fired on Fort Sumpter. Scholastic, 1995.

From Afar to Zulu: A Dictionary of African Cultures (with Joann Biondi). Walker, 1995.

The Harlem Renaissance. Millbrook, 1996.

Louis Farrakhan and the Nation of Islam. Walker, 1996.

Count Your Way Through Brazil/France/Greece/Ireland. With Kathleen Benson. Carolrhoda, 1996.

I am Rosa Parks. With Rosa Parks. Dial, 1997.

Bayard Rustin: Behind the Scenes of the Civil Rights Movement. Hyperion, 1997.

Power to the People: The Rise and Fall of the Black Panther Party. Simon & Schuster, 1997.

Spike Lee: By Any Means Necessary. Walker, 1997.

Black Star Biography Series (Series Editor). John Wiley & Sons, 1998.

African Beginnings. With Kathleen Benson. Lothrop, 1998.

Moaning Bones: African-American Ghost Stories. Lothrop, 1998.

Separate But Not Equal: The Dream and the Struggle. Scholastic, 1998.

Black, Blue & Gray: African-Americans in the Civil War. Simon & Schuster, 1998.

African-American Entrepreneurs. Wiley, 1998.

African-American Military Heroes. Wiley, 1998.

The Geography of Hope: Black Exodus from the South After Reconstruction. Millbrook Press, 1999.

Out of the Darkness: The Story of Blacks Moving North, 1890–1940. With Kathleen Benson. Marshall Cavendish, 1999.

Bound for America: The Forced Migration of Africans to the New World. Lothrop, 1999.

Carter G. Woodson: The Man Who Put "Black" in American History. Millbrook, 2000.

Toni Morrison: The Magic of Words. Millbrook Press, 2000.

One Nation Under a Groove: Rap Music and Its Roots. Hyperion, 2000.

One Love, One Heart: A History of Reggae. Hyperion, 2001.

Following Freedom's Star: The Story of the Underground Railroad. With Kathleen Benson. Marshall Cavendish, 2001.

Conjure Times: Black Magicians in America. With Kathleen Benson. Walker, 2001.

Toni Morrison: Telling a Tale Untold. Millbrook, 2002.

Champion: A Biography of Muhammad Ali. Walker & Company, 2002.

John Lewis in the Lead: A Story of the Civil Rights Movement. Illustrated by Benny Andrews. Lee & Low, 2006.

Hinds, Patricia Mignon

AUTHOR

Born in New York City, Hinds is a graduate of Hampton University and received her master's degree from the City University of New York. She began her book publishing career at Harper and Row and has been an editor at *Essence* magazine.

In 1980, she created her own corporate communications company, Mignon Communications, whose clients include an impressive list of Fortune 500 companies. Her company specializes in editorial services and book and magazine publishing. She has received three Communications Excellence to Black Audiences Awards for her work. She is also an educator on primary and college levels, having taught small business management and has been a writing professor.

Hinds has produced an educational television series titled *CAHOOTS*, and has served on the board of director of Cinque Gallery in New York City. In 1993, she was selected by Essence Communications to launch Essence Books and also to spearhead a new line of Essence children's books as the director of Essence books.

An avid support of several charities, Hinds lives in New York City.

BIBLIOGRAPHY
Animal Affairs. Dell, 1980.
Kittens Need Someone to Love. Western, 1981.
Puppies Need Someone to Love. Western, 1981.
Baby Calf. Longmeadow, 1988. Western, 1988.
Baby Pig. Longmeadow, 1988. Western, 1988.
A Day in the Life of Morgan Freeman. Macmillan, 1994.
What I Want to Be. Illustrated by Cornelius Van Wright. Golden, 1995.
My Best Friend. Illustrated by Cornelius Van Wright. Golden, 1996.

Holbert, Raymond

(1945–)

ILLUSTRATOR

Web site: www.memorybanque.com

"There has been a wonderful increase in the amount of books by African-American authors and illustrators over the past few years. Finally, there is an opportunity to see books that cover a more realistic representation of the diversity that exists in this country. Thanks to the worldwide web, it is also easier to locate the sources of these books. My career as an illustrator and artist began through an opportunity through Children's Book Press in San Francisco. There is a great opportunity to influence positive and inspiring thoughts and history through this medium designed to appeal to children and to offer them the opportunity to examine the world of books that inspires these influences. My inspiration is due to the severe shortage of books that expressed a specific point of view of my young life. I want to continue to see this publishing continue."

Educated at Laney College of Oakland, California and the University of California at Berkeley, Holbert received degrees in painting, drawing and printmaking from the Art Department. He has been the Chairman of the Art Department and has taught design, drawing, African American art history and illustration at City College of San Francisco for over thirty years.

He has illustrated two books by Willis Kirk on jazz drumming, and another on perspective drawing for artists and illustrators. He has worked in a variety of fields of illustration that run the gamut from children's books to scientific and technical illustration.

Married to Susan Demersseman, Holbert has three children and currently lives in Berkeley, California.

BIBLIOGRAPHY
The Barber's Cutting Edge. Children's Book Press, 1990.

Holley, Vanessa (Diane)

(1952–)

ILLUSTRATOR

E-mail: vanholley5@aol.com

Holley was born in Portsmouth, Virginia, the second of four children. She remembers loving to draw as early as the age of three. She studied commercial art and illustration at Pratt Institute in Brooklyn, New York and, while there, she worked as a freelance layout artist and illustrator for *Encore* magazine. This began her career as a professional illustrator.

Noted for her drawings of children, she is frequently commissioned as a portrait artist. Holley has exhibited her fine art extensively in the New York metropolitan area and has had several one-woman shows. She has work in the collections of Ossie Davis and Ruby Dee, the Pratt Institute, the Afro-American Historical Museum in Jersey City, New Jersey, and in numerous other private collections throughout the country.

As a children's-book illustrator, she is committed to using her art to uplift and inspire children. She believes that the African and African American experience is so rich in information and areas that need to be explored that it will take her a whole lifetime to express it through her art.

She lives in Jersey City, New Jersey.

BIBLIOGRAPHY

The Black Holocaust for Beginners. By S. E. Anderson. Writers & Readers, 1995.
Jazz for Beginners. By Ron David. Writers & Readers, 1995.
Kai: A Mission for Her Village (Girlhood Journeys Series). By Dawn C. Thomas. Simon & Schuster, 1996.
My Shoelaces are Hard to Tie! By Karla Roberson. Scholastic, 2004.

Hooks, Gwendolyn

(1951–)

AUTHOR

E-mail: grhooks@cox.net

"'Wow! What a glorious day!' That's how I greet each new day. I am constantly astonished by what life offers us. I'd like to think my writing reflects my astonishment and passion for life. If I can "fire up" a child to read more and explore life, then my books are a success."

Hooks was educated at Oklahoma State University and the University of Missouri-St. Louis where she earned a Bachelor of Science in Education: Secondary Mathematics.

She taught junior high and high school mathematics in Kansas, Missouri, and now Oklahoma. Between teaching assignments, Hooks was a financial manager for a home health agency and spent several years as a stay-at-home mom, raising three children.

Hooks served on PTA executive committees, school and community booster clubs, and is a sixteen-year member of Red Lands Council of Girl Scouts. She was her younger daughter's Girl Scout leader from her first day as a Daisy Girl Scout to her bridging ceremony to a Cadette Girl Scout.

In the early 1990s, Hooks began publishing adult magazine articles, but realized her passion was writing for children. Her passion led to her first book, *Can I Have a Pet?* in 2002. Hooks loves to share her joy of writing. She has presented writing programs at Encyclo-Media, Red Dirt Book Festival, Oklahoma Educators Association, Urban League, and the Oklahoma County Metropolitan Library System.

She is an active member of the Society of Children's Book Writers and Illustrators and Oklahoma City Kid Writers.

Hooks is married to Edmond L. Hooks, M.D. and lives in Oklahoma City with two of their children and Kitty Kat Hooks. Her older daughter teaches in Fort Worth, Texas.

BIBLIOGRAPHY

Can I Have a Pet? Illustrated by Lisa Cinelli. Bebop Books, 2002.

Three's a Crowd. Illustrated by Sylvia Walker. Scholastic/Color Bridge Books, 2004.

The Mystery of the Missing Dog. Illustrated by Nancy Devard. Scholastic/Color Bridge Books, 2004.

Nice Wheels! Children's Press, 2005.

Hoston III, James H.

(1963–)

ILLUSTRATOR

E-mail: jhprod@nyc.rr.com

Hoston was born in Freeport, Long Island, New York, the younger of two children. During his childhood, he was always drawing when he got the chance in between playing sports. He attributes his persistence to his mother, also artistic, and his uncle Edward who supplied him with endless materials.

During his elementary years, he won numerous awards and was once voted artist of the class. High school was primarily spent preparing for college and he had one art class during his junior and senior year. Several poster contests a year kept him in practice with his art. By the end of his senior year, he decided to pursue art.

First, he attended SUNY Farmingdale and received an Associate degree in advertising art and design. Next was Pratt Institute in Brooklyn where he studied Illustration and graduated with a BFA.

For the following five years he worked part-time at various jobs and pursued illustration in textbook drawings, black and white children's books for small publishers, some product illustrations for toy companies, and various magazine editorials.

In 1989 he applied for graduate school at the New York Academy of Art. He received an Andy Warhol scholarship for two years of study. (Andy Warhol was one of the founders of the school and a board member up until his death.) During this time, Hoston continued to illustrate and attend classes.

Upon graduation, he landed a job full-time at Marvel Comics working in a production capacity. He has done several paintings for Marvel as well as freelance coloring in numerous comic books and the prestigious Marvel Annual Report three years in a row. His graduate painting was featured in *American Artist* magazine in 1991 and he is currently represented by a gallery on Second Avenue in the East Village, Manhattan.

James Hoston's recent works were presented in May, 2005, by the Museum of American Illustration Society of Illustrators in New York.

Jim currently lives in Brooklyn and is single.

BIBLIOGRAPHY

The Original Freddie Ackerman. By Hadley Irwin. Margaret K. McElderry, 1992.

The Great Smith House Hustle. By Jane Louise Curry. Margaret K. McElderry, 1993.

Good Luck Gold. By Janet S. Wong. Margaret K. McElderry, 1994.

The Bicycle Thief. By Richard Brightfield. Macmillan, 1996.

Howard, Elizabeth Fitzgerald

(1927–)

AUTHOR

E-mail: lizfitzhow@aol.com

"There are so many wonderful, inspiring, funny, sad, heartwarming, heart-tickling, meaningful stories about Black families, waiting to be written down. Some of them are in my own family's treasury, and there is still a shortage—a dearth—of children's books about everyday Black families living ordinary lives during the early part of this century. I would like present-day children, Black and White, to know that Blacks have been a part of all of this country's growth since the beginning. And that there were Black grocers and doctors and postmen and teachers and porters and lawyers who celebrated holidays and sat in the balcony at the opera and went to church and sent their children to college—and hoped that the American dream included them. And lived as though it did, in spite of everything that might or might not have gone wrong. Of course, Virginia Hamilton and Patricia McKissack and others are telling this story with depth and flair. I hope that I am able in some small measure to contribute to this."

Thus has Elizabeth Fitzgerald Howard, professor emeritus of library science (West Virginia University) since 1993, stated her underlying philosophy in her works.

The author was born in Baltimore, Maryland. Howard earned her bachelor of arts degree from Radcliffe College in 1948, her master's degree in library science and her doctorate from the University of Pittsburgh in 1971 and 1977, respectively. In her senior year at Radcliffe, she was president of her class.

Her memberships include the American Library Association, the Society of Children's Book Writers and Illustrators, and Links,

Incorporated. In the American Library Association, Howard has served on the Caldecott Committee, the Hans Christian Andersen Committee, the Teachers of Children's Literature Discussion Group, and the American Library Association Children's Book Council Liaison Committee. She has served for many years on the board of trustees of Magee Women's Hospital in Pittsburgh, Pennsylvania, and has also been a member of the boards of QED Communications, Beginning with Books, the Ellis School, Three Rivers' Youth, and the Radcliffe Alumnae Association. She is married to Dr. Lawrence C. Howard and lives in Pittsburgh, Pennsylvania. They have three daughters and two grandchildren.

BIBLIOGRAPHY

The Train to Lulu's. Illustrated by Robert Casilla. Bradbury, 1988.

Chita's Christmas Tree. Illustrated by Floyd Cooper. Bradbury, 1989.

Aunt Flossie's Hats (and Crab Cakes Later). Illustrated by James Ransome. Clarion, 1991.

Mac and Marie and the Train Toss Surprise. Illustrated by Gail Gordon Carter. Four Winds, 1993.

Papa Tells Chita a Story. Illustrated by Floyd Cooper. Four Winds, 1995.

What's In Aunt Mary's Room? Illustrated by Cedric Lucas. Clarion, 1996.

When Will Sarah Come? Illustrated by Nina Crews. Greenwillow, 1999.

Virgie Goes to School. Illustrated by E.B. Lewis. Simon & Schuster, 2000.

Lulu's Birthday. Illustrated by Pat Cummings. Greenwillow, 2001.

Flower Girl Butterflies. Greenwillow, 2004.

Hudson, Cheryl Willis

(1948–)

AUTHOR

E-mail: justusbooks@aol.com

Web site: www.justusbooks.com

Author, publisher, and entrepreneur, Hudson has more than twenty-five years of experience creating books for children. A native of Portsmouth, Virginia, and graduate of Oberlin College in Ohio, Hudson began her career doing textbook design for publishers including Houghton Mifflin and Macmillan.

Noticing a lack of quality Black-interest books for her own two children, she set out to help fill the publishing industry void with her self-published first book, the AFRO-BETS® ABC Book. A year later, in 1988, she and her husband Wade Hudson founded Just Us Books, a publishing company that specializes in children's books that focus on African American experiences. As editorial director of Just Us Books, Hudson oversees the development of all the titles the company publishes. As an author, she crafts vibrant and engaging books that allow Black children to see themselves positively reflected in society.

Her book *Come By Here Lord: Everyday Prayers for Children* (Just Us Books) was recently named Children's Book of the Year by BlackBoard, Inc.

An active member of her community and publishing industry organizations, Hudson serves on the board of the Read Up! Book Club, a New Jersey children's literacy group; the Small Press Center, and the Langston Hughes Library at the Alex Haley Farm, operated by the Children's Defense Fund. A 2003 inductee of the International Hall of Fame for Writers of African Descent, Ms. Hudson also uses her experience to develop and conduct workshops on diversity in children's literature.

BIBLIOGRAPHY

AFRO-BETS ABC Book. Just Us Books, 1987, 1988.

Bright Eyes, Brown Skin. With Bernette Ford. Just Us Books, 1990.

Kwanzaa Sticker and Activity Book. Scholastic, 1994.

Hold Christmas in Your Heart. Scholastic, 1995.

How Sweet the Sound: African American Songs for Children. With Wade Hudson. Scholastic, 1995.

Many Colors of Mother Goose. Just Us Books, 1997.

In Praise of Our Fathers and Our Mothers. With Wade Hudson. Just Us Books, 1997.

Good Morning, Baby. Illustrated by Wade Hudson. Scholastic, 1997.

Good Night, Baby. Illustrated by Wade Hudson. Scholastic, 1997.

Let's Count, Baby. Illustrated by Wade Hudson. Scholastic, 1997.

Animal Sounds for Baby. Illustrated by Wade Hudson. Scholastic, 1997.

Glo Goes Shopping. Just Us Books, 1999.

Come By Here Lord, Everyday Prayers for Children. Just Us Books, 2001.

Langston's Legacy: 101 Ways to Celebrate the Life and Work of Langston Hughes. With Katura Hudson. Just Us Books, 2002.

Harlem Renaissance: Profiles in Creativity. Newbridge Educational Publishers, 2002.

Hands Can. Illustrated by John-Francis Bourke. Candlewick Press, 2003.

Hudson, Wade

(1946–)

AUTHOR

E-mail: justusbooks@aol.com

Web site: www.justusbooks.com

A native of Mansfield, Louisiana, Hudson began writing at a young age. After working for several civil rights organizations during the 1960s, he served as a newspaper reporter and public relations specialist. He is also a playwright and songwriter.

In 1988, Hudson's passion for writing and life-long mission to help foster positive self-image within the young Black community helped propel the launch of Just Us Books, an independent publisher that specializes in Black-interest children's books. Hudson serves as the company's president and CEO. He and his wife Cheryl have collaborated on a number of books. His newest published *Powerful Words* (Scholastic) chronicles more than two hundred years of extraordinary writing by African Americans.

An advocate of diversity in literature, he conducts workshops and presentations on topics such as "Building a Curriculum of Diversity," and "Introducing Authentic Multicultural Literature to Young Readers." He serves on the board of many organizations, including the Langston Hughes Library at the Alex Haley Farm, operated by the Children's Defense Fund and has received numerous honors, including the Stephen Crane Literary Award. In 2003 he was inducted into the International Hall of Fame for Writers of African Descent.

A highly sought-after marketing consultant, Hudson lives in New Jersey with his family.

BIBLIOGRAPHY

Beebe's Lonely Saturday. New Dimension, 1967.

Freedom Star. Macmillan, 1968.

AFRO-BETS® Book of Black Heroes from A to Z. With Valerie Wilson Wesley. Just Us Books, 1988.

AFRO-BETS® Alphabet Rap Song. Just Us Books, 1990.

Jamal's Busy Day. Illustrated by George Ford. Just Us Books, 1991.

AFRO-BETS® Kids: I'm Gonna Be! Illustrated by Culverson Blair. Just Us Books, 1992.

Pass It On: African American Poetry for Children. Compiled by Wade Hudson. Illustrated by Floyd Cooper. Scholastic, 1993.

I Love My Family. Illustrated by Cal Massey. Scholastic, 1993.

Great Black Heroes: Five Brave Explorers. Illustrated by Ron Garnett. Scholastic, 1994.

Great Black Heroes: Five Notable Inventors. Scholastic, 1995.

How Sweet the Sound: African-American Songs for Children. With Cheryl Willis Hudson. Illustrated by Floyd Cooper. Scholastic, 1995.

Kid's Book of Wisdom. With Cheryl Willis Hudson. Just Us Books, 1996.

Anthony's Big Surprise. Just Us Books, 1997.

In Praise of Our Fathers and Our Mothers. With Cheryl Willis Hudson. Just Us Books, 1997.

Robo's Favorite Places. Just Us Books, 1999.

Great Black Heroes: Five Bold Freedom Fighters. Scholastic, 2002.

Poetry From the Masters: The Pioneers. Just Us Books, 2003.

Book of Black Heroes: Scientists, Healers and Inventors. Just Us Books, 2003.

God Smiles When. Abingdon Press, 2003.

God Gave Me. Abingdon Press, 2003.

Powerful Words. Scholastic, 2004.

Roots Go Deep: African American Poems About Family. Scholastic, 2004.

Hyppolite, Joanne

(1969–)

AUTHOR

"I read tons of age-graded children's literature when I was young, and it taught me English, it taught me humor, and it taught me respect for the genre. I was also influenced by Haitian traditions, culture and language (kreyol). My mother's storytelling ('contes') and her memories of her life in Haiti are a great inspiration. I live and I write through them. I have been influenced by children's writer Kristin Hunter and other children's book authors."

Hyppolite was born in Haiti, and her family settled in the United States when she was four years old. She grew up in Boston, Massachusetts, and graduated in 1991 from the University of Pennsylvania with a BA in creative writing. In 1994, she received a master's degree in Afro-American studies from the University of California, Los Angeles. She is a doctoral student in Caribbean literature at the University of Miami. Hyppolite is the founder of Women Writers of Haitian Descent, a nonprofit literacy organization based in South Florida. Folklore, fiction, teaching, and reading stories to children have filled her college and literacy career. She is a regular speaker at libraries and schools across the country. The *Miami Herald* hailed her as a "hip, young Haitian-American who is setting new standards for children's literature."

Her fiction addresses the Haitian-American experience. *Seth and Samona*, her first novel, was published in 1995 and won the second annual Marguerite de Angeli Prize from Delacorte Press.

Hyppolite lives in Miramar, Florida.

BIBLIOGRAPHY
Seth and Samona. Illustrated by Colin Bootman. Delacourte, 1995.
Ola Shakes It Up. Delacorte, 1998.

Jackson, Garnet Nelson

(1944–)

AUTHOR

E-mail: kariskid@aol.com

The middle child of a family of three daughters, Jackson was born and reared in New Orleans, Louisiana, where she enjoyed a middle-class upbringing. Her early education consisted of private and Catholic schools.

Jackson began writing during her teen years, and, after having written several short stories, poems, and a book, she delayed her writing career and dedicated her early adulthood to teaching. During her college years, Jackson worked as a postal clerk. She received a Bachelor of Arts degree in Education from Dillard University in 1968 and began her teaching career in Flint, Michigan.

In 1980, she began writing poetry again. After joining the Rejoti Writers Club of New Jersey, she had several poems published and received an honorable mention for her poem "A Composite of Experiences," published in *The Griot Speaks* in 1986.

In 1989, after an unsuccessful search for books about African American achievers written for young children, she decided to write for her first-grade students. She wrote five biographies of great achievers that were enjoyed and appreciated by her students. In 1990, after seeking in vain for a publisher, she published them herself in the series African Like Me Books. They were later published by Modern Curriculum Press, Simon and Schuster's education group. They also published more than a dozen books she has written in a series entitled Beginning Biographies: African Americans. Jackson has also written a weekly column about issues concerning young children in the *Flint Journal* newspaper.

The many honors and awards she has received for her literary contributions include the National Association for the Advancement of Colored People's 1991 Harambee Medal; the Educator of the Year Award in 1991; a proclamation from the office of the mayor of Flint, Michigan, declaring February 26, 1992, as Garnet Jackson Day; and the Zeta Phi Beta Finer Womanhood Hall of Fame Award in 1993. She has completed a novel for adults and writes full time.

BIBLIOGRAPHY

I Am an African American Child. Illustrated by Inez Goodman. African Like Me Books, 1990.

The Little African King. Illustrated by Inez Goodman and Ken Ross. African Like Me Books, 1990.

Benjamin Banneker: Scientist. Illustrated by Rodney Pate. Modern Curriculum, 1993.

Elijah McCoy: Inventor. Illustrated by Gary Thomas. Modern Curriculum, 1993.

Frederick Douglass: Freedom Fighter. Illustrated by Keaf Holliday. Modern Curriculum, 1993.

Garrett Morgan: Inventor. Illustrated by Thomas Hudson. Modern Curriculum, 1993.

Phillis Wheatley: Poet. Illustrated by Cheryl Hanna. Modern Curriculum, 1993.

Rosa Parks: Hero of Our Times. Illustrated by Tony Wade. Modern Curriculum, 1993.

Charles Drew: Doctor. Illustrated by Gary Thomas. Modern Curriculum, 1993.

Mae Jemison: Astronaut. Illustrated by Fred Willingham. Modern Curriculum, 1994.

Maggie Walker: Business Leader. Illustrated by Keaf Holliday. Modern Curriculum, 1994.

Selma Burke: Artist. Illustrated by Cheryl Hanna. Modern Curriculum, 1994.

Shirley Chisholm: Congresswoman. Illustrated by Thomas Hudson. Modern Curriculum, 1994.

Thurgood Marshall: Supreme Court Justice. Illustrated by Higgins Bond. Modern Curriculum, 1994.

Toni Morrison: Author. Illustrated by Higgins Bond. Modern Curriculum, 1995.

George Washington: Our First President. Scholastic, 2000.

The First Thanksgiving. Scholastic, 2000.

Famous Explorers. Scholastic, 2000.

Martin Luther King Jr.: A Man of Peace. Scholastic, 2001.

James, Curtis E.

(1966–)

ILLUSTRATOR

E-mail: cjsstudio@aol.com

Web site: www.curtisejames.com

"Growing up in the south finding time between farming and school to do what I loved—draw—was difficult. I have never taken where I come from for granted and find beauty in everyday life. With the blessings God has given me I strive to depict the love and respect I have for humanity in each of my drawings. We as a people must use our gifts to empower and teach our youth."

James, originally from Albany, Georgia, moved to New York City in 1985 to attend Pratt Institute. There he received his BFA and MFA in Fine Arts. He has garnered several honors and awards, including a $50,000 scholarship from the Pratt Institute; the Silver Plate Award from the U.S. House of Representatives; the Albany Museum Purchase Award (at the ages of eighteen and nineteen, the youngest in the history of the museum to receive this award); the Gold Key Award from Savannah College; the Merit Award from Atlanta College of Arts, and the Outstanding Artist Award from the Georgia State Board of Education.

He has exhibited at the Historical Museum of Alabama; Albany Museum of Art, Georgia; Schomburg Center for Research in Black Culture; Cathedral of St. John the Divine; The Black Fine Art Show in New York and Chicago, as well as many other venues. His credits include: *Essence, Upscale, People, Chain Leader, Images, Art Trend,* and *Décor* magazines and *Artistic Impressions* catalogue.

James began illustrating in 1996 with *Vampire Bugs*. In 2003 he illustrated *Linda Brown, You Are Not Alone*, a Junior Library Guild Selection and a Bank Street 2004 Best Book of the Year and in 2005 *The School is Not White*. Curtis is currently working on *Freedom Ship*, a story about Robert Smalls' journey to freedom set in 1862.

Married with three children, two boys and a girl, he resides in Pennsylvania.

BIBLIOGRAPHY

Vampire Bugs. by Sharon Dennis Bantam Doubleday Dell Publishing Group, 1996.

Linda Brown, You Are Not Alone. by Joyce Carol Thomas Hyperion Books for Children, 2003.

The School Is Not White. by Doreen Rappaport Hyperion Books for Children, 2005.

Freedom Ship. by Doreen Rappaport Hyperion Books for Children. 2006

Johnson, Angela

(1961–)

AUTHOR

E-mail: ajohnson30@neo.rr.com

Web site: www.visitingauthors.com

"My writing has allowed a change to come over me. I no longer see the world as good or bad, with rules emblazoned in stone. I no longer have such a definite opinion on everything in the world. There is so much more gray in the spectrum of life. Thankfully this will make my writing grow."

Johnson was born in Tuskegee, Alabama, and attributes her story-telling skills to her father and grandfather, both of whom frequently told stories to the children in the family. She began writing poetry in Windham High School in Ohio and continued while attending Kent State University. Her first book, *Tell Me a Story, Mama*, is described in a *School Library Journal* review as a "touching picture book in both language and art."

Johnson believes that there should be more Black-oriented literature for children and senses the need for Black children to see their own images in books. She placed her own Aunt Rosetta as a character in *Tell Me a Story, Mama*.

Her book *When I Am Old with You* won a 1991 Coretta Scott King Honor Book Award and the American Library Association Social Responsibilities Round Table Award, and, that same year, she also won the Ezra Jack Keats New Writer Award. She received the Northern Ohio Live Writers Award in 1991 and the Alabama Author Award in 1993, and, in 1994, *Toning the Sweep* won the Coretta Scott King Award, and the PEN-Norma Klein Award in 1995.

She has been a Volunteers in Service to America (VISTA) volunteer at the King-Kennedy Community Center, a volunteer at the Kent Head Start Program, and also worked as a nanny for four years in Kent, Ohio.

She won the Coretta Scott King Award for *Heaven* and a Coretta Scott King Honor recognition for *The Other Side* in 1999. Also, *The First Part Last* won a MacArthur Fellowship in 2003, the Michael Printz award and the Coretta Scott King Award in 2004.

Johnson is single and lives and writes full time in Kent, Ohio.

BIBLIOGRAPHY

Tell Me a Story, Mama. Illustrated by David Soman. Orchard, 1989.

Do Like Kyla. Illustrated by James Ransome. Orchard, 1990.

When I Am Old with You. Illustrated by David Soman. Orchard, 1990.

One of Three. Illustrated by David Soman. Orchard, 1991.

The Leaving Morning. Illustrated by David Soman. Orchard, 1992.

The Girl Who Wore Snakes. Illustrated by James Ransome. Orchard, 1993.

Julius. Illustrated by Dav Pilkey. Orchard, 1993.

Toning the Sweep. Orchard, 1993.

Joshua by the Sea. Illustrated by Rhonda Mitchell. Orchard, 1994.

Joshua's Night Whispers. Illustrated by Rhonda Mitchell. Orchard, 1994.

Mama Bird, Baby Bird. Illustrated by Rhonda Mitchell. Orchard, 1994.

Rain Feet. Illustrated by Rhonda Mitchell. Orchard, 1994.

Humming Whispers. Orchard, 1995.

Shoes Like Miss Alice's. Illustrated by Ken Page. Orchard, 1995.

The Aunt in Our House. Illustrated by David Soman. Orchard, 1996.

Daddy Calls Me Man. Illustrated by Rhonda Mitchell. Orchard, 1997.

The Rolling Store. Illustrated by Peter Cat. Orchard, 1997.

Heaven. Simon & Schuster, 1998.

Songs of Faith. Orchard Books, 1998.

The Wedding. Illustrated by David Soman. Orchard Books, 1999.

Down the Winding Road. Illustrated by Shane Evans. D.K., 2000.

Those Building Men. Illustrated by Barry Moser. Blue Sky Press, 2001.

Looking for Red. Simon & Schuster, 2002.

I Dream of Trains. Illustrated by Loren Long. Simon & Schuster, 2003.

The First Part Last. Simon & Schuster, 2003.

A Cool Moonlight. Dial Books, 2003.

Just Like Josh Gibson. Illustrated by Beth Peck. Simon & Schuster, 2004.

Violet's Music. Illustrated by Laura Huliska-Beth. Dial Books, 2004.

A Sweet Smell of Roses. Illustrated by Eric Valesquez. Simon & Schuster, 2004.

Bird. Dial Books, 2004.

Johnson, Cathy Ann

(1964–)

AUTHOR/ILLUSTRATOR

E-mail: cjlurit1@aol.com

"There is a definite need for lighthearted, whimsical, imaginative illustrations for children of color. It is important to me to create images that create a solid partnership with literary works that evoke an emotional interest, and provide an element of escape for the reader. Too often children of color are restricted to in the box thinking, and bound by the reality of cultural categorization. I believe when you offer any child an imaginative escape, when you offer a child an unusual creative adventure, it opens their minds. It gives them the opportunity to activate their creative genius. The utilization of the mind, particularly the creative mind, continues to develop throughout childhood, and extends well into the adult years. In my personal opinion there is a parallel with the next major scientist, the cure for cancer, financial genius, and ending world hunger, that lies within the child that can think outside of the box. It lies in the child that is able to look past traditional cultural casting, and begin to creatively conceive themselves in new roles, and exploring new solutions to old challenges. Literature is part of the solution; it is a much-needed tool in the creative development for Children of Color. Offering a body of imaginative, culturally relevant stories and images would assist in opening their world, and developing out of the box thinking. I am committed to contributing a body of work that would impact the literary world for all children, with a personal interest and passion for children of color."

Johnson was born in 1964 in Columbus, Ohio. After high school she attended Columbus College of Arts and Design where she received her bachelor of fine arts degree. After graduating from college, she and her son relocated to Kansas City, Missouri, where she pursued a career at Hallmark Card, Inc. as a designer/illustrator.

She began working for publishing companies in high school. Her first assignment was for the Franklin County Department of Education, designing characters and books for their early learner reading promotion. Since then she has worked for various companies. Her influence on juvenile products can be seen on various educational, trade and mass-market books; toy designs, cards, ornaments, party designs, and more.

Johnson has been the presenter in children's literary workshops with many writers and illustrators, including the Juvenile Writers of Kansas City and the Art of Crafting Early Readers conducted with Scholastic Library Children's Press. She has performed storytelling workshops with the Kansas City Children's Jazz Museum, Kaleidoscope (Hallmark Greeting Cards creative arts and crafts center). She is working on a children's literary workshop for the urban schools of Recife, Brazil.

She and her son have collaborated on a new series of books that is currently being considered for publication.

Johnson lives in Kansas City, Missouri.

BIBLIOGRAPHY

The Dashiki. By Gaylia Taylor. Bebop Books, 2004.

A Heart for Jesus. By Juanita Bynum. Charisma Kias/Strang Communication, 2004.

The Girls in the Circle. By Nikki Giovanni. Color Bridge Books/Sterling Publishing, 2004.

You Say Hola, I Say Hello. By Elizabeth Zapata. Children's Press, 2005.

Our Special Sweet Potato. By Andrea Davis Pinkney. McGraw-Hill Publishing, 2005.

Little Lamb Easter Surprise. By Christine Taylor Butler. Color Bridge Books/ Sterling Publishing, 2005.

My Nana and Me. By Irene Smalls. Little Brown Publishing, 2005.

Pop, Pop and Me a Recipe. By Irene Smalls. Little Brown Publishing, 2006.

Johnson, Charles

(1948–)

AUTHOR/ILLUSTRATOR

E-mail: chasjohn@u.washington.edu

Web site: www.oxherdingtale.com

"The experience I work to create for young readers is the same feeling of enchantment that so delighted me when I was in my teens. Back then, when I turned to the first page of a novel or a story, I knew nothing at all about the writer, his or her previous works, of whether the book was literary or pulp fiction. All I knew then was that sometimes from the first page—often from the first sentence—of a story, a kind of spell was cast over me. It was the experience of mystery and wonder, and needing to know what happens next because I was certain the outcome had meaning for my own life."

Born in 1948 in Evanston, Illinois, Johnson received his BA and MA degrees in journalism and philosophy at Southern Illinois University (which sponsors the national "Charles Johnson Student Fiction Award"), and his PhD in philosophy at the State University of New York at Stony Brook. At age twenty-one, he created, hosted, and coproduced an early how-to-draw series for public television, *Charlie's Pad* (1970). As a professional cartoonist since the age of seventeen, he has published over one thousand drawings and illustrations as well as two books of comic art, *Black Humor* (1970) and *Half-Past Nation Time* (1972).

Johnson, a 1998 MacArthur Fellow, received the National Book Award for his novel *Middle Passage* (1990), and is a 2002 recipient of the Academy Award for Literature from the American Academy of Arts and Letters. In 2003, he was elected to membership in the American Academy of Arts and Sciences. While not primarily a writer of children's literature, some of his titles are appropriate reading for young adults. Among his sixteen published books are three other novels, three collections of short stories, and two books on aesthetics.

His work has appeared in numerous publications in America and abroad, and has been translated into nine languages. A literary critic, screenwriter, philosopher, and international lecturer, he is the S. Wilson and Grace M. Pollock Endowed Professor of English at the University of Washington in Seattle. Additional information on his work can be found at the Web site for the Charles Johnson Society at the American Literature Association.

He and Joan, his wife of thirty-five years, live in Seattle with their two children and Nova, a West Highland White Terrier ("a Westie").

BIBLIOGRAPHY

Dr. King's Refrigerator and Other Bedtime Stories. Scribner, 2005.
Soulcatcher and Other Stories. Harcourt, 2001.
King: The Photobiography of Martin Luther King, Jr. Viking Studio, 2000.

Johnson, Dinah (Dianne)

(1960–)

AUTHOR

E-mail: dinah@dinahjohnson.com

Web site: www.dinahjohnson.com

"As Dianne I am an English professor. But as Dinah—the name my parents have always called me—I write books for young people and visit schools all around the country. I write about things for which I have a passion: my family, my dolls, and African American culture. I love starting with a blank white page, using my imagination, and finally having a book to share with my friends of every age and background. And I always remember what Frederick told us: 'Once you learn to read you will be forever free.'"

Dinah Johnson was born in the historic city of Charleston, South Carolina, on August 6, 1960. The child of an Army colonel, Douglas L. Johnson, and lifelong educator, Beatrice Taylor, she grew up in ten of the United States, Germany, and Iran and continues to travel the world with her siblings, Debora, Douglas, Loretta, and sister-in-law Sonia King. She graduated from Spring Valley High School in Columbia, South Carolina, went to college at Princeton University, earned a MA in African American studies and PhD at Yale University, and then returned home to teach English at the University of South Carolina.

Johnson began writing every day when she was twelve years old, inspired by her favorite teacher, Carol Johnson. Dinah published her first children's book in 1995. But in addition to writing children's books, as Johnson has made a significant contribution to the scholarship devoted to recovering the history of African American children's literature. Editing *The Best of the Brownies' Book* was a particular labor of love. She has also served as chair of the advisory board of the Children's Defense Fund's Langston Hughes Library.

Dinah Johnson and children's book illustrator, the late Tom Feelings are the parents of beloved daughter, Niani Sekai Feelings, and Dinah is the aunt of cherished nephew and niece, Richard Vig Ross, and Taelor Marie Johnson.

She lives in Columbia, South Carolina.

BIBLIOGRAPHY

Telling Tales. Greenwood, 1980.

Presenting Laurence Yep. Author Dianne Johnson-Feelings. Twayne, 1995.

The Best of the Brownies' Book. Author Diane Johnson-Feelings. Oxford University Press, 1996.

All Around Town: The Photographs of Richard Samuel Roberts. Photographed by Richard Roberts. Henry Holt, 1998.

Sunday Week. Illustrated by Tyrone Geter. Henry Holt, 1999.

Quinnie Blue. Illustrated by James Ransome. Henry Holt, 2000.

Sitting Pretty: A Collection of Black Dolls. Photographed by Myles C. Pinkney. Henry Holt, 2000.

Collected Works of Langston Hughes, Volume II — Works for Children and Adults: Poetry, Fiction and Other Writing. (Editor) University of Missouri Press, 2003.

Black Magic. Illustrated by R. Gregory Christie. Henry Holt, 2006.

Johnson, Dolores

(1949–)

AUTHOR/ILLUSTRATOR

E-mail: dolojo2@yahoo.com

Johnson was born in New Britain, Connecticut, the third of thee children. She attended public schools until she went to college in Boston, Massachusetts, and studied art at Boston University School of the Arts, graduating with a bachelor of fine arts degree. Within a year of graduating from college, she moved to Los Angeles, California. Johnson had been a sculpture major in college and found few jobs available in her field; her first jobs were clerical. Eventually, she found work as a production artist and production manager at various advertising agencies.

Johnson started making pottery and stained glass windows at home; then she did some painting and writing until a friend suggested that she pursue the writing and illustration of children's books. After taking courses, she found an agent and submitted manuscripts and dummies to publishers until she was finally awarded a contract in 1989 to illustrate her first book, *Jenny*, written by Beth P. Wilson

She has continued to write and/or illustrate many other books, including *What Will Mommy Do When I'm at School?*, *What Kind of Baby-Sitter Is This?*, and *Your Dad Was Just Like You* (books about contemporary children and their worlds); *Now Let Me Fly: The Story of a Slave Family*, and *Seminole Diary: Remembrances of a Slave* (period fiction); and *The Children's Book of Kwanzaa* and *Bessie Coleman: She Dared to Fly* (nonfiction).

Johnson teaches children's-book illustration in the Otis College of Art and Design Continuing Education Program in Los Angeles, and UCLA Extension in Los Angeles.

She lives in Los Angeles, California.

BIBLIOGRAPHY

Jenny. By Beth P. Wilson. Macmillan, 1990.

What Will Mommy Do When I'm at School? Macmillan, 1990.

What Kind of Baby-Sitter Is This? Macmillan, 1991.

The Best Bug to Be. Macmillan, 1992.

Who Fed the Chickens? By Ella Jenkins. Scott Foresman, 1992.

Calvin's Christmas Wish. By Calvin Miles. Viking, 1993.

Your Dad Was Just Like You. Macmillan, 1993.

Now Let Me Fly: The Story of a Slave Family. Macmillan, 1993.

Papa's Stories. Macmillan, 1994.

Seminole Diary: Remembrances of a Slave. Macmillan, 1993.

Bessie Coleman: She Dared to Fly. Marshall Cavendish, 1996.

Big Meeting. By Dee Palmer Woodtor. Atheneum, 1996.

The Children's Book of Kwanzaa: A Guide to Celebrating the Holiday. Atheneum, 1996.

Grandma's Hands. Benchmark, 1998.

My Mom Is My Show-and-Tell. Benchmark, 1999.

We Play Music. Lee & Low, 2002.

Johnson, Gail

(1955–)

AUTHOR

E-mail: gjohnson@jhsph.edu

Web site: www.thewritestuff.com

"It seems the vast majority of books written for African American children are of some historical significance, often illustrating the Black experience in America. Such books tend to be of a serious nature. Of course, these stories need to be told. But there's also room for stories that are just plain fun that children can relate to, with situations they can see themselves in. These are the kinds of stories I like to write."

Johnson (pen name G. Francis Johnson) was born in Derby, England, but grew up in Brooklyn, New York, where she lived for over thirty years. She attended the University of Hartford where she majored in psychology.

Johnson has been writing in one form or another most of her life. She began writing for children over eight years ago and has written for Highlights for Children. She was a finalist for the 2002 SCBWI/Judy Blume Contemporary Novel Grant for her middle grade story, *Isabelle's Garden.*

Johnson currently lives in Abingdon, Maryland, with her two sons.

BIBLIOGRAPHY

Has Anybody Lost a Glove? Illustrated by Dimitrea Tokunbo. Boyds Mills Press, 2004.

Johnson, Hannibal B.

(1959–)

AUTHOR

E-mail: hjohnsonok@aol.com

Web site: www.hannibalbjohnson.com

"My parents instilled in me a sense of the majesty of Black history and the nobility of Black history-makers. As a writer, I feel compelled to give voice to the remarkable power of our traditions and culture. Children and young adults need books that connect with them with their roots. We cannot blaze the trails to our future unless we first retrace the footsteps of our past."

Johnson is a graduate of Harvard Law School. He did his undergraduate work at The University of Arkansas, where he completed a double major in economics and sociology. Johnson is an attorney, author, and independent consultant. He has also served as an adjunct professor at The University of Tulsa College of Law, Oklahoma State University, and the University of Oklahoma.

Past president of Leadership Tulsa, past president of the Metropolitan Tulsa Urban League, and past president of the Northeast Oklahoma Black Lawyers Association, he is also the director of Anytown, Oklahoma, a statewide human relations camp for teens sponsored by The National Conference for Community and Justice ("NCCJ"). Johnson served as Chairman of the board of directors of The Community Leadership Association, an international leadership organization, during 2001–2002. A founding director of the Oklahoma Appleseed Center for Law and Justice, he serves on the board of directors of the Oklahoma Department of Libraries and Tulsa Community College Foundation. He is a member of the Rotary Club of Tulsa.

Johnson's honors include the Don Newby/Ben Hill award from Tulsa Metropolitan Ministry; theKeeping The Dream Alive award from the Dr. Martin Luther King, Jr. Commemoration Society; the Outstanding Service to the Public Award from the Oklahoma Bar Association; the Ten Outstanding Young Tulsans award from the Tulsa Jaycees; and the Distinguished Leadership Award from the National Association for Community Leadership. In 2004, Mr. Johnson graduated with the inaugural class of the national Connecting Community Fellowship Program based in Richmond, Virginia.

He lives in Tulsa, Oklahoma.

BIBLIOGRAPHY

Black Wall Street—From Riot to Renaissance in Tulsa's Historic Greenwood District. Eakin Press, 1998.

Up From the Ashes—A Story About Community. Eakin Press, 1999.

Acres of Aspiration—The All-Black Towns in Oklahoma. Eakin Press, 2002.

Mama Used to Say—Wit & Wisdom From the Heart & Soul. HAWK Publishing, 2003.

Jones, K. Maurice

(1958–)

AUTHOR

"I am a literary freedom fighter. Reading is certainly fundamental. As an African American author, I testify that reading has always been my gateway to the actualization of dreams. Reading affords one the freedom and power to envision life beyond their most grandiose imaginations."

An editor, journalist, poet, and performance artist, Jones was born in Highland Park, Michigan. He grew up addicted to the rhythm, blues, and jazz soul of Motown. He began his career as an editor for the *Cass Technician* at Cass Technical High School in Detroit, Michigan, and has been writing ever since. His first book, the award-winning *Say It Loud! The Story of Rap Music*, was published in 1994. It was voted a Best Book for Young Adults, nonfiction, by the American Library Association.

A graduate of the University of Michigan and the Columbia School of Journalism, Jones has traveled, reported, and lectured extensively throughout southern Africa and the Caribbean. He has taught at the College of New Rochelle, Hunter College, and the Africa Literature Center in Kitwe, Zambia. His articles have appeared in the *Rochester Times Union, Black Enterprise, Essence*, the *Michigan Chronicle, Monthly Detroit*, the *Detroit News*, the *Quarterly Black Book Review, Ebony Man*, and *Scholastic* magazine, where he holds the position of media editor.

Jones has appeared at the Nuyorican Poets Café in New York City with percussionist Eli Fountain and tap dancer Savion Glover in "an experimental fusion of jazz, tap, and verse." He is co-chair of the Africa Outreach Committee for the New York chapter of the National Association of Black Journalists; other affiliations include UNICEF's (United Nations Children's Fund) Day of the African

Child, TransAfrica, Fellowship Chapel United Church of Christ in Detroit, and St. Paul Community Baptist Church in Brooklyn, New York.

Jones lives in New York City.

BIBLIOGRAPHY

Say It Loud! The Story of Rap Music. Millbrook, 1994.

Spike Lee and the African American Filmmakers: A Choice of Colors. Millbrook, 1996.

Jordan, June (Meyer)

(1936–2002)

AUTHOR

Jordan was born in New York City. She attended Barnard College and the University of Chicago and then taught English at Connecticut College, City College, City University of New York, Sarah Lawrence College, and the State University of New York (SUNY) at Stony Brook.

Her publications include essays, poetry, newspaper articles, and books for young people. Her work has appeared in the *New York Times, Partisan Review,* the *Village Voice,* and the *Nation.* She has worked in films, with Mobilization for Youth, and as codirector of the Voice of the Children and its writers' workshop. Among her awards are a Rockefeller Foundation fellowship in creative writing, the Rome Prize fellowship in environmental design, 1970–1971, and a C.A.P.S. grant in poetry. *His Own Where,* published in 1971, was a National Book Award finalist and an American Library Association Best Book for Young Adults. *The Voice of the Children* was a 1971 Coretta Scott King Honor Book.

In 1982, Jordan was awarded a National Endowment of the Arts fellowship in poetry. In 1985, she received a New York Foundation of the Arts fellowship and an award from the Massachusetts Council on the Arts in contemporary arts. In 1986, she received an achievement award for national reporting from the National Association of Black Journalists. Jordan was an associate professor of English at SUNY at Stony Brook from 1982 to 1987 and a director of its Creative Writing Program. Since 1989, she had been at the University of California, Berkeley, as professor of African American studies and of English.

She was a member of several organizations, including the Center for Constitutional Rights, the New York Foundation of the Arts (where she served on the board of governors), and the Nicaraguan Culture Alliance (where she was also on the board of directors).

A full-length documentary, *A Place of Rage,* on June Jordan and Angela Davis was produced by England's TV Channel 4, directed by Pratibha Pama.

In 2002 to 2003, Jordan presented *Kissing God Goodbye* at the Vienna Festival in Vienna, Austria.

She was the Founder and Director of Poetry for the People at the University of California at Berkeley.

Jordan died on June 14, 2002 in Berkeley California. She had published twenty-eight books of poetry, political essays, and children's fiction and read her works throughout the United States and Europe.

BIBLIOGRAPHY

Who Looks at Me. Crowell, 1969.

Soulscript: Afro-American Poetry. Edited by June Jordan. Doubleday, 1970.

The Voice of the Children. Collected with Terri Bush. Holt, 1970.

His Own Where. Crowell, 1971.

Some Changes. Dutton (Second Edition), 1971.

Dry Victories. Holt, 1972.

Fannie Lou Hamer. Crowell, 1972.

New Life: New Room. Crowell, 1975.

Kimako's Story. Houghton, 1981.

Joseph, Lynn

AUTHOR

The author was born and reared on the island of Trinidad in the West Indies. She moved to the United States with her family and received a bachelor's degree from the University of Colorado. In 1994 she won the Book America's Award presented by the Consortium of Latin American Studies for *The Mermaid's Twin Sister*.

She lives in Hollis, New York, with her family and is also an attorney for the City of New York.

BIBLIOGRAPHY

Coconut Kind of Day. Illustrated by Sandra Speidel. Lothrop, 1990.

A Wave in Her Pocket: Stories from Trinidad. Illustrated by Brian Pinkney. Clarion, 1991.

An Island Christmas. Illustrated by Catherine Stock. Clarion, 1992.

Jasmine's Parlour Day. Illustrated by Ann Grifalconi. Lothrop, 1994.

The Mermaid's Twin Sister: More Stories from Trinidad. Illustrated by Donna Perrone. Houghton, 1994.

Fly, Bessie, Fly. Illustrated by Yvonne Buchanan. Simon & Schuster, 1998.

Jump Up Time. Illustrated by Linda Saport. Houghton Mifflin, 1998.

Color of My Words. (Reprint). Harper Trophy, 2002.

Keens-Douglas, Ricardo

AUTHOR

"At night, my family would sit on the veranda telling stories and jokes. We had picnics on the beach and ate mangoes until our bellies were full. There was always laughter and a strong sense of living."

Keens-Douglas was born in Grenada, the Isle of Spice. As the youngest of seven children, he has fond memories of growing up. He is a storyteller, playwright, radio and television show host and actor. Now he is exploring new ground—as an author of children's books. His first title, The Nutmeg Princess, teaches an important message to children: "Follow your dreams, and if you believe in yourself all things are possible."

He attended the Dawson Theatre School and has appeared in films and on radio and television across the country, including the Stratford Shakespearean Company. He performed his famous creation story, *Mama God, Papa God*, for Princess Diana aboard the British royal yacht *Britannia* during her 1991 visit to North America.

The biggest influence in his work is the oral tradition of story telling. The sounds of words are like a song to him. He also shares his stories with workshops in schools and universities, encouraging the use of imagination and the expression of cultural pride.

As a storyteller, Keens-Douglas has thrilled audiences in the United States and the Caribbean and at international storytelling festivals. His storytelling cabaret production of *Once Upon an Island* was a Sterling Award nominee for Best Touring Production in Edmonton, Alberta, Canada, in 1991. In 2002, he was inducted into the Caribbean Hall of Fame for Excellence.

Many of Keens-Douglas's stories are now in print and are anthologized in *Take Five* and *Fiery Spirits*. Three fables for young readers, *The Nutmeg Princess, LaDiablesse and the Baby*, and *Freedom Child of the Sea*, have been translated into French and Spanish.

Keens-Douglas currently divides his time between his home in Toronto and Grenada. He is the host of the Caribbean version of *Who Wants To Be a Millionaire.*

BIBLIOGRAPHY

The Nutmeg Princess. Annick Press, 1992.

Freedom Child of the Sea. Annick Press, 1995.

LaDiablesse and the Baby. Annick Press, 1995.

Grandpa's Visit. Annick Press, 1996.

The Miss Meow Pageant. Annick Press, 1998.

Mama God, Papa God: A Caribbean Tale. Crocodile Books, 1999.

The Trial of the Stone: A Folk Tale. Annick Press, 2000.

Anancy and the Haunted House. Annick Press, 2002.

Tales from the Isle of Spice: A Collection of New Caribbean Folk Tales. Annick Press, 2004.

Lauture, Denizé

(1946–)

AUTHOR

Lauture was born in Haiti, the first of thirteen children, and emi-grated from Haiti to the United States in 1968. He was then twenty-two years old, a welder, and without a high school diploma.

He worked as a welder in Harlem, New York, and attended evening classes at the City College of New York. He earned a bache-lor of arts degree in sociology, a master of science degree in bilingual education, and a master of arts in Spanish literature from Lohman College. His poetry has been published in many countries, includ-ing the West Indies, Spain, and Canada. In the United States, his poetry has appeared in various literary magazines, including *Cal-laloo, Black American Literature Forum, African Commentary, Présence Africaine*, and *Artist and Influence*. The main source for his children's books is his childhood in rural Haiti.

Father and Son was one of five books nominated to receive the National Association for the Advancement of Colored People's (NAACP) 1993 Image Award. Lauture teaches at Saint Aquinas Col-lege in Sparkill, New York, where he was the recipient of the 1994 Board of Trustees' Award for Excellence. *Running the Road to ABC* won the 1997 Coretta Scott King Honor Award for illustration.

He has two sons, Charles and Conrad, and lives in the Bronx, New York.

BIBLIOGRAPHY

Father and Son. Illustrated by Jonathan Green. Philomel, 1993.

Running the Road to ABC. Illustrated by Reynold Ruffins. Simon & Schuster, 1996.

Mothers & Daughters. Illustrated by Vladimin Cybil Chanlier. educaVision, 2004.

Lester, Julius (Bernard)

(1939–)

AUTHOR

E-mail: jbles@charter.net

The author was born in Saint Louis, Missouri, but his family moved to Kansas City, Missouri, and then to Nashville, Tennessee, during his early adolescence. Lester earned his bachelor's degree in English in 1960 at Fisk University. He attributes his interest in Southern rural traditions and Black folklore to his father, a Methodist minister and a captivating storyteller.

Lester has had a varied work experience. Since 1971, he has been a professor at the University of Massachusetts, Amherst, where he teaches in the Judaic Studies, English, and History Departments. He hosted a radio talk show on WBAI-FM in New York City from 1968 to 1975 and a live television talk show on WNET from 1971 to 1973.

His political activities include experience in the late 1960s as a field secretary and head of the Photo Department for the Student Non-Violent Coordinating Committee (SNCC). In 1967, he took photographs of North Vietnam to show the effects of U.S. bombing there, and also attended the Organization of the Latin American Solidarity Conference in Cuba with SNCC activist Stokely Carmichael.

As a father, he felt the need to write the sort of books unavailable during his own childhood. Lester has also written books for adults and articles that have appeared in newspapers and journals such as the *Village Voice*, *The New Republic*, *Ebony*, the *New York Times Book Review Forward*, and *Parents' Choice*. He has also written poetry. His interest in music is evident in his work with folk-singer Pete Seeger on the instructional book, *The 12-String Guitar as Played by Leadbelly.*

To Be a Slave was a Newbery Honor Book in 1969, and *Long Journey Home: Stories from Black History* (1972) and *Black Folktales* (1969) were on the *New York Times* list of Outstanding Books of the Year. *Long Journey Home* was nominated for a National Book Award in 1973, and *John Henry*, illustrated by Jerry Pinkney, received both the Caldecott Honor Book Award and the Boston Globe-Horn Book Award in 1995. In addition, Lester won Coretta Scott King Honor Book Awards for *This Strange New Feeling* in 1983 and *The Tales of Uncle Remus: The Adventures of Brer Rabbit* in 1988.

Lester has five children and lives in Belchertown, Massachusetts.

BIBLIOGRAPHY

To Be a Slave. Illustrated by Tom Feelings. Dial, 1968.

Black Folktales. Illustrated by Tom Feelings. R. W. Baron, 1969.

The Knee-High Man and Other Tales. Illustrated by Ralph Pinto. Dial, 1972.

Long Journey Home: Stories from Black History. Dial, 1972.

Two Love Stories. Dial, 1972.

Who I Am. Photopoems by Julius Lester and David Gahr. Dial, 1974.

This Strange New Feeling. Dial, 1982.

The Tales of Uncle Remus: The Adventures of Brer Rabbit. Illustrated by Jerry Pinkney. Dial, 1987.

More Tales of Uncle Remus: Further Adventures of Brer Rabbit, His Friends, Enemies and Others. Illustrated by Jerry Pinkney. Dial, 1988.

How Many Spots Does a Leopard Have? Illustrated by David Shannon. Scholastic, 1989.

Further Tales of Uncle Remus: The Misadventures of Brer Rabbit, Brer Fox, Brer Wolf, the Doodang and Other Creatures. Illustrated by Jerry Pinkney. Dial, 1990.

John Henry. Illustrated by Jerry Pinkney. Dial, 1994.

The Last Tales of Uncle Remus. Illustrated by Jerry Pinkney. Dial, 1994.

The Man Who Knew Too Much: A Moral Tale from the Baila of Zambia. Illustrated by Leonard Jenkins. Clarion, 1994.

Othello: A Novel. Scholastic, 1995.

Sam and the Tigers. Illustrated by Jerry Pinkney. Dial, 1996.

From Slave Ship to Freedom Road. Illustrated by Rod Brown. Dial, 1997.

Black Cowboy, Wild Horses: A True Story. Illustrated by Jerry Pinkney. Dial, 1998.

When the Beginning Began: Stories about God, the Creatures, and Us. Illustrated by Emily Lisker. Silver Whistle-Harcourt, 1999.

What a Truly Cool World. Illustrated by Joe Cepeda. Scholastic, 1999.

Pharaoh's Daughter. Silver Whistle-Harcourt, 2000.

Albidaro and the Mischievous Dream. Illustrated by Jerry Pinkney. Phyllis Fogelman, 2000.

Ackamarackus: Julius Lester's Sumptuously Silly Fabulously Funny Fables. Illustrated by Emile Chollat. Scholastic, 2001.

The Blues Singers: Ten Who Shook the World. Hyperion/Jump at the Sun, 2001.

Why Heaven is Far Away. Illustrated by Joe Cepeda. Scholastic, 2001.

When Dad Killed Mom: A Novel. Harcourt-Silver Whistle, 2001.

Shining. Illustrated by John Clapp. Harcourt-Silver Whistle, 2003.

Let's Talk About Race. Illustrated by Karen Barbour. HarperCollins/Amistad, 2004.

Day of Tears: A Novel is Dialogue. Hyperion/Jump at the Sun, 2005.

The Old African. Illustrated by Jerry Pinkney. Dial Books, 2005.

Lindamichellebaron

(1950–)

AUTHOR

E-mail: harlinjacquepub@aol.com

Web site: www.lindamichellebaron.com

One of two children, Lindamichellebaron was born in New York City, the daughter of a pastor.

She has authored and published two books of poetry, one in 1971 while still a junior at New York University, and the other in 1977. Shortly after, she received the Martin Luther King Service Award for Achievement in Arts and Letters for the year 1978.

Lindamichellebaron, a former New York City public school teacher, earned her master's degree in reading and her doctorate in cross categorical studies from Columbia University's Teachers College.

President and founder of Harlin Jacque Publications, a publishing and educational consulting firm established over two decades ago, she visits public schools, colleges, conferences, and organizations to share positive approaches to academic achievement and personal growth. She artfully weaves a range of instructional and inspiration styles that creates interactive experiences for adults and children of all ages.

She became an educational sales representative for the McGraw-Hill publishing company in 1978, and her reputation as a "take care of business" salesperson allowed her to be welcomed at two other major publishing houses, Harcourt Brace Jovanovich and Silver Burdett. In 1988, she began working for herself as a publisher, performing artist, motivational speaker, consultant, and "edu-tainer."

She received the New York State Small Business Development Center's Entrepreneur of the Year Award in 1993 and the Business Recognition Award for Outstanding Business Achievement and Its Impact on Community Life, presented in 1991 by the Black Business and Professional Women. She received the 1992 National Association for the Advancement of Colored People's (NAACP) President's Award and was named Educator of the Year in 1995 by the New York Association of Black Educators.

Lindamichellebaron appears nationally as a keynote speaker at colleges and universities and social and political organizations and has been featured on both radio and television. She is on the board of directors for the multicultural Publishing Exchange and Black Women in Publishing, and she is a member of many professional and social organizations, including the Theta Iota Omega chapter of Alpha Kappa Alpha sorority.

Lindamichellebaron lives in Garden City, New York.

BIBLIOGRAPHY

Black is Beautiful. Lindamichellebaron, 1971.

Going Through Changes. Illustrated by Leola Young. Lindamichellebaron, 1977.

Rhythm and Dues. Illustrated by Jorge Domenech. Harlin Jacque, 1981, 1990, 1995.

The Sun is On. Illustrated by Jorge Domenech. Harlin Jacque, 1981, 1990, 1995.

For the Love of Life. Harlin Jacque Publications, 2002.

Anthony Ant and Grady Grasshopper. Illustrated by Zeph Ernest. Harlin Jacque Publications, 2004.

Lindsey, Kathleen Dorothy

(1949–)

AUTHOR

Web site: www.Katlindsey.com

"My writing career started at four years old. To keep me quiet my mother would give me old junk mail to carry to church and I would scribble on every inch of those papers creating stories. That was the easy part. The hard part was finding someone that would take the time to listen. Many of my stories are historical fiction about families working together for a common goal. This is one way of preserving my family's legacy through patience, understanding and most of all, hard work!"

After completing her High School education, Kathleen Lindsey, or "Kat" as she prefers to be called, was employed at her local school district. For ten years she worked as a teacher's assistant for the reading department and four years as a teacher's aide with handicapped/mentally challenged elementary and high school students. She became very interested in literacy for young children, taking courses to improve her writing skills.

Lindsey served as president of a local quilting guild and began teaching quilting in craft stores, libraries, schools, churches, and community centers. Quilting took on a new perspective when she was featured in *Good Housekeeping Magazine*, January of 1996.

In 1988, after the death of her son, Lindsey worked with many families through the organization, M.A.D.D., Mothers Against Drunk Driving. As a volunteer for Gloucester County Chapter of Victims, she gave lectures on the dangers of drinking and driving to families, groups of D.U.I. offenders, and High School students. She used her quilting as a sharing experience to cope with grief. Together, members composed a quilt to represent their loved ones.

This quilt is displayed at many conferences and formal presentations given by M.A.D.D.

Lindsey used her family recipe for Sweet Potato Pie that has been passed down for generations as the theme for a prize-winning quilt. The Sweet Potato Pie Quilt has been admired by thousands of children and adults over the past five years and is featured in her first children's picture book for readers of all ages, called *Sweet Potato Pie*, published by Lee & Low Books in September of 2003. She also plans to put the story on audiocassette with a raised picture of the quilt to be as a hands-on experience for the blind.

Lindsey gives presentations for TV documentaries, colleges, churches, schools (pre-kindergarten to twelfth grade), and various historical societies. A student thesis has been written telling about her quilting and how her life is parallel to that of her ancestors. Recently, she gave a performance for *Overbrook School for the Blind* in Philadelphia. In addition, Lindsey has presented her program for the Commissioner of Education in Trenton, New Jersey.

One of her latest most prized achievements was to pose for a 70-foot high mural in Philadelphia, Pennsylvania on the I. Goldberg store in center city. She depicts the famous Underground Railroad conductor, Harriet Tubman.

In January, 2004 she received a Proclamation from the Mayor and Borough Council of Clayton, New Jersey and was honored for her numerous achievements.

In March, 2004 Lindsey performed at the New Jersey Avenue School in Atlantic City, New Jersey and shared the stage with Miss Erica Dunlap, Miss America 2004.

Kathleen Lindsey lives with her husband, David, and their two youngest children in Clayton, New Jersey.

BIBLIOGRAPHY

Sweet Potato Pie. Illustrated by Charlotte Riley-Webb. Lee & Low, 2003.

Little, Lessie Jones

(1906–1986)

AUTHOR

Little was born in Parmele, North Carolina. A 1924 graduate of Higgs Roanoke Seminary, she also attended North Carolina State Normal School (now Elizabeth City State University). After graduation, she began teaching in her home state, and two years later she married her childhood sweetheart, Weston W. Little, Sr. They moved to Washington, D.C., in 1929 and later became parents of five children.

Little's daughter, children's author Eloise Greenfield, has noted that her mother had a special love for people and for the arts and enjoyed bringing these together through her writing.. Although Little entered this field late in her life (she was almost seventy), she was diligent in studying the craft and took seriously what she saw as her responsibility to pass on to children messages of truth and hope.

She developed a Harriet Tubman crossword puzzle, which appeared in *Ebony Jr.'s* June/July 1973 issue, and this experience became the stimulus for writing. Her own book of poetry, *Love: A Lamp Unto My Feet*, was published in 1982.

Among her awards during her brief writing career are the Boston Globe-Horn Book Honor Book Award in 1980 for *Childtimes: A Three-Generational Memoir* which she coauthored with her daughter, and the 1988 Parents Choice Award for *Children of Long Ago*.

She died leaving several unpublished manuscripts—picture books and poetry for children and a novel for adults.

BIBLIOGRAPHY

I Can Do It by Myself. With Eloise Greenfield. Illustrated by Carole Byard. Crowell, 1978.

Childtimes: A Three-Generation Memoir. With Eloise Greenfield. Illustrated by Jerry Pinkney. Harper, 1979.

Children of Long Ago (New edition). Illustrated by Jan Spivey Gilchrest. Lee & Low, 2000.

Lloyd, Errol

(1943–)

AUTHOR/ILLUSTRATOR

Lloyd was born in Jamaica and attended Munro College, Jamaica, London University, and the Council of Education in London, England. He became interested in art when he was about sixteen years old. He had already decided on a legal career, and he did start to study law in 1964, but his love of art outweighed this pursuit and he never completed his studies.

His illustrations for *My Brother Sean*, written by Petronella Breinburg, were commended for the Kate Greenaway Medal in England in 1974.

BIBLIOGRAPHY

My Brother Sean. By Petronella Breinburg. Bodley Head, 1973.

Shawn Goes to School. By Petronella Breinburg. HarperCollins, 1973.

Doctor Shawn. By Petronella Breinburg. HarperCollins, 1975.

Shawn's Red Bike. By Petronella Breinburg. Crowell, 1976.

Nimi at Carnival. Crowell, 1978.

Nima on Time. Random House, 1981.

Nandy's Bedtime. Bodley Head, 1982.

Y Has a Long Tail. Penguin Books Ltd., 1988.

Sasha and the Bicycle Thieves. Barron's, 1989.

Ravi at the FunFair. Blackie Children's Books, 1990.

Don't Do That! Cambridge University Press, 1991.

The Big Gold Robbery (Yellow Bananas). Egmont Children's Books, 1993.

Many Rivers to Cross. Egmont Children's Books, 1996.

Oxford Reading Tree: Treetops True Stories: This Is Me! Oxford University Press, 2003.

Lyons, Kelly Starling

(1971–)

AUTHOR

E-mail: email@Kellystarlinglyons.com

Web site: http://www.kellystarlinglyons.com

"As a child growing up in a predominantly white neighborhood, I rarely found books at my elementary school about young people who looked like me. Instead, I entered the world of white children and talking animals. Magic lived for me in those pages then as it does now. But as a Black girl, I longed for something to connect with my spirit in a different way. A few years ago while working as a feature writer for Ebony magazine, I discovered it—multicultural children's books. That literary landscape swept me into familiar and new places. It became a channel that transported me back to the enchantment of youth. Reading those stories was like peering into a mirror displaying the desires, fears, struggles and joys of young folks I knew and the girl I used to be. Right then, I decided that one day I would add my voice.

"I am inspired by trailblazers like Virginia Hamilton, Walter Dean Myers, Patricia and Fred McKissack, and contemporary writers who infuse their stories with power and purpose. The tales they create send young people on a journey. Kids enter the world of their characters, experience their emotions, and see their surroundings. Our children hunger for that kind of quality writing that speaks to who they are. We can motivate them to read by continuing to make books that tell their stories, visiting schools and community centers to make personal connections and raise the profile of children's literature by Black authors and letting kids know that they matter."

For Pittsburgh native, Lyons, the love of writing started as a child. Her aspiration first took her to Syracuse University where she earned a bachelor of arts in African American studies and a master of science in Magazine Journalism.) Next, Lyons became a journalist who specialized in feature writing about relationships, personal struggles and communities of color. She has worked for the *Syracuse Newspapers*, *Ebony* magazine, and *The News Observer* in Raleigh, North Carolina. and been a fellow at the *Casey Journalism Center*. Lyons, now a freelance writer and children's book author, belongs to the Society of Children's Book Writers and Illustrators, the Author's Guild, online forum for the African-American Children's Book Writers and Illustrators and Delta Sigma Theta Sorority, Inc. Her first book, *Eddie's Ordeal*, title #4 in the middle-grade series *NEATE*, was published in 2004 by Just Us Books. Lyons lives with her husband and young daughter in Raleigh, North Carolina.

BIBLIOGRAPHY

Eddie's Ordeal. Just Us Books, 2004.

Magubane, Peter

(1932–)

ILLUSTRATOR/AUTHOR

Photographer Magubane was born in Johannesburg, South Africa. He started his career in 1956 as a photographer in Vrededorp, now Pageview, a suburb in Johannesburg on the magazine *Drum* and was a staff member of the *Rand Daily Mail*, a Johannesburg newspaper. For more than twenty years, he was the only major Black South African news photographer. His experiences, recorded in *Magubane's South Africa*, portray his arrests, banning orders, solitary confinement, and other experiences under the apartheid system. He became more attracted to photography after usng a Brownie as a schoolboy. Magubane's photographs have documented the struggle for liberation in South Africa for more than fifty years. As a visiting scholar at UCLA, Magubane was honored at a reception at the newly renovated African-American Museum in Exposition Park. The reception was cosponsored by the Museum, the UCLA Center for American-American Studies, the Black Photographers of California, and the UCLA Center for African Studies. More than one hundred people attended the invitation-only event.

His *Black Child* won the 1983 Coretta Scott King Award for illustration.

He still has a home in Dupkloof, a section of the Black township of Soweto, outside Johannesburg, South Africa.

BIBLIOGRAPHY
Black Child. Knopf, 1982.

Massey, Calvin (Cal)

(1926–)

ILLUSTRATOR

E-mail: cal@calmassey.com

Web site: www.calmassey.com

"I paint because I have to; it's my way of communicating with the world around me."

Massey was born in Philadelphia, Pennsylvania. He attended and graduated from the Hussian School in Philadelphia in 1950, majoring in life drawing and illustration. He later joined the faculty for a three-year tenure.

His illustrations have appeared in the *Saturday Evening Post* and have been used by several publishing companies, including Scott Foresman, Random House, Scholastic, and Just Us Books. Among his designs and sculptures, he has created the crest and class rings for the United States Naval Air Force Military Academy, the MacArthur Memorial Medal, and a bas-relief sculpture commemorating the restoration of Ellis Island for the Statue of Liberty Foundation. He designed fifty medallions for the Madison Collection from 1990 to 1991.

Massey has had several one-man shows: at John Wanamaker's Fine Arts Gallery in 1979, the Makler Gallery in Philadelphia, Pennsylvania, in 1979, and Swarthmore College between 1983 and 1984, among others. He was commissioned to do a portrait of Gloria Chisum in 1993 for the Philadelphia Library, and his work can be found in many private collections.

Massey's exhibitions have been seen in the Philadelphia Library in 1993,, Shows 2 and 3 at the Washington Arts Festival in 1992 and

1993 and several one-man shows, among them the Prestige Fine Gallery in 1992 and the Heritage Celebration in New York in 1993.

When not painting, Massey lends his artistic touch to baking breads and pastries; plays a mean jazz piano, and is a student of Siddha Yoga and Theosophical concepts.

Massey lives in Moorestown, New Jersey.

BIBLIOGRAPHY

Tom B and the Joyful Noise. By Jerome Cushman. Westminster, 1970.

What Harry Found When He Lost Archie. By Jean Horton Berg. Westminster, 1970.

My First Kwanzaa Book. By Deborah M. Newton Chocolate. Scholastic, 1992.

I Love My Family. By Wade Hudson. Scholastic, 1993.

Jesus Feeds a Crowd. American Bible Society, 2002.

Mathenge, Judy (Wanjiku)

(1971–)

ILLUSTRATOR

Born in Nairobi, Kenya, Mathenge went to Nairobi Primary School and Kenya High School for Girls. Inspired by her secondary school art teacher, and encouraged by her father to pursue a career in art, she entered Kenyatta University and graduated in 1994 with a bachelor's degree in fine art. Mathenge has been associated with the publishing house Jacaranda Designs since it first began operation in 1991, working part-time as an illustrator until her graduation, when she became a full-time member of the art staff.

In 1995, she was selected as the illustrator for the book *What Causes Bad Memories* by the trauma team of UNICEF (United Nations Children's Fund), which was working with displaced and orphaned children in Rwanda. A trained and qualified teacher and artist, Mathenge was selected to run the Healing Arts Program, which organizes groups of Kenyan secondary school art students to paint the walls in the children's wards of Nairobi hospitals.

At the Pan African Book Fair in Nairobi, she conducted a painting workshop in 1994 and was a facilitator in computer graphic design in 1995.

She lives in Nairobi, Kenya.

BIBLIOGRAPHY

Mcheshi Goes to the Market. By The Jacaranda House Team. Jacaranda Designs, 1993.

Beneath the Rainbow: Princess Rainbow. By Kariuki Gakuo. Jacaranda Designs, 1994.

Mcheshi Goes on a Journey. By The Jacaranda House Team. Jacaranda Designs, 1994.

Zamani: Flight of the Firehawk. By Tom Nevin. Jacaranda Designs, 1995.

What Causes Bad Memories. By UNICEF, UNICEF, 1995.

Mcheshi Goes to School. By The Jacaranda House Team. Jacaranda Designs, 1995.

Mcheshi Goes to a Farm. By The Jacaranda House Team. Jacaranda Designs, 1995.

Mathis, Sharon (Yvonne) Bell

(1937–)

AUTHOR

Mathis was born in Atlantic City, New Jersey, the first of four children. As a child and young adult, she enjoyed reading her books on an iron fire escape suspended above the back yard. The books of Black writers were greatly appreciated in Mathis's home, and she had the additional advantage of watching her mother draw pictures and create poems.

Mathis graduated from Morgan State University, Baltimore, Maryland, in 1958, and in 1975 she received a master of science degree in library science from Catholic University in Washington, D.C. After five years as a fifth-grade teacher for the archdiocese of Washington, ten years as a special-education teacher, and twenty years as a school library media specialist, Mathis retired from the District of Columbia public schools in 1995.

A former columnist for *Ebony, Jr.* magazine, Mathis has contributed fiction to *Negro Digest*, *Essence* and *Scholastic* magazines. She has reviewed books for the *Washington Post* and *Black Books Bulletin*. *Sidewalk Story* was a Child Study Association of America's Children's Book of the Year in 1970. Several of her works have been American Library Association Notable Books. *The Hundred Penny Box* was a Newbery Honor Book in 1976, and *Ray Charles* won the Coretta Scott King Award in 1974 for both text and illustration. *Red Dog, Blue Fly* won the American Bookseller Association Pick of the List in 1991 and Bank Street College's Children's Books for the year 1991.

The divorced mother of three daughters, she lives in Fort Washington, Maryland.

BIBLIOGRAPHY

Brooklyn Story. Illustrated by Charles Bible. Hill & Wang, 1970.

Sidewalk Story. Illustrated by Leo Carty. Viking, 1971.

Teacup Full of Roses. Viking, 1972.

Ray Charles. Illustrated by George Ford. Crowell, 1973.

Listen for the Fig Tree. Viking, 1974.

The Hundred Penny Box. Illustrated by Leo and Diane Dillon. Viking, 1975.

Cartwheels. Illustrated by Norma Holt. Scholastic, 1977.

Red Dog, Blue Fly. Illustrated by Jan Spivey Gilchrist. Viking, 1991.

Running Girl: The Diary of Ebonee Rose. Browndeer, 1997.

Mbugua, Kioi wa

(1962–)

AUTHOR

Mbugua was born in Ngong near Nairobi, Kenya, the third in a family of seven children. He grew up in an ethnically mixed environment among the Kikuyu and the culture loving Maasai peoples. This played an essential role in his development, inculcating a deep appreciation of cultural diversity and a love of the rich, traditional African heritage.

Mbugua graduated from Nairobi University in 1988 with a bachelor's degree in African languages. He worked for two years as a journalist with the Kenya News Agency and continues to contribute articles, short stories, and book reviews. He is an active member of the Kenya Oral Literature Association, an organization that promotes professional collection and publication of Kenyan folklore.

In 1991, he received a postgraduate diploma in film production from the Kenya Institute of Mass Communication. In 1995, he worked as a script consultant on two educational video productions: *Roots of Rhythm* and *Envision: The Malaysia Child of Kenya.*

Since 1991, he has been a resident writer and editor with Jacaranda Designs and has actively participated in training workshops for African writers and illustrators from other countries. Mbugua has translated several of their books into Swahili and is a senior member of the editorial board.

He lives in Naiobi, Kenya.

BIBLIOGRAPHY

Inkishu: Myths and Legends of the Maasai. Jacaranda Designs, 1994.
Inkishu: Nkai's Great Gift. Illustrated by Kang'ara wa Njambi. Jacaranda Designs, 1994.

Inkishu: The Forest of the Lost Child. Illustrated by Samwel Ngoje. Jacaranda Designs, 1994.

Fumo Liyongo: A Hero of Swahili. Jacaranda Designs, 1996.

Fumo Liyondo: A Hero of Swahili. Illustrated by Mazola Mwashigadi. Jacaranda Designs, 2001.

McConduit, Denise Walter

(1950–)

AUTHOR

E-mail: denisemcconduit@yahoo.com

Web site: www.denisemcconduit.com

"When I write children's books, I try to create something that will reach children and adults on many levels. African American children in inner cities can be exposed to both negative and positive elements in their environment. It is important for them to see their life experiences, culture and adventures captured in literature. The D..J. series is about a little boy from New Orleans who likes to have fun. D.J. has taught me how to look at things through the eyes and heart of a child. Writing for children is rewarding because one story can change a child forever. Stories are powerful because as human beings our lives are formed around our own personal or family stories. We mark our passages of life in terms of stories. To me, writing books for children is an honor, privilege, and a responsibility."

McConduit has written stories about the rich culture of New Orleans. She has been invited to speak at numerous book conferences, schools, and libraries throughout Louisiana and the United States. Some of her publications include *Essence Magazine, Black New Orleans Magazine*, and the *New Orleans Tribune*.

The character of D.J. is based on her own son, Darrell James McConduit. It was his real-life experience as a page in the famous New Orleans Zulu parade that gave her the idea to write the book, *D.J. and the Zulu Parade*. Her second book, *D.J. and the Jazz Fest*, takes young readers on D.J.'s adventure to his first visit to the New Orleans Jazz & Heritage Festival with his mother, who wanted him to learn about jazz music. In her newest book, *D.J. and the*

Debutante Ball, Mom is determined to send him to an etiquette school to learn about manners. Although the etiquette school visit was disastrous, D.J. does finally learn about manners from his grandfather, who was a former World War II veteran. Children love to read about New Orleans culture and McConduit has been able to capture some of the city's unique experiences and put them into context for children.

A native of New Orleans, McConduit graduated from St. Mary's Academy and is currently pursuing a degree in English Literature from the Southern University of New Orleans. She serves on the Advisory Board of the Friends of the New Orleans Public Library and is a member of the Society of Children's Book Writers. She lives in New Orleans and has four grown children and four exceptional grandchildren.

BIBLIOGRAPHY

D.J. and the Zulu Parade. Illustrated by Emile Henriquez and Lucian Barbarin. Pelican, 1995.

D.J. and the Jazz Fest. Illustrated by Emile Henriquez. Pelican, 1997.

D.J. and the Debutante Ball. Illustrated by Emile Henriquez. Pelican, 2004.

McDonald, Janet

AUTHOR

E-mail: projectfille@hotmail.com

Web site: www.projectgirl.com

"Children everywhere, growing and grown, are enriched by good literature. If the stories written recount the lives of people who think, dream and do with dash and defiance, that is great. If those people happen to look or live like the reader, that's even better. In writing about "growing up urban" I aim to incite and inspire, amuse and instruct. You'll find in my books references to Doestoevsky and Missy Elliott, Shakespeare and Snoop Dogg, Darwin and do-rags. Because, in literature as in life, it really is all good."

One of seven children, Janet McDonald grew up in Brooklyn, New York. She holds a bachelor's degree in French Literature from Vassar College, a master's in journalism from Columbia University School of Journalism and a JDoctor degree from New York University School of Law. She practiced law in New York, Seattle, and Paris, and is a member of MENSA, the international IQ society.

McDonald moved to Paris in 1995 where her career an as international corporate lawyer took her from Brooklyn to Bermuda, Europe to India, with stops along the way in England, Germany, Italy, Norway, Spain, and Slovenia. She began writing fiction for young adults in 2001 and has garnered widespread critical acclaim, winning in 2002 for *Chill Wind* the American Library Association's Coretta Scott King/John Steptoe New Talent Award. Her books have been included on a number of "best books" lists by the American Library Association, the New York Public Library and the Chicago Public Library.

An enthusiastic correspondent, McDonald welcomes e-mail and letters from readers.

BIBLIOGRAPHY

Spellbound. Francis Foster Books/Farrar Straus & Giroux, 2001.

Chill Wind. Frances Foster Books/Farrar Straus & Giroux, 2002.

Twists and Turns. Frances Foster Books/Farrar Straus & Giroux, 2003.

Skin Deep. Puffin/Penguin, 2004.

Brother Hood. Frances Foster Books/Farrar Straus & Giroux, 2004.

Harlem Hustle. Frances Foster Books/Farrar Straus & Giroux, 2006.

McKissack, Fredrick (Lemuel)

(1939–)

AUTHOR

"If you don't know the stories and lore of your people, then it is difficult to participate in the culture."

McKissack, a civil engineer, was born in Nashville, Tennessee. He has owned his own construction company for many years. Now, he believes, his writing "builds bridges with books." He comes from a long line of builders. His great-grandfather, Moses McKissack, was the first licensed Black architect in the state of Tennessee and the founder of a company that bore his name as partner. His grandfather was one of the first African American builders known particularly for his design of doors. His father, Lewis Winter McKissack, was also an architect.

McKissack attended Tennessee State University (formerly Tennessee Agricultural and Industrial State University) and obtained his bachelor of science degree in civil engineering in 1964. He is a member of the African Method Episcopal Church, where he is a steward on the church board and a member of the male chorus. He also belongs to the National Writers Guild and the Society of Children's Book Writers and Illustrators and is co-owner of All-Writing Services with his wife, Patricia.

He has shared honors with his wife for many books, including *Abram, Abram, Where Are We Going?*, which won the C.S. Lewis Silver Medal Award from the Christian Educators Association in 1985; *A Long Hard Journey: The Story of the Pullman Porter*, which won the Jane Addams Children's Book Award and the Coretta Scott King Award in 1990; *Sojourner Truth: Ain't I a Woman?*, which won a Boston Globe-Horn Book Award in 1993 and was a Coretta Scott

King Honor Book that same year; and *Christmas in the Big House, Christmas in the Quarters*, which won the Coretta Scott King Award in 1995. *Rebels Against Slavery: American Slave Revolts* was named a 1997 Coretta Scott King Author Honor Book.

McKissack has been called "one of the best" researchers in the business, and with good reason. The photo research for the book *A Long Hard Journey: The Story of the Pullman Porter* has been widely acclaimed because of the previously unpublished photographs he secured from a private collection. In 1993, he was honored as Tennessee Author of the Year by the *Nashville Banner* newspaper for his research.

In addition to writing, McKissack and his wife are often speakers at educational meetings, workshops, and seminars. Both received honorary doctorate degrees in 1994 from the University of Missouri.

He lives in Chesterfield, Missouri, a suburb of St. Louis.

BIBLIOGRAPHY

Abram, Abram, Where Are We Going? With Patricia C. McKissack. David Cook, 1984.

It's the Truth, Christopher. With Patricia C. McKissack. Augsburg, 1984.

Lights Out, Christopher. With Patricia C. McKissack. Illustrated by Bartholomew. Augsburg, 1984.

Michael Jackson: Superstar. With Patricia C. McKissack. Children's Press, 1984.

Paul Laurence Dunbar: A Poet to Remember. With Patricia C. McKissack. Children's Press, 1984.

The Civil Rights Movement in America from 1865 to the Present. With Patricia C. McKissack. Children's Press, 1987, 1991.

Frederick Douglass: The Black Lion. With Patricia C. McKissack. Children's Press, 1987.

Constance Stumbles. With Patricia C. McKissack. Children's Press, 1988.

Messy Bessey. With Patricia C. McKissack. Illustrated by Richard Hackney. A Big Book. Children's Press, 1988.

God Made Something Wonderful. With Patricia C. McKissack. Illustrated by Ching. Augsburg, 1989.

A Long Hard Journey: The Story of the Pullman Porter. With Patricia C. McKissack. Walker, 1990.

Taking a Stand Against Racism and Racial Discrimination. With Patricia C. McKissack. Watts, 1990.

W.E.B. Du Bois. With Patricia C. McKissack. Watts, 1990.

Carter G. Woodson. With Patricia C. McKissack. Enslow, 1991.

Frederick Douglass: Leader Against Slavery. With Patricia C. McKissack. Enslow, 1991.

George Washington Carver: The Peanut Scientist. With Patricia C. McKissack. Enslow, 1991.

Ida B. Wells-Barnett: A Voice Against Violence. With Patricia C. McKissack. Enslow, 1991.

Louis Armstrong: Jazz Musician. With Patricia C. McKissack. Enslow, 1991.

Marian Anderson: A Great Singer. With Patricia C. McKissack. Enslow, 1991.

Martin Luther King, Jr.: Man of Peace. With Patricia C. McKissack. Enslow, 1991.

Mary Church Terrell: Leader for Equality. With Patricia C. McKissack. Enslow, 1991.

Ralph J. Bunche: Peacemaker. With Patricia C. McKissack. Enslow, 1991.

Booker T. Washington: Leader and Educator. With Patricia C. McKissack. Enslow, 1992.

Jesse Owens: Olympic Star. With Patricia C. McKissack. Enslow, 1992.

Langston Hughes: Great American Poet. With Patricia C. McKissack. Enslow, 1992.

Madam C. J. Walker: Self-Made Millionaire. With Patricia C. McKissack. Enslow, 1992.

Paul Robeson: A Voice to Remember. With Patricia C. McKissack. Enslow, 1992.

Satchel Paige: The Best Arm in Baseball. With Patricia C. McKissack. Enslow, 1992.

Sojourner Truth: Ain't I a Woman? With Patricia C. McKissack. Scholastic, 1992.

Zora Neale Hurston: Writer and Storyteller. With Patricia C. McKissack. Enslow, 1992.

Tennessee Trailblazers. With Patricia C. McKissack. March Media, 1993.

African-American Inventors. With Patricia C. McKissack. Millbrook, 1994.

Christmas in the Big House, Christmas in the Quarters. With Patricia C. McKissack. Scholastic, 1994.

The Royal Kingdoms of Ghana, Mali and Songhay: Life in Medieval Africa. With Patricia C. McKissack. Holt, 1994.

Red-Tail Angels: The Story of the Tuskegee Airmen of World War II. With Patricia C. McKissack. Walker, 1995.

Rebels Against Slavery: American Slave Revolts. With Patricia C. McKissack. Scholastic, 1996.

Ma Dear's Apron. Illustrated by Floyd Cooper. Knopf, 1997.

Can You Imagine? Photographs by Miles Pinkney. Owen, 1997.

Let my People Go: Bible Stories Told by a Freeman of Color. Illustrated by James E. Ransome. Atheneum, 1998.

Run Away Home. Scholastic, 1998.

McKissack, Patricia (Carwell)

(1944–)

AUTHOR

"Good books—fiction and nonfiction—written for, by, and about African Americans are needed if we are to help young readers develop a healthy self-image and an open attitude about other cultures different from their own. That is my goal. To reach it, however, I begin by writing an appealing story. When youngsters have an enjoyable reading experience, they are most likely to choose a similar book . . . and another. By providing interesting and lively written materials for children, the above goal can be achieved."

The author was born in Nashville, Tennessee. McKissack attended Tennessee Agricultural and Industrial State University), now Tennessee State University, where she obtained her bachelor of arts degree in 1964. She earned a master of arts in 1975 from Webster University in St. Louis, Missouri, and married writer Fredrick McKissack in 1964. From 1968 to 1975, she worked as a junior high school teacher in Kirkwood, Missouri, and in 1975 she was a part-time instructor in English at Forest Park College in St. Louis.

McKissack is co-owner of All-Writing Services with her husband and has been an instructor of children's literature at the University of Missouri. She was a writer for a preschool series, *L Is for Wishing*, broadcast by KWMU radio from 1975 to 1977. She has written radio and television scripts and been a contributor to the magazines *Friend, Happy Times,* and *Evangelizing Today's Child*.

McKissack won the Helen Keating Ott Award from the National Church and Synagogue Librarians Association in 1980 for her editorial work at Concordia Publishing House and Coretta Scott King Award in 1993 for her book *The Dark-Thirty: Southern*

Tales of the Supernatural. In addition, in 1989 Jerry Pinkney won a Caldecott Honor Book Award and the Coretta Scott King Award for his illustration of McKissack's book *Mirandy and Brother Wind.*

McKissack has also shared honors with her husband on many books, including *Abram, Abram, Where Are We Going?*, which won the C.S. Lewis Silver Medal Award from the Christian Educators Association in 1985; *A Long Hard Journey: The Story of the Pullman Porter,* which won the Jane Addams Children's Book Award and the Coretta Scott King Award in 1990; *Sojourner Truth: Ain't I a Woman?*, which won a Boston Globe-Horn Book Award in 1993 and was a Coretta Scott King Honor Book that same year; and *Christmas in the Big House, Christmas in the Quarters,* which won the Coretta Scott King Award in 1995.

McKissack's memberships include Alpha Kappa Alpha sorority, the Tennessee State Alumni Association, the Authors Guild, and the Society for Children's Book Writers and Illustrators.

In 1991, McKissack wrote her first movie script with award-winning author, Marvis Jukes. The movie, produced by Disney Educational Productions, titled *Who Owns the Sun,* won several major film awards and a starred review from Kirkus. In 1994 she and her husband received honorary doctorate degrees from the University of Missouri.

McKissack lives in St. Louis, Missouri, with her husband, Fredrick McKissack. They have three adult sons. Their oldest son Fredrick, Jr., co-author with her of *Black Diamond: The Story of the Negro Baseball League,* is an editor for *The Progressive Magazine* n Madison, Wisconsin. Their son Robert wrote a text for the educational division of Houghton Mifflin Publishers, and John Patrick is an engineer in Memphis, Tennessee.

BIBLIOGRAPHY

Who Is Who? Illustrated by Elizabeth M. Allen. Children's Press, 1983.

Abram, Abram, Where Are We Going? With Fredrick McKissack. David Cook, 1984.

It's the Truth, Christopher. With Fredrick McKissack. Augsburg, 1984.

Lights Out, Christopher. With Fredrick McKissack. Illustrated by Bartholomew. Augsburg, 1984.

Michael Jackson: Superstar. With Fredrick McKissack. Children's Press, 1984.

Paul Laurence Dunbar: A Poet to Remember. With Fredrick McKissack. Children's Press, 1984.

Flossie and the Fox. Illustrated by Rachel Isadora. Dial, 1986.

When Do You Talk to God? Prayers for Small Children. Illustrated by Gary Gumble. Augsburg, 1986.

The Civil Rights Movement in America from 1865 to the Present. With Fredrick McKissack. Children's Press, 1987, 1991..

Frederick Douglass: The Black Lion. With Fredrick McKissack. Children's Press, 1987.

Constance Stumbles. Illustrated by Tom Dunnington. With Fredrick McKissack. Children's Press, 1988.

Messy Bessey. With Fredrick McKissack. Illustrated by Richard Hackney. A Big Book. Children's Press, 1988.

Mirandy and Brother Wind. Illustrated by Jerry Pinkney. Knopf, 1988.

Monkey-Monkey's Trick: Based on an African Folk Tale. Illustrated by Paul Meisel. Random House, 1988.

God Made Something Wonderful. With Fredrick McKissack. Illustrated by Ching. Augsburg, 1989.

Jesse Jackson: A Biography. Scholastic, 1989.

Nettie Jo's Friend. Illustrated by Scott Cook. Knopf, 1989.

James Weldon Johnson: Lift Every Voice and Sing. Children's Press, 1990.

A Long Hard Journey: The Story of the Pullman Porter. With Fredrick McKissack. Walker, 1990.

Taking a Stand Against Racism and Racial Discrimination. With Fredrick McKissack. Watts, 1990.

W.E.B. Du Bois. With Fredrick McKissack. Watts, 1990.

Who Is Coming? Illustrated by Clovis Martin. Children's Press, 1990.

Carter G. Woodson. Illustrated by Ned Ostendorf. With Fredrick McKissack. Enslow, 1991.

Frederick Douglass: Leader Against Slavery. Illustrated by Ned Ostendorf. With Fredrick McKissack. Enslow, 1991.

George Washington Carver: The Peanut Scientist. Illustrated by Ned Ostendorf. With Fredrick McKissack. Enslow, 1991.

Ida B. Wells-Barnett: A Voice Against Violence. Illustrated by Ned Ostendorf. With Fredrick McKissack. Enslow, 1991.

Louis Armstrong: Jazz Musician. Illustrated by Ned Ostendorf. With Fredrick McKissack. Enslow, 1991.

Marian Anderson: A Great Singer. Illustrated by Ned Ostendorf. With Fredrick McKissack. Enslow, 1991.

Martin Luther King, Jr.: Man of Peace. Illustrated by Ned Ostendorf. With Fredrick McKissack. Enslow, 1991.

Mary Church Terrell: Leader for Equality. Illustrated by Ned Ostendorf. With Fredrick McKissack. Enslow, 1991.

Ralph J. Bunche: Peacemaker. Illustrated by Ned Ostendorf. With Fredrick McKissack. Enslow, 1991.

Booker T. Washington: Leader and Educator. With Fredrick McKissack. Enslow, 1992.

The Dark-Thirty: Southern Tales of the Supernatural. Illustrated by Brian Pinkney. Knopf, 1992.

Jesse Owens: Olympic Star. With Fredrick McKissack. Enslow, 1992.

Langston Hughes: Great American Poet. With Fredrick McKissack. Enslow, 1992.

Madam C. J. Walker: Self-Made Millionaire. With Fredrick McKissack. Enslow, 1992.

A Million Fish . . . More or Less. Illustrated by Dena Schutzer. Knopf, 1992.

Paul Robeson: A Voice to Remember. With Fredrick McKissack. Enslow, 1992.

Satchel Paige: The Best Arm in Baseball. With Fredrick McKissack. Enslow, 1992.

Sojourner Truth: Ain't I a Woman? With Fredrick McKissack. Scholastic, 1992.

Zora Neale Hurston: Writer and Storyteller. With Fredrick McKissack. Enslow, 1992.

Tennessee Trailblazers. With Fredrick McKissack. March Media, 1993.

African-American Inventors. With Fredrick McKissack. Millbrook, 1994.

Black Diamond: The Story of the Negro Baseball League. With Fredrick McKissack, Jr. Scholastic, 1994.

Christmas in the Big House, Christmas in the Quarters. Illustrated by John Thompson. With Fredrick McKissack. Scholastic, 1994.

The Royal Kingdoms of Ghana, Mali and Songhay: Life in Medieval Africa. With Fredrick McKissack. Holt, 1994.

Red-Tail Angels: The Story of the Tuskegee Airmen of World War II. With Fredrick McKissack. Walker, 1995.

Rebels Against Slavery: American Slave Revolts. With Fredrick McKissack. Scholastic, 1996.

Ma Dear's Apron. Illustrated by Floyd Cooper. Knopf, 1997.

Let my People Go: Bible Stories Told by a Freeman of Color. Illustrated by James E. Ransome. Atheneum, 1998.

The Honest to Goodness Truth. Illustrated by Giselle Potter. Atheneum, 2000.

Abby Takes a Stand. Viking, 2005.

Porch Lies: Tales of Slicksters, Tricksters, and Other Wiley Characters. Illustrated by Andre Carriho. Swartz & Wade, 2006.

Away West. Illustrated by Gordon James. Viking, 2006.

McPherson, Miles

(1960–)

AUTHOR

Web site: www.therocksandiego.org

McPherson is president and founder of *Miles Ahead Ministries* and speaks to hundreds of thousands of teens and adults each year. A former defensive back with the San Diego Chargers, he is a nationally known evangelist and the founder of The Rock Church, which meets at San Diego University.

In his ministry, McPherson has talked to young people from all walks of life—one on one and in youth rallies of thousands. He knows what makes them tick, especially rebellious teenagers. That's because he was one. As a junior in high school he started smoking marijuana, which led to cocaine use as a rookie in the NFL. In 1984, however, he committed his life to the Lord. From that point on, he was delivered from his drug habit, stopped using foul language, and was reunited with his girlfriend, Debbie, who is now his wife.

After earning a Master of Divinity from Azusa Pacific University, he began his ministry and is now a featured speaker at some of the nation's largest youth and adult events. His *Miles Ahead Crusades*, which target unsaved teenagers, have been used to bring over twenty-seven thousand young people to Christ since 1996.

McPherson and his wife make their home in San Diego with their three children.

BIBLIOGRAPHY
Bad to the Bone. Bethany House Publishers, 1999.

Medearis, Angela Shelf

(1956–)

AUTHOR

Web site: www.medearis.com

"I love introducing children all over the world to all the different aspects of African-American history, folklore and culture. I love picture books because they are a challenge to convey complex ideas in a simple form for children. I really enjoy factually and vividly presenting history in a thirty-two or forty-eight page book. It's wonderful to be able to hold a child's attention and teach them something important.

"Picture books are a child's first step into a lifetime of reading. That's why I feel that my job is important. I want to write about history in such an interesting and exciting way that the memory of reading my book and the information it contained about a particular historical event will linger with them for a lifetime. I love children and I like to write books especially for them. I really love writing books. I enjoy that wonderful feeling you get when you have a great idea and can't wait to get started to work on it. I enjoy thinking about all of the children that have read my work. I have books in Africa and England and other places. It's fun to think that someone, somewhere, is reading one of my books or checking them out of the library.

"Most people think I'm funny. I like to make people laugh. I really, really like to make kids laugh. It's one of the happiest sounds in the world."

Medearis was born in Hampton, Virginia, and attended Southwest Texas University for one year. *Picking Peas for a Penny*, written in rhyme, and the sequel, *Dancing with the Indians*, are based on family stories told to her by her mother. *Dancing with the Indians* was a Reading Rainbow selection and winner of the Violet Crown Literary Award and the Notable Social Studies Book Award. *The Zebra-Riding Cowboy* was an ABA Pick of the List. *The Singing*

Man, which was a Coretta Scott King Honor Book Award winner for illustration in 1995, has received numerous awards.

She has been a freelance writer and also a staff writer for *CRISIS* magazine. From 1988 to 1989 she produced a radio program, *The Children's Radio Bookmobile*, featuring a wide range of topics and focusing on authors with diverse ethnic backgrounds.

She is the founder of Book Boosters, a multicultural, multiethnic reading motivational/tutorial program designed for elementary students in the Austin, Texas, Independent School District, and was curator of two African American history exhibits for the George Washington Carver Museum in Austin.

Medearis has been a popular speaker at literary conferences and at educational workshops and a consultant for publishing companies. Since 1966 Medearis has been the owner and President of DIVA Productions, Inc., a multimedia company in which she creates, writes, directs, and produces concepts, scripts, and videos for film television and stage. She is also creator and executive producer and host of *Angela's Notebook*, an educational television show about writing, reading, authors, and illustrators and is the executive producer of *The Scribble Show*, a children's program about reading, writing, math, and science applications in daily life.

She holds positions on the board of McGraw Hill and the Scholastic Advisory Board.

She is a member of the Society of Children's Book Writers and Illustrators, the Texas Library Association, and the Texas Institute of Letters.

She and her husband, Michael, daughter Deanna, and granddaughter Anysa live in Austin, Texas.

BIBLIOGRAPHY

Picking Peas for a Penny. State House, 1990.
Dancing with the Indians. Holiday House, 1991.
The Zebra-Riding Cowboy. Illustrated by Maria Cristina Brusca. Holt, 1992.
Come This Far to Freedom: A History of African Americans. Illustrated by Terea D. Shaffer. Atheneum, 1993.
Annie's Gifts. Illustrated by Anna Rich. Just Us Books, 1994.
Dare to Dream: The Story of Coretta Scott King. Illustrated by Anna Rich. Lodestar, 1994.
Little Louis and the Jazz Band: The Story of Louis Armstrong. Lodestar, 1994.
Our People. Illustrated by Michael Bryant. Atheneum, 1994.
The Seven Days of Kwanzaa. Scholastic, 1994.

The Singing Man. Illustrated by Terea Shaffer. Holiday House, 1994.

Bye, Bye Babies. Candlewick, 1995.

Eat, Babies, Eat. Illustrated by Patrice Aggs. Candlewick, 1995.

Poppa's New Pants. Illustrated by John Ward. Holiday House, 1995.

Sharing Danny's Dad. Illustrated by Jan Spivey Gilchrist. HarperCollins, 1995.

Skin Deep and Other Teenage Reflections. Illustrated by Michael Bryant. Macmillan, 1995.

The Adventures of Sugar and Junior. Illustrated by Nancy Poydar. Holiday House, 1995.

The Freedom Riddle. Illustrated by John Ward. Lodestar, 1995.

The 100th Day. Scholastic, 1995.

Too Much Talk. Illustrated by Stefano Vitale. Candlewick, 1995.

Treemonisha. Illustrated by Michael Bryant. Holt, 1995.

We Play on a Rainy Day. Scholastic, 1995.

The Ghost of Sifty-Sifty Sam. Scholastic, 1996.

Here Comes the Snow. Illustrated by Maxie Chambliss. Scholastic, 1996.

Nannie. Atheneum, 1996.

Haunts. Illustrated by Trina Schart Hyman. Holiday House, 1996.

Shari and the Musical Monster. Atheneum, 1996.

We Eat Dinner in the Bathtub. Scholastic, 1996.

Dance. With Michael R. Medearis. Holt, 1997.

Music. With Michael R. Medearis. Holt, 1997.

Rum-A-Tum Tum. Illustrated by James Ransome. Holiday House, 1997.

Princess of the Press: The Story of Ida B. Wells-Barnett. Lodestar, 1997.

Poppa's Itchy Christmas. Illustrated by John Ward. Holiday House, 1998.

Best Friends in the Snow. Bt. Bound, 1999.

The Spray-Paint Mystery. Bt. Bound, 1999.

Seeds Grow. Bt. Bound, 2000.

Seven Spools of Thread: A Kwanzaa Story. Illustrated by Daniel Minter. Albert Whitman and Co., 2000.

What Did I Do to Deserve a Sister Like You? Illustrated by Mark Galbreath. Eakin Press, 2001.

With Friends Like These, Who Needs Enemies? Scholastic, 2003.

Best Friends Forever. With Robert Papp. Scholastic, 2004.

Lucy's Quiet Book. Illustrated by Lisa Campbell Ernst. Harcourt Children's Books, 2004.

Snug in Mama's Arms. Illustrated by John Sanford. School Specialty Children's Publication, 2004.

I'd Still Pick You. School Specialty Publication, 2005.

On the Way to the Pond. With Lorinda Bryan Cauley. Harcourt Children's Books, 2006.

Medina, Tony

(1966–)

AUTHOR

E-mail: tonymedina@erols.com

Web site: www.tonymedina.net

Medina was born in the South Bronx, New York, raised in the Throgs Neck Housing Projects, and currently lives in Harlem and the Washington, D.C., metropolitan area. He is the author of twelve books for adults and children. Named by *Writer's Digest* as one of ten poets to watch in the new millennium, Medina's poetry, fiction, and essays appear in over twenty anthologies and two CD compilations. His children's books, *DeShawn Days* (Lee & Low Books, 2001) and *Love to Langston* (Lee & Low Books, 2002), both illustrated by R. Gregory Christie, have garnered several awards, including the Parent's Guide Children's Media Award (2001), the Paterson Prize for Books for Young People (2002), and the Rhode Island Children's Book Award (2003). Among his three anthologies, *In Defense of Mumia* (Writers & Readers, 1996) won the American Booksellers Association's Firecracker Alternative Book Award and *Bum Rush the Page: A Def Poetry Jam* (Three Rivers Press, 2001) was named a Best Book of 2002 by *The Washington Post's Book World*. His work has recently been published in *African American Literature* (Penguin Academics), edited by Keith Gilyard and Anissa Wardi. Medina, who has taught English and Creative Writing at several colleges and universities for ten years, has recently earned his MA and PhD in poetry and American and African American literature from Binghamton University, SUNY. Currently, Medina is assistant professor of Creative Writing at Howard University in Washington,

D.C., where he served as Writer-in-Residence from 2003 to 2004. He lives in New York City.

BIBLIOGRAPHY

Christmas Makes Me Think. Illustrated by Chandra Cox. Lee & Low, 2001.

DeShawn Days. Illustrated by R. Gregory Christie. Lee & Low, 2001.

Love to Langston. Illustrated by R. Gregory Christie. Lee & Low, 2002.

Follow-up Letters to Santa From Kids Who Never Got a Response. Just Us Books, 2003.

Miller, Robert Henry

(1944–)

AUTHOR

E-mail: rmiller@comcast.net

"When I first endeavored to write about African American cowboys, I must admit, secretly as a youngster, I frequently envisioned myself as a western hero. The fantasy of rescuing damsels in distress and saving a town from evil men has always intrigued me. In some small way I'm doing that now as I write about the heroics of African American pioneers and mountain men but especially the 'cowboys'.

"When I visit classrooms across the country, it's apparent my books are rescuing young African American boys and girls from the ignorance of not knowing that the American frontier was settled by people who looked like them. To see ourselves as heroes in the shaping of America is vital, in my view."

Miller was born in San Antonio, Texas. He holds a bachelor of science degree in urban studies and a master's degree in communications. He has worked as a U.S. marshal in Washington, D.C., and as an international account executive for a major hotel chain.

The Reflections of a Black Cowboy series was the American Booksellers Association's Pick of the List in 1991. The series was also reviewed in *School Library Journal* in 1991 and the *Multicultural Review* in 1994.

Miller has traced the African American cowboy roots from ancient Egypt to the American west. He has written articles for Greenwood Press and is working on other projects.

Miller received a PhD in 2002 from Temple University in Philadelphia, Pennsylvania. He is an assistant professor in the Department of Religion.

Miller is single and lives in Camden, New Jersey.

BIBLIOGRAPHY

Cowboys. Illustrated by Richard Leonard. Reflections of a Black Cowboy Series. Silver Burdett, 1992.

Mountain Men. Illustrated by Richard Leonard. Reflections of a Black Cowboy Series. Silver Burdett, 1993.

Pioneers. Illustrated by Richard Leonard. Reflections of a Black Cowboy Series. Silver Burdett, 1993.

Buffalo Soldiers: The Story of Emanuel Stance. Illustrated by Michael Bryant. Reflections of a Black Cowboy Series. Silver Burdett, 1994.

The Story of Nat Love. Illustrated by Michael Bryant. Stories from the Forgotten West Series. Silver Burdett, 1994.

John Baptist DuSable: Founder of Chicago. Illustrated by Richard Leonard. Stories from the Forgotten West Series. Silver Burdett, 1995.

The Story of Stagecoach Mary Fields. Illustrated by Richard Leonard. Stories from the Forgotten West Series. Silver Burdett, 1995.

A Pony for Jeremiah. Illustrated by Mneka Bennett. Silver Burdett, 1997.

Minter, Daniel

(1961–)

ILLUSTRATOR

E-mail: art@danielminter.com

Web site: www.danielminter.com

"I am attracted to children's books for their narrative structure and their ability to present our culture to young people in an easily accessible format. The illustrations in children's books are an excellent extension of the story telling nature of my fine art paintings and sculptures. Young people respond to work that represents them and their ideas. They want to be able to place themselves in the story and one of the easiest ways of doing that is use words and images that look like them and their friends.

"My art work is a study of memory. The many ways in which memory is embedded into our past, present and future. It is the interconnection of time that contains the essence of what memory has left behind. These concepts are the inspiration for my paintings and sculpture."

Minter was born in Ellaville, a small rural community in southern Georgia. Upon graduating from high school, he moved to Atlanta, where he then graduated from The Art Institute of Atlanta. Shortly after, Minter began working professionally as an illustrator, arts educator, painter and sculptor. His work has taken him from Atlanta, Seattle, Salvador, and Brazil to Brooklyn, Chicago and Portland, Maine, where he currently resides.

Minter began illustrating children's books with the 1994 publication of *The Footwarmer and the Crow*. In 2003 Minter was chosen by the U.S. Postal Service to create the 2004–2005 Kwanzaa Stamp. Current children's book exhibits include This is Our Land at the Meridian International Center in Washington, D.C., and Picture

Stories for the Smith Kramer Fine Art Services, a traveling exhibit in various cities.

BIBLIOGRAPHY

The Foot Warmer and the Crow by Evelyn Coleman. Simon & Schuster, 1994.

The Riches of Osceola McCarty. By Evelyn Coleman. Albert Whitman & Company, 1998.

Bubber Goes to Heaven. By Arna Bontemps. Oxford University Press, 1998.

Seven Spools of Thread. By Angela Shelf Medearis. Albert Whitman & Company, 2000.

New Year Be Coming. By Katharine Boling. Albert Whitman & Company, 2002.

The First Marathon – The Legend of Pheidippides. By Susan Reynolds. Albert Whitman & Company, 2006.

Mitchell, Margaree King

(1953–)

AUTHOR

E-mail: margareeKm@aol.com

"I knew it was important that children view themselves positively. I thought if I could somehow write a book that would inspire children to achieve their dreams, then maybe children would be motivated to stay in school and look to the future for a better life for themselves. Shortly after Uncle Jed's Barbershop was published, I was invited to read the book to seven- and eight-year-olds during story hour at a public library. As I was leaving, a little girl was waiting for me by the door. She said to me, 'I liked your story about Uncle Jed. I want to be a doctor when I grow up. But my grandmamma keeps telling me that I will never be one. Now I know I can be a doctor.' I knew then that I had achieved my goal in writing Uncle Jed's Barbershop."

Mitchell was born and reared in Holly Springs, Mississippi, growing up on her grandfather's farm. She received a bachelor's degree in 1975 from Brandeis University.

Uncle Jed's Barbershop was the winner of the 1995 Living the Dream Award, and the 1994 Coretta Scott King Honor Book Award for illustration by James Ransome. It was an American Library Association Notable Children's Book and an American Booksellers Association Pick of the List, and it was selected as one of Thirty-Three Favorite Reads of 1994 by librarians. The book was also featured as a *Reading Rainbow* book on the Public Broadcasting System (PBS) in 1995 and was mentioned in the 1995 movie *Losing Isaiah*. *Granddaddy's Gift* won a 1998 Skipping Stones Award, a 1998 Teacher's Choice Award from the International Reading Association, and a 2002 SCERUS Award given by the Southern Consortium for Educational Research in the Urban South.

A member of the Society of Children's Book Writers and Illustrators, Mitchell is a full-time writer.

She lives in Houston, Texas.

BIBLIOGRAPHY

Uncle Jed's Barbershop. Illustrated by James Ransome. Simon & Schuster, 1993.

Granddaddy's Gift. Illustrated by Larry Johnson. BridgeWater, 1997. (Reissue Scholastic, 2004.)

Mollel, Tololwa Marti

(1952–)

AUTHOR

E-mail: ujuto@freenetedmonton.ab.ca

"Writing for children for me is both challenging and rewarding. You have to find a way of writing about a big idea in simple terms. You have to be innovative in order to catch a child's attention. At the same time, the story has to appeal to you the writer, first. Simple and clear doesn't mean being frivolous. Writing for children is a good way to learn the fundamentals of fiction and story making. You have to put everything that you put in adult fiction and then some. When I first started writing, I used to write everything. I wrote short stories for adults, I wrote a novella. However, it wasn't until my first son was born that I decided to write for children. I remember reading to my son some stories that I enjoyed as a kid (like The Little Red Hen, The Lion and the Rat, The Emperor's New Clothes, etc.) and the writer in me appreciating the brilliant simplicity of the tales. I remember saying to myself that I would like to be able to write with such conciseness and evocative clarity, and it seems to me that writing for children offers an opportunity for doing that."

Mollel is a storyteller born in Arusha, Tanzania, in East Africa, and author of several children's books who credits his upbringing, his grandfather, and growing up in an oral culture as major influences. In 1991, *The Orphan Boy* won a Parents Choice Storybook Award, was a Notable Children's Book in the Language Arts, a Notable Children's Trade Book in the Field of Social Studies, and the American Bookseller Pick of the List for that year. The book was also a 1992 American Library Association Notable Children's Book. He has done readings, storytelling, talks, and workshops in and outside of schools in Edmonton, Alberta, Canada, across Canada, and in the United States.

Mollel received his bachelor of arts degree from the University of Dar-es-Salaam in Tanzania and his master of arts from the University of Alberta, and he is working on his doctoral thesis on African drama. He was a university lecturer, an actor with Paukwa Theater, and codirector of a children's theatrical group in Tanzania from 1979 to 1986. He has won the Writer's Guild of Alberta's R. Ross Annett Children's Prize for *Big Boy* in 1955; shortlisted on Ontario's Silver Birch Award for *The Flying Tortoise* in 1994; Florida Reading Association Award for *Rhinos for Lunch and Elephants for Supper*, and received a Governor General's Award (for Paul Morin's illustrations) for *Orphan Boy*.

He is married with two sons, Lese and Emeka, and lives in Edmonton, Alberta, Canada, with his family.

BIBLIOGRAPHY

The Orphan Boy. Illustrated by Paul Morin. Oxford University Press, 1990. Houghton, 1991.

The Princess Who Lost Her Hair. Illustrated by Charles Reasoner. Troll, 1992.

A Promise to the Sun: An African Story. Illustrated by Beatriz Vidal. Joy Street, 1992.

Rhinos for Lunch and Elephants for Supper! Illustrated by Barbara Spurll. Clarion, 1992.

The King and the Tortoise. Illustrated by Kathy Blankley. Houghton, 1993.

The Flying Tortoise: An Igbo Tale. Illustrated by Barbara Spurll. Clarion, 1994.

Big Boy. Illustrated by E.B. Lewis. Clarion, 1995.

Ananse's Feast. Illustrated by Andrew Glass. Houghton Mifflin, 1997.

Kele's Secret. Illustrated by Catherine Stock. Lodestar, 1997.

Kitoto the Mighty. Illustrated by Kristi Frost. Stoddard, 1997.

Song Bird. Illustrated by Rosanne Litzinger. Clarion, 1999.

Monk, Isabell (O'Connor)

AUTHOR

Monk has been involved in volunteer work as an acting coach, reader, writing artist, and mentor in dozens of Twin Cities schools and volunteer literacy organizations for more than a decade. She has held "Storytelling" residencies in association with the Children's Theater Company (two years) at Marcy Open and Tuttle Elementary Schools. At the Dowling School, her own residency program blended the use of classic children's literature and science for three years.

The Stepping Stone Children's Theater in St. Paul produced *The Story of Hope*, a play, in the winter of 2001, also in February 2006, which was written by Isabell Monk and Matt Vaky. The set was designed by Janice Porter.

Monk performs a thirty-five minute piece, *Dream Keeper*, for schools and libraries in the Twin Cities metro area and was a member of the Guthrie Theater's Acting Company for nine seasons. She is a 1998 McKnight Fellow and a 1999 Twentieth Century Fox Fellow and received her BFA degree at Towson State University and her MFA degree at the Yale University School of Drama.

Since 1981 Monk has been in nearly sixty productions on the main stage as well as the Guthrie Lab.

Monk has been awarded the Parent's Choice Honor Award for Picture Book *Family* in 2001, the Midwest Emmy for Mother in KTCA's *Things that Matter* in 1991, and the Obie Award for Gloucester in *Lear* in 1990.

She lives in Minneapolis, Minnesota.

BIBLIOGRAPHY

Hope. Illustrated by Janice Lee Porter. Carolrhoda Books (Lerner Publishing), 1999.

Family. Illustrated by Janice Lee Porter. Carolrhoda (Lerner Publishing), 2001.

Blackberry Stew. Illustrated by Janice Lee Porter. Carolrhoda (Lerner Publishing), 2005.

Moore, Johnny Ray

(1955–)

AUTHOR

E-mail: Jmoore92591@nc.rr.com

"As guardians of our children, we must give them the opportunity to absorb, and then experience, the beauty of the English language. We can do this by reading to them, religiously, while they are infants. We cannot wait for our children to get beyond the infant stage, and then, try to motivate them to read. Also, by reducing the hours our children spend watching television, listening to music, and playing computer games, we will be able to get them to read more. My writing career began when I tried my hand at writing poetry while in the second grade.

"Furthermore, my goal as a poet and children's author is to pour my mind, body, and soul into every piece I write."

Moore graduated from Vaiden Whitley High School in 1974. He was in the Army from 1976 to 1980. While in the Army, he studied writing for children with The Institute of Children's Literature and completed this course in July 1980.

Moore is a member of The Society of Children's Books Writers and Illustrators. He lectures and does readings and signings, whenever and wherever he can.

He works full time for the postal service and is also a Notary Public.

Moore and his lovely wife have three charming daughters and live in Raleigh, North Carolina.

BIBLIOGRAPHY

Howie Has a Stomachache. Illustrated by Lynne Srba. Seedling Publications (Continental Press), 1996.

A Leaf. Illustrated by Kristin Rauchenstein. Seedling Publications (Continental Press), 1999.

The Story of Martin Luther King, Jr. Illustrated by Amy Wummer. Candy Cane Press (Imprint of Ideals Publications), 2001.

Meet Martin Luther King, Jr. Illustrated by Amy Wummer. Ideals Children's Books, 2002.

Mordecai, Pamela Claire

(1942–)

AUTHOR/ILLUSTRATOR

Mordecai was born in Kingston, Jamaica, the second of five children. She went to Convent of Mercy Alpha from 1946 to 1959, then to Newton College, a liberal arts school in Massachusetts, where she received her bachelor of arts degree in English in 1963. She returned to Jamaica in 1963 to teach, first in high school, then at Mico, Jamaica's largest teachers college. At Mico, she was motivated to write poems for children when she discovered that the trainee teachers could find few Caribbean poems to use in their teaching-practice lessons.

In 1974, she was hired by the University of the West Indies, where she spent the next fourteen years as publications officer in the faculty of education She now operates a Canadian branch of Sandberry Press with her husband, Martin Mordecai.

In addition to authoring and coauthoring many textbooks, Mordecai has edited and coedited five anthologies on writings by Caribbean women. Mordecai received the Institute of Jamaica's Tercentenary Medal in 1980 and, in 1993, the inaugural Vic Reid Award for Children's Literature for *Ezra's Goldfish and Other Storypoems*.

Although Mordecai has lived in Canada since 1994, the Caribbean experience continues to be the focus of most of her poetry and stories and the materials she creates for the classroom. As a former language arts teacher with a PhD in English, she was editor of the *Caribbean Journal of Education* for fourteen years.

Mordecai has three children and lives in Toronto, Ontario, Canada.

BIBLIOGRAPHY

Storypoems: A First Collection. Ginn, 1987.

Don't Ever Wake a Snake. Sandberry, 1991.

Ezra's Goldfish and Other Storypoems. National Book Development Council, 1995.

Morninghouse, Sundaira

(Carletta Carrington Wilson)

(1951–)

AUTHOR

"I have had the unique opportunity to share the treasures of the literary world in a personal and professional manner. In my work as a librarian, I have been amazed at how far we've come in the development of literature for African American children and how far we've yet to go in terms of the range of themes, subjects, and artistic exploration of the African American experience, in particular, and the African diaspora as a whole."

Sundaira Morninghouse is the pseudonym used by Carletta Carrington Wilson. She has published fiction, poetry, and essays under her given name since 1984 and created the name Sundaira Morninghouse to be used for works intended for children. *Habari Gani? What's the News?* Received the Midwest Book Achievement Award for Best Children's Book in 1993.

Wilson was born in Philadelphia, Pennsylvania, and received her bachelor's degree in fine arts from Cheyney University of Pennsylvania and her master's degree in library science from the University of Washington. She has worked as a museum educator, an art and creative writing teacher, and a children's and visual arts and literature librarian.

She decided to write books for children when she became inspired by a children's-literature course while working on her master's degree. Recognizing how few poetry titles were available for preschool African American children, she began writing what was to become her first children's book, *Nightfeathers*.

She has contributed to *Make Things Fly: Poems About the Wind*, edited by Dorothy M. Kennedy, 1998 and *Poetry Works! The*

First Verse Idea Book by Babs Bell Hajdusiewicz, Modern Curriculum Press, 1993.

She lives in Seattle, Washington.

BIBLIOGRAPHY

Nightfeathers. Illustrated by Jody Kim. Open Hand, 1989.

Habari Gani? What's the News? Illustrated by Jody Kim. Open Hand, 1992.

Moss, Onawumi Jean

AUTHOR

E-mail: ojmoss@amherst.edu

Web site: www.amherst.edu/storytelling

Moss, storyteller and educator, is associate dean of students at Amherst College in Massachusetts. Her first stories were learned from her parents and in church. Her mother, a home missionary, was a self-taught Bible historian and provided her with the historical context for the stories she learned in Sunday School. Her father was a teller of eerie, sometimes funny, ghost stories.

Over the years her own interests expanded, providing Moss with wider perspectives on the importance and use of story. As she became deeply involved in learning about her cultural heritage, she realized that use of story as a means of imparting valued knowledge and traditions was accessible to her.

During her career she has performed at public and private schools (K–12), colleges, universities, conventions, conferences, festivals, churches, libraries, and on television. Moss has told wondrous tales at the National Storytelling Association's Swappin' Ground (1992), and Exchange Place (1995). She has also swapped stories and been a featured teller at the National Association of Black Storytellers Conference (1992, 1993, 1994, 1995, 1997, and 2000). Moss holds memberships in the National Storytelling Network (NSN), the National Association of Black Storytellers (NABS), and the League for the Advancement of New England Storytelling (LANES).

Moss is the founder and producer of the dynamic Keepers of the Word Storytelling Festival at Amherst College, host to the country's best yarn spinners since 1993.

BIBLIOGRAPHY

Precious and the Boo Hag. With Patricia C. McKissack. Illustrated by Kyrsten Brooker. Simon & Schuster, 2005.

Muse, Daphne

AUTHOR

E-mail: msmusewriter@aol.com

Web site: www.daphnemuse.com

"While the oral tradition came with us across the water, now more than two centuries of the written tradition in Black children's literature is part of the cultural canon and curriculum of child care centers, schools and teacher training programs across the country and around the world. The treasure chest of Black children's books contains a wealth of picture books, poetry collections, biographies and novels educating the minds and nurturing the hearts of children from points all over the globe."

Muse is a writer, social commentator, and poet. She is the author of many children's books as well as a writer for a series of curriculum projects for Scholastic, Inc., Major League Baseball's *Breaking Barriers* and Norman Lear's *Declaration of Independence Road Trip.* In 2002 she was appointed as an Adjunct Associate Professor in the English Department at the University of California, Berkeley where she taught *Theorizing Children's Literature: A Survey of Gender, Class, and Ethnic Diversity in Books for Young Readers (K–12) 1817 to the Present.* From 1975–1983 and 1991–1993, Muse developed and taught survey and writing courses in multicultural children's literature at Mills College.

Muse was born in Washington, D.C. *Children of Africa* launched her more than three-decade commitment to, and published work in, multicultural children's literature. As an educational consultant, she has worked on major curriculum projects for the California State Department of Education, the Hitachi Foundation and several school districts throughout the country. Her reviews and critical essays have appeared in the *New Advocate, Black Scholar,* and *Black Issues in Book Reviews.*

As a featured speaker, she has conducted workshops and made presentations at Rutgers, case Western Reserve, Stanford, University of California, Berkeley, Mills College, University of San Francisco, the Yoshiyama Awards, and the American Library Association. Her work has taken her to England, Tanzania, Guyana, and throughout the United States. Muse currently serves as a member of the board of ARTAIDSART. Based in False Bay, just outside of Capetown, South Africa, the cross cultural project promotes education and sustainable economic development through collaborative art programs.

Muse lives in Oakland, California with her husband, David Landes. She is the mother of Anyania Muse and grandmother to Maelia Sakae Jones and Elijah Lateef Jones.

BIBLIOGRAPHY

Sa Yaa Watofo. Drum & Spear Press, 1970.
Children of Africa. Drum & Spear Press, 1970.
Prejudice: A Story of Collection. Hyperion, 1995.
The New Press Guide to Multicultural Resources for Young Readers. The New Press, 1997.
The Entrance Place of Wonders: Poems of the Harlem Renaissance. Abram, 2006.

Myers, Walter Dean

(1937–)

AUTHOR

Myers was born in Martinsburg, West Virginia. He speaks of his adoptive parents fondly; the Dean family adopted him informally after his mother's death. He attended City College in New York City and received his bachelor's degree in communications from Empire State College in 1984. In 1981, he received a fellowship from the New Jersey State Council of the Arts; in 1982, a grant from the National Endowment of the Arts.

Myers is a member of the Harlem Writers Guild and P.E.N. International. He has written articles for magazines and was an editor for Bobbs-Merrill publishing house.

Although most of his books are about the Black experience or have urban settings, a few of his books have been based on travels to the East and Africa. His book *Motown and Didi: A Love Story* won the Coretta Scott King Award for fiction in 1985, as did *The Young Landlords* in 1980, *Fallen Angels* in 1989, and *Now Is Your Time! The African American Struggle for Freedom* in 1992. *Malcolm X: By Any Means Necessary* was a Coretta Scott King Honor Book in 1994, as was *Somewhere in Darkness* in 1993 and *Fast Sam, Cool Clyde, and Stuff* in 1976. *Scorpions* was a Newbery Honor Book in 1989.

His *Where Does the Day Go?*, another prize-winning book, was submitted to Parents Magazine Press in the late 1960s by the Council on Interracial Books for Children. He has published a series of books under the title of *Eighteen Pine Street*. Myers was named the 1997 recipient of the Coretta Scott King Author Award Winner for *Slam!* His book, *Harlem*, illustrated by Christopher Myers, won the 1998 Coretta Scott King Honor Book Illustrator Award and a 1998 Caldecott Honor Book Award.

Monster was a Finalist selection at the National Book Awards in 1999. The first Michael L. Printz Award was given in recognition for his book *Monster* in 2000 and a Coretta Scott King Honor Award also in 2000. Also in the year 2000, Myers' book *145th Street Stories* was selected for a Boston Globe-Horn Book Honor Award and also in 2003, *Blues Journey* was selected.

Myers lives in Jersey City, New Jersey, and has three children, Karen, Michael, and Christopher.

BIBLIOGRAPHY

Where Does the Day Go? Illustrated by Leo Carty. Parents, 1969.

Fly Jimmy Fly! Illustrated by Moneta Barnett. Putnam, 1974.

Fast Sam, Cool Clyde, and Stuff. Viking, 1975.

It Ain't All for Nothin'. Viking, 1978.

The Young Landlords. Viking, 1979.

The Black Pearl and the Ghost. Illustrated by Robert Quackenbush. Viking, 1980.

The Golden Serpent. Illustrated by Alice and Martin Provensen. Viking, 1980.

Hoops. Delacorte, 1981.

The Legend of Tarik. Viking, 1981.

Won't Know Till I Get There. Viking, 1982.

Tales of a Dead King. Morrow, 1983.

Motown and Didi: A Love Story. Viking, 1984.

Mr. Monkey and the Gotcha Bird. Illustrated by Leslie Morrill. Delacorte, 1984.

Crystal. Viking, 1987.

Fallen Angels. Scholastic, 1988.

Me, Mop, and the Moondance Kid. Illustrated by Rodney Pate. Delacorte, 1988.

Scorpions. Harper, 1988.

The Mouse Rap. Harper, 1989.

Now Is Your Time! The African-American Struggle for Freedom. HarperCollins, 1991.

Me, Mop, and the Nagasaki Knights. Illustrated by Rodney Pate. Delacorte, 1992.

A Place Called Heartbreak: A Story of Vietnam. Illustrated by Frederick Porter. Steck-Vaughn, 1992.

The Righteous Revenge of Artemus Bonner. HarperCollins, 1992.

Somewhere in the Darkness. Scholastic, 1992.

Brown Angels: An Album of Picture and Verse. HarperCollins, 1993.

Dangerous Games. Bantam, 1993.

Fashion by Tasha. Bantam, 1993.

HeartBreak. Illustrated by Leonard Jenkins. Steck-Vaughn, 1993.

Malcolm X: By Any Means Necessary. Scholastic, 1993.

Young Martin's Promise. Illustrated by Higgins Bond. Steck-Vaughn, 1993.

Darnell Rock Reporting. Delacorte, 1994.

The Glory Field. Scholastic, 1994.

The Dragon Takes a Wife. Illustrated by Fiona French. Scholastic, 1995.

Glorious Angels: A Celebration of Children. HarperCollins, 1995.

One More River To Cross. Harcourt, 1995.

Shadow of the Red Moon. Illustrated by Christopher Myers. Scholastic, 1995.

The Story of the Three Kingdoms. Illustrated by Ashley Bryan. HarperCollins, 1995.

How Mr. Monkey Saw the Whole World. Illustrated by Synthia Saint James. Doubleday, 1996.

Smiffy Blue, Ace Crime Detective: The Case of the Missing Ruby and Other Stories. Illustrated by David J. Sims. Scholastic, 1996.

Slam! Scholastic, 1996.

Toussaint L'Ouverture: The Fight for Haiti's Freedom. Illustrated by Jacob Lawrence. Simon & Schuster, 1996.

Harlem. Illustrated by Christopher Myers. Scholastic, 1997.

Amistad: A Long Road to Freedom. Dutton, 1997.

Angel to Angel. HarperCollins, 1998.

At Her Majesty's Request. Scholastic, 1999.

The Journal of Joshua Loper: Black Cowboy. Scholastic, 1999.

Monster. HarperCollins, 1999.

The Journal of Scott Pendleton Collins. Scholastic, 1999.

Malcolm X: A Fire Burning Brightly. HarperCollins, 2000.

The Blues of Flats Brown. Illustrated by Nina Laden. Holiday House, 2000.

145th Street: Short Stories. Delacorte, 2000.

The Greatest: The Life of Muhammad Ali. Scholastic, 2000.

Patrol. Illustrated by Ann Grifalconi. HarperCollins, 2002.

Three Swords for Granada. Holiday House, 2002.

Handbook for Boys. HarperCollins, 2002.

A Time to Love: Stories from the Old Testament. Illustrated by Christopher Myers. Scholastic, 2003.

Blues Journey. Illustrated by Christopher Myers. Holiday House, 2003.

Dream Bearer. HarperCollins, 2003.

The Beast. Scholastic, 2003.

Shooter. HarperCollins, 2004.

I've Seen the Promised Land: Martin Luther King. Illustrated by Leonard Jenkins. HarperCollins, 2004.

Constellation. Holiday House, 2004.

Antarctica. Scholastic, 2004.

Here in Harlem. Holiday House, 2004.

Jazz. Illustrated by Christopher Myers. Holiday House, 2006.

Negatu, Tewodros

(1973–)

ILLUSTRATOR

Negatu was born in the capital city of Ethiopia, Addis Ababa. At ten years old, he won a school art competition and also won third prize in a national Red Cross art competition.

Upon leaving secondary school, he was among the top 15 percent of artists in the country to be chosen to study graphic arts at the Addis Ababa School of Fine Art. Four years later in 1991, Negatu graduated with an advanced diploma. While at college, he won first prize for his painting in a national competition held by the Italian Cultural Center.

After graduation, he worked for the Swedish International Development Agency as a cartoonist and illustrator for developmental magazines. For political reasons, after the arrest of his father, Negatu was forced to flee Ethiopia in January 1993, and he traveled alone to Kenya, where he has refugee status.

In 1994, he illustrated the cover of *Meskel: An Ethiopian Family Saga (1926–1981)*, and his artwork appears in the anthology *Zamani*.

Negatu lives in Nairobi, Kenya.

BIBLIOGRAPHY

Zamani: The Mouse Who Would Be King. By Tom Nevin. Jacaranda Designs, 1995.

Nelson, Kadir

(1974–)

ILLUSTRATOR

E-mail: office@kadirnelson.com

Web site: www.kadirnelson.com

"I have had conversations with a number of African-American authors and have found that we have similar aspirations in regard to working in the field of children's literature.

We all strive to create quality children's books with characters of color for children to identify with, learn from and admire. The reason being, we didn't have very many of them available to us as young children and feel that we may have missed something. We want to insure that this void will be filled for our children and the children of the world. We all learn from diversity as it helps us understand the differences among us. But truthfully, it's just so much more fun! I mean who has ever heard of an African-American family of giants as in Hewitt Anderson's Great Big Life? Or, how about a tall tale set in the old west with the lead character being a twelve-year-old confident African-American girl who rides atop a longhorn steer and lassos rain clouds? Or of a little girl who grew up among worldly men like Paul Robeson, Duke Ellington, and WEB Dubois? These are the stories that we are so eager to share with the world, and we are able to do so by way of children's literature."

Kadir Nelson began drawing at the age of three, displaying artistic acumen before he could write or spell. At age eleven, Nelson was apprenticed by his uncle, an artist and an art instructor. "My uncle gave me my foundation in art," says the artist. Nelson experimented with several different media and later began painting in oils at age sixteen under the encouragement and tutelage of his uncle and his high school art teacher. He began entering his paintings in art competitions and ultimately won an art scholarship to study at Pratt Institute in Brooklyn, New York. Upon graduating with honors with a Bachelor of Arts degree in Communications Design, Nelson began his professional career as an artist, publishing his work in the limited edition print market and receiving commissions from publishers and production studios such as Dreamworks, Nike, *Sports Illustrated*, Coca-Cola, the *New York Times*, *The New Yorker*, and Major League Baseball, among others.

Nelson also exhibited his work in galleries and museums throughout the United States and abroad, including the Simon Weisenthal Center; Museum of Tolerance; The Museum of African-American History in Detroit; The Negro Leagues Baseball Museum in Kansas City, Missouri; the Studio Museum in Harlem, New York; The Bristol Museum in England; The Citizen's Gallery of Yokohama, Japan; and the Center for Culture of Tijuana, Mexico.

In 1999 Nelson began illustrating for children, collaborating with several notable authors for books, including Debbie Allen's *Dancing in the Wings*, Jerdine Nolen's *Thunder Rose*, Deloris and Roslyn Jordan's *New York Times* best seller *Salt in his* Shoes, Spike and Tonya Lee's *Please, Baby, Please* and Will Smith's *Just the Two of Us*, for which Nelson won an NAACP Image Award. Currently, Nelson is planning a tribute book about the Negro Baseball Leagues which he is both authoring and illustrating to be published by Jump at the Sun, an imprint of Hyperion.

Nelson has received numerous awards for his work in illustration including gold and silver medals from the New York Society of Illustrators, the Nebraska Golden Sower Award for *Salt in His Shoes*, the Coretta Scott King Illustrator Honor and Award for *Thunder Rose* and *Ellington was not a Street*, and the Jane Addams illustrator honor for *The Village That Vanished*, among others. Most notably, Nelson was the "Conceptual Artist" for Steven Spielberg's feature film, *Amistad*, and the animated feature *Spirit: Stallion of the Cimarron*.

Nelson is married with two children and lives in San Diego, California.

BIBLIOGRAPHY

Brothers of the Night. By Debbie Allen. Dial, 1999.
Big Jabe. By Jerdine Nolen. HarperCollins, 2000.
Dancing in the Wings. By Debbie Allen. Dial, 2000.

Salt in His Shoes. By Deloris and Roslyn Jordan. Simon and Schuster, 2000.

Just the Two of Us. By Will Smith. Scholastic, 2001.

Please, Baby, Please. By Spike and Tonya Lee. Simon and Schuster, 2002.

The Village that Vanished. By Ann Grifalconi. Dial, 2002.

Under the Christmas Tree. By Nikki Grimes. HarperCollins, 2002.

Thunder Rose. By Jerdine Nolen. Harcourt, 2003.

Ellington was not a Street. By Ntozake Shange. Simon and Schuster, 2004.

Tales from Shakespeare. By Tina Packer. Scholastic, 2004.

He's Got the Whole World in his Hands. By Kadir Nelson. Dial, 2005.

Hewitt Anderson's Great Big Life. By Jerdine Nolen. Simon and Schuster, 2005.

Please, Puppy, Please. By Spike and Tonya Lee. Simon and Schuster, 2005.

The Real Slam Dunk. By Charisse Richardson. Dial, 2005.

Nelson, Marilyn

(1946–)

AUTHOR

E-mail: hogan@frontstreetbooks.com

Nelson was born in Cleveland, Ohio, and comes from a long line of teachers on her mother's side. Her father was a career Air Force officer who wrote poetry and plays. Nelson grew up on air bases all over the country and wrote her first poem at age eleven.

She earned her BA. from the University of California, Davis, and holds postgraduate degrees from the University of Pennsylvania (MA, 1970), the University of Minnesota (PhD, 1979), and honorary doctorates from Kutztown University in Pennsylvania and Simpson College in Iowa.

Nelson was named Poet Laureate of Connecticut in June, 2001. Other honors include two Pushcart prizes, two creative writing fellowships from the National Endowment for the Arts, a Fulbright Teaching Fellowship, the 1990 Connecticut Arts Award, and a Guggenheim Fellowship. She was professor of English at the University of Connecticut in Storrs from 1978 to 2002, and professor of English at the University of Delaware from 2002 to 2004. Since September 2004 she is Emeritus Professor at the University of Connecticut and Director of Soul Mountain Retreat, a writers' colony.

Among the many awards she has received are a Lenore Marshall Poetry Prize finalist, a National Book Award finalist and a PEN Winship Award Winner.

When she has the time and the energy, Nelson is a quilt maker.

Nelson was honored by Front Street and Boyds Mills Press publishers at a reception in 2005 held at Roosevelt University in Chicago, Illinois.

BIBLIOGRAPHY

The Cat Walked Through the Casserole and Other Poems for Children (Marilyn Waniek) (with Pamela Espeland). Carolrhoda, 1984.

The Field of Praise: New and Selected Poems. Louisiana State University Press, 1997.

Carver: A Life in Poems. Front Street Books, 2001.

A Wreath for Emmett Till. Houghton Mifflin, 2005.

Fortune's Bones: The Manumission Requiem. Front Street, 2005.

The Ladder (Translated from the Danish of poet Halfadan Rasmussen). Candlewick Books, 2005.

Nelson, Vaunda Micheaux

(1953–)

AUTHOR

E-mail: vaundanelson@hotmail.com

"I grew up the fifth and youngest child in a rural community near Pittsburgh. I feel lucky to be able to say I had a wonderful childhood. Our extended family spent Sundays together, went on picnics, and the cousins took turns spending the night at each other's houses. Things seemed simpler then. Being black, we had some obstacles growing up, but family gave me the strength to deal with whatever came my way.

"My love of books began at bedtime, which was story time at our home. My mother read to us every day, and my father wrote and recited poetry. They taught me the power of language and inspired me to write. Through my work both as a writer and a children's librarian, I hope to provide children with some of what my parents gave me—the opportunity to grow through story.

"I write for children, but first I write for myself. It's my way of sorting things, my way of coping with the world. Writing helps me to understand because it forces me to really look at things closely and to think about more than one way of seeing. My stories often grow from personal experience, but it's not simply a matter of telling about something that has happened to me; it's more about facing the questions I still have and allowing my characters to help me find answers."

Nelson's first book, *Always Gramma*, was selected by the Children's Book Council as a Notable Children's Trade Book in the Field of Social Studies. *Mayfield Crossing* won the Georgia Children's Book Award in 1995, and *Beyond Mayfield* received a 1999 Parents' Choice Gold Award. In 2004, *Almost to Freedom* received a Coretta Scott King Honor for illustration. In addition, her poetry has been published in *Cricket* and *Cicada* magazines.

The author holds master's degrees from The Bread Loaf School of English at Middlebury College, Vermont, and from the University of Pittsburgh School of Library and Information Science. She has been a teacher, a newspaper reporter, a bookseller, a school librarian, and has twice been a member of the Newbery Award Committee.

Currently, Nelson is a youth services librarian at Rio Rancho Public Library in New Mexico, where she lives with her husband, Drew, also a writer.

BIBLIOGRAPHY

Always Gramma. Illustrated by Kimanne Uhler. Putnam, 1988.

Mayfield Crossing. Putnam, 1993.

Possibles. Putnam, 1995.

Beyond Mayfield. Putnam, 1999.

Ready? Set, Raymond! Illustrated by Derek Anderson. Random House, 1999.

Almost to Freedom. Illustrated by Colin Bootman. Carolrhoda, 2003.

Juneteenth (Co-Author Drew Nelson). Illustrated by Mark Schroder. Carolrhoda, 2006.

Nolen, Jerdine

(1953–)

AUTHOR

Web site: www.jerdinenolan.com

"I can't ever recall a time when I wasn't writing. From as early as I can remember, I have been writing something. I collected words. I simply like the sound of words and the feelings they evoke as they come out of me. I even like the sound the pencil makes as it travels across the page. Writing is fun work. It takes patience to get the right story. Once you have the story idea, it is important to revise/revisit the work to make it the best that it could be. It is like sculpting or wiring the pieces together in a way so the words on the page have enough life … they could stand up and walk around all on their own. That is why my motto is:
   "Hold fast to your dreams as you would your balloons!"

Nolen was born in Crystal Springs, Mississippi, and raised in Chicago, Illinois. The author received a bachelor's degree in special education from Northeastern Illinois University in 1981 and a master's in interdisciplinary arts education from Loyola University. She lectures on a variety of topics related to her books and other books for children, as well as on writing and the writing process.

Her professional experience includes being an elementary teacher in Evanston, Illinois, an artist in residence at the Chicago Office of Fine Arts, and a special-education teacher in the Baltimore County public schools in Maryland. She works part-time for the Baltimore County public schools as a specialist in the Language Arts Department.

In 1994, she was featured in *People* magazine and was the recipient of the Apple for the Teacher Award presented by Iota Phi Lambda sorority. Her book *Harvey Potter's Balloon Farm* was named an American Library Association Notable Book, an IRA/CTC Children's Choice, and will be produced by Disney Studios as a live-action film.

She has been an educator for a number of years as a classroom teacher, curriculum writer, staff developer, family involvement specialist, and administrator. She also enjoys lecturing on a variety of topics related to books and the writing process.

Her professional affiliations include memberships in the National Education Association and the Chicago Reading Round Table, and she was a cofounder of Black Literary Umbrella.

Nolen lives near Columbia, Maryland with her husband Anthony, their two children, two cats, and the occasional giant pumpkins that grow in the yard.

BIBLIOGRAPHY

Harvey Potter's Balloon Farm. Illustrated by Mark Buchner. Lothrop, 1994.

Raising Dragons. Illustrated by Elise Primavera. Harcourt, 1998.

Momma's Kitchen. Illustrated by Colin Bootman. Amistad (Reprint), 2001.

Max and Jax in Second Grade. Illustrated by Karen Lee Schmidt. Silver Whistle, 2002.

Plantzilla. Illustrated by David Catrow. Silver Whistle (2002).

Irene's Wish. Illustrated by Martin Matje. Silver Whistle, 2003.

Laura McGill's Pickle Museum. Illustrated by Debbie Tilley. Silver Whistle, 2003.

Thunder Rose. Illustrated by Kadir. Silver Whistle, 2003.

Big Jabe. Illustrated by Kadir Nelson. Amistad (Reprint), 2004.

Hewitt Anderson's Great Big Life. Illustrated by Kadir Nelson. Simon & Schuster/Paula Wiseman Books, 2005.

O'Keragori, Abel

(1952–)

AUTHOR/ILLUSTRATOR

O'Keragori was born in the town of Kisii in the western province of Kenya. In primary school, his artistic talents emerged as he explored the world of art through painting, clay modeling, woodcarving, and papier-mâché. He passed art at ordinary and advanced levels but could not find employment as an artist in Africa. Inspired by an excellent math teacher, he made the decision to study accounting.

Combining his career with painting was challenging, but his reputation grew as the quality of his art work became widely appreciated. His first solo exhibition at the prestigious Signature Gallery in Nairobi, Kenya, met with enthusiastic reviews, and he has since participated in more than thirty group shows both in Kenya and internationally. In 1993, he gave up his career and become a professional artist.

During a visit to his grandmother at the family homestead in Kisii, O'Keragori collected a series of ancient stories from the oral traditions of his tribe. He felt strongly that these should be preserved for future generations and presented them to the publishers Jacaranda Designs in Nairobi. They invited him to work on a book as both author and artist, and his first publication, *Totems of the Kisii*, appeared in 1994. The book was launched at the National Arts at the National Arts Festival in 1995 to much acclaim.

O'Keragori has won many national prizes for his artwork and has exhibited at the National Museum, the French Cultural Center, and the National Arts Festival. His work is held in collections in the United Kingdom, the United States, Germany, and France.

He lives in Nairobi, Kenya.

BIBLIOGRAPHY

Totems of the Kisii. Jacaranda Designs, 1994.

Olaleye, Isaac O.

(1941–)

AUTHOR

E-mail: leyeola@hotmail.com

"Usually, children who lack interest in reading is a legacy from a home where reading is not held in high value. Home is children's first world, where they learn what becomes memorable to them for the rest of their lives, including the love for books. Solution: Read to them before they are born. Play book recordings in vehicles. They are listening—in the womb. Introduce to them as soon as they are born the exciting world of creating worlds with words. They may taste the book or chew it to make sure it is good. If they sink their teeth into books as toddlers, they are likely to sink their minds into them as adults. I try to put everything into my books to incite children to be literary and useful citizens of tomorrow. And I espouse the sentiments expressed by Doctor Maria Montessori, an educationalist with special interest in children: 'We know how to find pearls in the shells of oysters, gold in the mountains and coal in the bowels of the earth, but we are unaware of the spiritual gems, the creative nebulae, that the child hides in himself when he enters this world.' I hope my books spark or enhance that 'creative nebulae' in children of all colors and cultures. Reading and writing children's books and interacting with the young ones have become to me like a lifetime celebration of youth."

Olaleye is a graduate of Thurrock Technical College, England, where he majored in transport management. He worked for Pan Am Airways and he has done various kinds of jobs.

He plunged into writing children's books in 1991 and had his first book, *Bitter Bananas*, published in 1994. It got a starred review from *School Journal* and was recognized by Ohio Teachers' and Pupils' Reading Title; and Read Alouds—Too Good to Miss List, Indiana Department of Educators. The second book, *The Distant Talking Drum*, published in 1995, was an ALA Notable book,

NCSS-CBC Notable Children's Trade Book in the field of social studies, and an IRA Book for Global Society Award. His other books have also won awards.

He gets a kick out of playing soccer and was a coach for AYSO in Los Angeles, California. He is single (at present) and lives in Chula Vista, California.

BIBLIOGRAPHY

Bitter Bananas. Illustrated by Ed Young. Boyds Mills Press, 1994.

The Distant Talking Drum. Boyds Mills Press, 1995.

Lake of the Big Snake. Boyds Mills Press, 1998.

Bikes for Rent. Orchard Books, 2001.

In The Rainfield Who Is The Greatest? Blue Sky Press, 2002.

Onyefulu, Ifeoma (Ebele)

(1959–)

AUTHOR/ILLUSTRATOR

"In my opinion, there is a void in the realm of literature for Black children, for example, the absence of 'fun to read books.' I think it will be fun to tell stories like in the good old days. Children like to be entertained as well as allowing them to use their imaginations when stories are told. As a child, I enjoyed listening to stories that stretched my imagination—stories that drew wonderful, colorful pictures in my mind. I also think that women are not represented enough as heroes.

"My approach is to keep it simple but colorful and fun to read. Children have a huge hunger for knowledge, always asking question after question. Therefore, children's book illustrations should meet that requirement. And I think some books are now beautifully illustrated, especially the skin tones."

Onyefulu was born in Nigeria, her father a lawyer and her mother a businesswoman. Using simple clear writing, Onyefulu reveals the rich diversity of African life and culture, exploring familiar themes like the alphabet, numbers, colors, and family and children can effortlessly absorb information about another culture finding similarities and enjoying the differences. After completing a business management course, she trained as a photographer and contributed to a number of magazines. She is married and has two children, Emeka and Ikenna, and lives in London.

BIBLIOGRAPHY

A is for Africa. Cobblehill, 1993.
Emeka's Gift: An African Counting Story. Cobblehill, 1995.
Ogbo: Sharing Life in an African Village. Gulliver, 1996.
Chidi Only Likes Blue. NAL/Dutton, 1997.

Grandfather's Work. Millbrook Press, 1998.

Ebele's Favourite: A Book of African Games. Antique Collectors' Club, 2000.

Welcome Dede: An African Naming Ceremony. Frances Lincoln, 2003.

An African Christmas. Frances Lincoln, 2005.

My Grandfather Is a Magician: Work and Wisdom in an African Village. 2006.

Owens, Vivian W.

AUTHOR

E-mail: escharpub@earthlink.net

Web site: www.escharpublications.com

Owens wrote the book *Nadanda the Wordmaker*, and it won a Writer's Digest Best Book Award. In order to provide helpers for parents and other child caregivers, she wrote *Parenting for Education* and *Create a Math Environment*, books selected as Resources in Education. She also developed a radio program for parents prior to the books. Having taught mathematics to junior high school student with success in bringing them up to grade level, Owens taught chemistry, physics, and mathematics in the private and public school systems of Virginia. For many years, she wrote newspaper and magazine articles with a theme of parenting for education, encouraging parents to work in their homes to improve their children's academic performance. Over the years, Owens appeared as the guest of the Virginia Festival of the Book, the American Association of University Women's Author's Brunch, and the Authors Pavilion of the Congressional Black Caucus, to name a few. She is the author of nine books, including her adult publications.

Owens lives in Mount Dora, Florida.

BIBLIOGRAPHY

Create a Math Environment. Eschar, 1992.
Nadanda, the Wordmaker. Illustrated by Richard Jesse Watson. Eschar, 1994.
The Rose Bush Witch. Eschar, 1996.
Chemistry Quickies. Eschar, 1998.
I Met a Great Lady. Illustrated by Richard Jesse Watson. Eschar, 1998.
I Met a Great Man. Illustrated by Richard Jesse Watson. Eschar, 1998.

The Mount Dorans: African American History Notes of a Florida Town. Eschar, 2000.

How Oswa Came to Own All Music. Illustrated by John D. Owens, III. Eschar, 2003.

Page, Mark

(1974–)

ILLUSTRATOR

Web site: www.mpagestudio.com

"As an illustrator, I relish occasions to illustrate African American Children in a positive light and in settings that expand their imaginations. Much of the literature written in the fantasy and fairytale genre lacks the presence of Black children. I feel minority kids need to see themselves in these unusual and fanciful settings and I love to produce work that does this in a way that sparks in a child creativity and wonder."

Page started drawing at a very early age. Imitating his older brother, Christian, Page began to draw cartoon characters from television and heroes from the pages of comic books. As he became a little older his eagerness to learn more about art was apparent. All throughout middle school and high school he was immersed in any art classes he could take and even enrolled on the weekends in the "Saturday High" program at the Pasadena Art Center, College of Design. After graduating from high school, Page became a full-time student at the Art Center, where he majored in illustration.

Since completing his college education, he has worked in the film industry, and also for The Walt Disney Company as an imaginer, designing rides and attractions for Disney theme parks. He continues to do design work in the field of entertainment along with fulfilling a lifelong dream of illustrating books for children.

Mark Page lives in Upland, California with his wife Nikki and their little dog Lola.

BIBLIOGRAPHY

No Boys Allowed. By Christine Taylor-Butler. Scholastic, 2003.
The King's Big Foot. By Loretta West. Rigby, 2003.
The Two Tyrones. By Wade Hudson. Scholastic, 2004.

Parker, Toni Trent

(1947–2005)

AUTHOR

Web site: www.blackbookgalore.com

Parker was born in Winston-Salem. She received a bachelor's degree in History from Oberlin College and also did graduate work at the University of California Berkeley.

Parker and two friends, Donna Rand and Sheila Foster, established a company to help promote the visibility of Black children in children's books: Black Books Galore! Children's picture books featuring or including minority children were largely absent before the 1960s. She created sales and raised awareness which helped bring more books with Black children into the mainstream.

In 1998 she established Kids Cultural Books, a nonprofit organization that holds book festivals around the country to bring multicultural books and their authors together with children. They received the Parenting Leaders award from *Parenting* magazine. The organization received a grant from the John D. and Catherine T. MacArthur Foundation in 2000.

In 2004, the John F. Kennedy Center for the Performing Arts recognized Parker for "her commitment to diversity in children's literature" for her assistance in the creation, development and implementation of the Kennedy Center Multicultural Children's Book Festival," and created a Toni Trent Parker Reading Room in her honor.

Parker is survived by her husband, Judge Barrington D. Parker, Jr. of Stamford, Connecticut, who is on the 2nd U.S. Circuit Court of Appeals, and their daughters Christine, Kathleen, and Jennifer and family. Parker died at fifty-eight years old at her home in Stamford.

BIBLIOGRAPHY

Black Books Galore! Guide to Great African American Children's Books. With Donna Rand and Sheila Foster. John Wiley & Sons, Inc., 1998.

Black Books Galore! Guide to Great African American Children's Books About Boys. With Donna Rand. John Wiley & Sons, Inc., 2001.

Black Books Galore! Guide to Great African American Children's Books About Girls. With Donna Rand. John Wiley & Sons, Inc., 2001.

Being Me: A Keepsake Scrapbook for African American Girls. Scholastic, 2002.

Hugs and Hearts. Illustrated by Earl Anderson. Cartwheel, 2002.

Painted Eggs and Chocolate Bunnies. Illustrated by Earl Anderson. Cartwheel, 2002.

Snowflake Kisses and Gingerbread Smiles. Illustrated by Earl Anderson. Cartwhell, 2002.

Sweets and Treats. Illustrated by Earl Anderson. Cartwheel, 2002.

Sienna's Scrapbook. Illustrated by Janell Genovese. Chronicle Books, 2005.

Pinkney, Andrea Davis

(1963–)

AUTHOR

Pinkney was born in Washington, D.C., the eldest of three children. Her mother was constantly reading books, and her father was, and still is, a master storyteller. She credits these influences as the "gentle hands" that helped shape her into a teller of her own stories for young readers.

Pinkney holds a bachelor's degree in journalism from Syracuse University's Newhouse School of Public Communications. She began her career as a gardening editor for a small home-decorating magazine in New York City, where she met illustrator Brian Pinkney, who worked in the Art Department at the sports-and-fishing magazine across the hall. Years later, he became her husband.

While working at the magazine, she spent nights and weekends writing short stories, essays, poems and whatever came to mind, for fun. One weekend, she wrote an essay about her experiences as an African American girl growing up in Wilton, Connecticut where there were only a few Black families. On a whim, she sent the piece to the *New York Times*, which published it within one week's time! Years later, she used her *New York Times* essay as the basis for her first young adult novel, *Hold Fast To Dreams*, which was named Pick of the List by the American Booksellers Association (ABA) in 1995. She won the 2001 Coretta Scott King Author Award for *Honor, Let It Shine!* Stories of Black Women Freedom Fighters.

She has written articles for *American Visions*, *Essence*, *Executive Female*, and *Highlights for Children* magazines. She is also the award-winning author of several children's picture books, all illustrated by her husband, Brian Pinkney. *Alvin Ailey*, published in 1993, was a National Association for the Advancement of Colored

People (NAACP) Image Award nominee and winner of the Parenting Publication Award Gold Medal. *Dear Benjamin Banneker*, published in 1994, was named an ABA Pick of the List title, a Child Study Children's Book Committee Best Books for Children, the winner of the Carter G. Woodson Honor Award, and *New York Times* Bookshelf Selection. *Seven Candles for Kwanzaa*, published in 1993, was also named an ABA Pick of the List book.

She is formerly a senior editor at *Essence* magazine, as well as an editor for the book publishers Simon & Schuster and Scholastic. The series she envisioned for promoting Black heritage, *Jump at the Sun*, was very well received. She became both a publisher of children's books and vice president at Houghton Mifflin, a publishing company with an unparalleled publishing history of more than 170 years with a long-standing tradition.

Her parents were deeply involved in the civil rights movement. As a result, Pinkney was exposed to the movement at an early age and attended many annual conferences of the National Urban League during her summer vacations.

She lives with her husband, Brian Pinkney, in Westchester County in New York and they have four children and seven grandchildren.

BIBLIOGRAPHY

Alvin Ailey. Hyperion, 1993.

Seven Candles for Kwaanza. Dial, 1993.

Dear Benjamin Banneker. Illustrated by Brian Pinkney. Gulliver Books, 1994.

Bill Pickett, Rodeo Ridin' Cowboy. Illustrated by Brian Pinkney. Gulliver Books, 1996.

I Smell Honey. Illustrated by Brian Pinkney. Red Wagon Books, 1997.

Pretty Brown Face. Illustrated by Brian Pinkney. Red Wagon Books, 1997.

Solo Girl. Hyperion, 1997.

Shake, Shake, Shake. Illustrated by Brian Pinkney. Red Wagon Books, 1997.

Watch Me Dance. Illustrated by Brian Pinkney. Red Wagon Books, 1997.

Duke Ellington: The Piano Prince and His Orchestra. Jump at the Sun, 1998.

Look at Me. Red Wagon Books, 1998.

Raven in a Dove House. Gulliver Books, 1998.

Hold Fast to Dreams. Bt. Bound, 1999.

Silent Thunder: A Civil War Story. Jump at the Sun, 1999.

Let it Shine! Stories of Black Women Freedom Fighters. Illustrated by Stephen Alcorn.

Heinemann Library, 2000.

Dear Mr. President: Abraham Lincoln: Letters from a Slave Girl. Winslow
  Press, 2001.

Mim's Christmas Jam. Illustrated by Brian Pinkney. Gulliver Books, 2001.

Ella Fitzgerald: The Tale of a Vocal Virtuosa. Jump at the Sun, 2002.

Fishing Day. Illustrated by Shane Evans. Jump at the Sun, 2003.

Sleeping Cutie. Illustrated by Brian Pinkney. Gulliver Books, 2004.

Peggony-Po. Illustrated by Brian Pinkney. Jump at the Sun, 2006.

Pinkney, Brian

(1961–)

AUTHOR/ILLUSTRATOR

Pinkney grew up in an artistic family. His father, Jerry Pinkney, is an award-winning illustrator of children's books and his mother, Gloria Jean Pinkney, an award-winning children's book writer. From an early age, Pinkney knew he wanted to be an illustrator and later began to write also. He holds both a bachelor of fine arts degree from the University of the Arts in Philadelphia and a master's degree in illustration from the School of Visual Arts in New York City. His illustrating career began with assignments for publications such as the *New York Times*, *Woman's Day*, *Ebony Man*, *Business Tokyo*, and *Amtrak Express* magazines. His illustrations have also appeared in numerous textbooks. As a children's book illustrator Pinkney has completed over twenty children's books. He was awarded the Caldecott Honor Award and the Coretta Scott King Honor Award for *The Faithful Friend* and is also a four-time winner of the Parent's Choice Award for illustrations that appeared in *The Boy and the Ghost*, *The Ballad of Belle Dorcas*, *Where Does the Trail Lead?* And *Sukey and the Mermaid*. *Sukey and the Mermaid* was also awarded the 1993 Coretta Scott King Honor Award for illustration, American Bookseller Pick of the List, *Parenting* magazine, Ten Best Books of 1992, Booklists, "Editors Choice for 1992," and *School Library Journal* Best Books 1992.

Pinkney has also illustrated several picture books written by his wife Andrea Davis Pinkney.

Pinkney's works have been exhibited at The Detroit Institute of Art, The Society of Illustrators; The Cleveland Museum of Art; the Cinque Gallery, New York; Montclair Art Museum, New Jersey; the Art Center of Battle Creek, Michigan; The National Arts

Club, New York; The Walters Art Gallery, Baltimore, Maryland; and The Schomburg Center for Research and Development in Black Culture, New York, among others.

He lives with his wife in Brooklyn, New York.

BIBLIOGRAPHY

Cendrillon. By Robert D. San Souci. Simon & Schuster, 1988.

The Boy and the Ghost. By Robert D. San Souci. Simon and Schuster, 1989.

The Ballad of Belle Dorcas. By William H. Hooks. Knopf, 1990.

Harriet Tubman and Black History Month. By Polly Carter. Silver Burdett Press, 1990.

Where Does the Trail Lead? By Burton Albert. Simon and Schuster, 1991.

The Lost Zoo. By Christopher Cat and Countee Cullen. Modern Curriculum Press, 1991.

A Wave in Her Pocket. By Lynn Joseph. Clarion, 1991.

Sukey and the Mermaid. By Robert D. San Souci. Four Winds Press, 1992.

The Elephant's Wrestling Match. By Judy Sierra. Lodestar, 1992.

The Dark Thirty. By Patricia C. McKissack. Knopf, 1992.

Happy Birthday, Martin Luther King. By Jean Marzollo. Scholastic, 1993.

Cut from the Same Cloth. By Robert D. San Souci. Philomel, 1993.

Alvin Ailey. By Andrea Davis Pinkney. Hyperion, 1993.

Seven Candles for Kwanzaa. By Andrea Davis Pinkney. Dial, 1993.

Dear Benjamin Banneker. By Andrea Davis Pinkney. Harcourt Brace and Co., 1994.

Max Found Two Sticks. By Brian Pinkney. Simon and Schuster, 1994.

The Dream Keeper and Other Poems. By Langston Hughes. Knopf, 1994.

Day of Delight. By Maxine Rose Schur. Dial, 1994.

The Faithful Friend. By Robert D. San Souci. Simon and Schuster, 1995.

Jojo's Flying Side Kick. By Brian Pinkney. Simon and Schuster, 1995.

When I Left My Village. By Maxine Rose Schur. Dial, 1995.

Wiley and the Hairy Man. By Judy Sierra. Lodestar, 1996.

Bill Pickett: Rodeo Ridin' Cowboy. By Andrea Davis Pinkney. Harcourt Brace and Co., 1996.

In the Time of the Drums. By Kim Siegelson. Hyperion, 1999.

Cosmo and the Robot. Greenwillow, 2000.

Mim's Christmas Jam. By Andrea Davis Pinkney. Gulliver Books, 2001.

Thumbelina. By Hans Christian Anderson. Greenwillow, 2003.

Ella Fitzgerald. By Andrea D. Pinkney. Hyperion, 2002.

The Stone Lamp. By Karen Hesse. Hyperion, 2003.

Sleeping Cutie. Harcourt, 2004.

Pinkney, Gloria Jean

(1941–)

AUTHOR

Pinkney was born in Lumberton, North Carolina, and treasures many childhood memories of family reunions. Her first picture book, *Back Home*, is based on an early experience of a trip back to her hometown. It won the 1992 American Library Association Notable Children's Book Award, was also selected as the *Booklist* Children's Editors Choice, and was listed among the New York Public Library's 100 Titles for Reading and Sharing.

Pinkney has worked as a model, a window designer, an arts and crafts instructor, a silversmith, and an artist representative. She is a member of Black Women in Publishing and the Society of Children's Book Writers and Illustrators. She is married to artist Jerry Pinkney, who illustrated *Back Home* and her second book, *The Sunday Outing*.

Several years ago while looking for a new direction in her writing, Pinkney found herself increasingly drawn to the Holy Scriptures. Early one morning, she committed her vocation to writing inspirational stories from life experiences. With *In the Forest of Your Remembrance* Pinkney shows how she came to recognize the many miraculous events in her life.

Pinkney and her husband have four children, Troy Bernardette, Brian, Scott, and Myles, all involved in some aspect of the creative arts. They live in Croton-on-Hudson, New York.

BIBLIOGRAPHY

Back Home. Illustrated by Jerry Pinkney. Dial, 1992.
The Sunday Outing. Illustrated by Jerry Pinkney. Dial, 1994.

In the Forest of Your Remembrance. Illustrations by Jerry Pinkney, Brian Pinkney and Myles C. Pinkney. Phyllis Fogelman Books, 2001.

Music from Our Lord's Holy Heaven. Illustrated by Jerry Pinkney and Myles C. Pinkney. HarperCollins, 2005.

Pinkney, Jerry

(1939–)

ILLUSTRATOR

Pinkney states that he took an interest in drawing at a very early age and then realized that he would rather sit and draw than do almost anything else. He was born in Philadelphia and while growing up in the Germantown section of the city his interest in art was supported by his family, especially his mother who made it clear to everyone that if art was what he wanted to pursue, then that's what she wanted to happen. His father also became supportive, and when he wanted to take art classes after school his father found a way for him to attend.

In junior high school, Pinkney had a newsstand and took a drawing pad with him to work every day and sketched people passing by. That was how he met cartoonist John Liney, who encouraged him to draw and showed him the possibilities of making a living as an artist.

He studied at the Philadelphia Museum College of Art (now the University of the Arts). In 1968, he and his family moved to Boston, Massachusetts, and he began his career as an illustrator-designer for the Rustcraft Publishing Company. He was next employed by the Barker-Black Studio, where he illustrated his first children's book, *The Adventures of Spider: West African Folk Tales*. Then he and two other artists opened Kaleidoscope Studio and he opened his own studio in Boston in 1968. In 1971, he moved to the New York area and began to freelance out of his studio in Croton-on-Hudson.

Since 1964, Pinkney has illustrated more than seventy-five children's books and twelve novels for adults. He has had the rare distinction of receiving three Caldecott Honor Medals, four Coretta Scott King Awards, and two Coretta Scott King Honor Book

Awards, two *New York Times* Best Illustrated Awards, two Christopher Awards, and the Boston Globe-Horn Book Award for illustration, among numerous other commendations. His works have been honored by the American Institute of Graphic Arts and the New York Art Directors Club, the Council on Interracial Books for Children, and the National Conference of Christians and Jews. In addition, he has been honored for his body of work with a citation for children's literature from Drexel University.

He has been a visiting critic for the Rhode Island School of Design, an associate professor at Pratt Institute, Brooklyn, New York, an associate professor of art at the University of Delaware, and a visiting professor in the Department of Art at the University at Buffalo, New York.

Best noted for his book illustrations, Pinkney has also designed twelve stamps for the United States Postal Service and served on the United States Postal Service Citizen Stamp Advisory Committee. Pinkney won the Coretta Scott King Illustrator Award for *Minty: A Story of Young Harriet Tubman.*

He and his wife, author Gloria Jean Pinkney, have collaborated on many books. They live in Westchester County, New York, and have four children and seven grandchildren. Their son Brian is also a children's-book illustrator and author.

BIBLIOGRAPHY

The Adventures of Spider: West African Folk Tales. By Joyce Arkhurst. Little Brown, 1964.

The Year Around. By Helen Jill Fletcher. Fletcher, McGraw-Hill, 1965.

More Adventures of Spider: West African Folk Tales. By Joyce Arkhurst. Scholastic, 1971.

Femi and Old Granddaddie. By Adjai Robinson. Coward, 1972.

J.D. By Mari Evans. Doubleday, 1973.

Kasho and the Twin Flutes. By Adjai Robinson. Coward, 1973.

The Great Minu. By Beth P. Wilson. Follett, 1974.

Song of the Trees. By Mildred D. Taylor. Dial, 1975.

Roll of Thunder, Hear My Cry. By Mildred D. Taylor. Dial, 1976.

The Winthrop Covenant. By Louis Auchincloss. Franklin Library, 1976.

Yagua Days. By Cruz Martel. Dial, 1976.

Mary McLeod Bethune. By Eloise Greenfield. Crowell, 1977.

Childtimes: A Three-Generation Memoir. By Lessie Jones Little and Eloise Greenfield. Harper, 1979.

Tales from Africa. By Lila Green. Silver Burdett Press, 1979.

The Flowering of New England 1815–1865 (100 Greatest Masterpieces of American Literature). By Van Wyck Brooks. Franklin Library, 1979.

Count on Your Fingers, African Style. By Claudia Zaslafsky. Crowell, 1980.

Jahdu. By Virginia Hamilton. Greenwillow, 1980.

The Patchwork Quilt. By Valerie Flournoy. Dial, 1985.

Forever Friends (formerly *Breadsticks and Blessing Places*). By Candy (Marguerite) Dawson Boyd. Macmillan, 1985.

Half a Moon and One Whole Star. By Crescent Dragonwagon. Macmillan, 1986.

The Adventures of Spider: West African Folktales. By Joyce Cooper Arkhorst. Scholastic, 1987.

The Little Match Girl. By Hans Christian Andersen. Putnam, 1987.

The Tales of Uncle Remus: The Adventures of Brer Rabbit. Volume One. By Julius Lester. Dial, 1987.

Wild Wild Sunflower Child Anna. By Nancy White Carlstrom. Macmillan, 1987.

The Green Lion of Zion Street. By Julia Fields. Macmillan, 1989.

Mirandy and Brother Wind. By Patricia C. McKissack. Knopf, 1988.

More Tales of Uncle Remus: Further Adventures of Brer Rabbit, His Friends, Enemies and Others. By Julius Lester. Dial, 1988.

Planet of Junior Brown. By Virginia Hamilton. G. K. Hall & Co., 1988.

Rabbit Makes a Monkey of Lion. By Verna Aardema. Dial, 1989.

The Talking Eggs. By Robert D. San Souci. Dial, 1989.

Turtle in July. By Marilyn Singer. Macmillan, 1989.

Further Tales of Uncle Remus: The Misadventures of Brer Rabbit, Brer Fox, Brer Wolf, the Doodang and Other Creatures. By Julius Lester. Dial, 1990.

Homeplace. By Crescent Dragonwagon. Macmillan, 1990.

Pretend You're a Cat. By Jean Marzollo. Dial, 1990.

Their Eyes Were Watching God. By Zora Neale Hurston. HarperCollins, 1991.

In for Winter, Out for Spring. By Arnold Adolf. Harcourt, 1991.

The Man Who Kept His Heart in a Bucket. By Sonia Levita. Dial, 1991.

Tonweya and the Eagles, and Other Lakota Tales. By Rosebud Yellow Robe. Dial, 1991.

David's Songs: His Psalms and Their Story. By Colin Eisler. Dial, 1992.

Back Home. By Gloria Jean Pinkney. Dial, 1992.

Drylongso. By Virginia Hamilton. Harcourt, 1992.

Rikki-Tikkik-Tavi. By Rudyard Kipling. Harcourt, 1992.

I Want to Be. By Thylias Moss. Dial, 1993.

New Shoes for Sylvia. By Johanna Hurwitz. Morrow, 1993.

A Starlit Somersault Downhill. By Nancy Willard. Little Brown, 1993.

Turtle in July. By Marilyn Singer. Turtleback Books, 1994.

The Hired Hand. By Robert D. San Souci. Dial, 1994.

John Henry. By Julius Lester. Dial, 1994.

The Last Tales of Uncle Remus. By Julius Lester. Dial, 1994.

The Sunday Outing. By Gloria Jean Pinkney. Dial, 1994.

The Jungle Book (Books of Wonder). By Rudyard Kipling. HarperCollins, 1995.

Tanya's Reunion. By Valerie Flournoy. Dial, 1995.

Minty: A Story of Young Harriet Tubman. By Alan Schroeder. Dial, 1996.

The Patchwork Quilt. By Valerie Flournoy. Scholastic, 1996.

Sam and the Tigers. Retold by Julius Lester. Dial, 1996.

A Starlit Somersault Downhill. By Nancy Willard. Little Brown, 1996.

The Hired Hand: An African-American Folktale. By Robert D. San Souci. Dial, 1997.

Black Cowboy, Wild Horses. By Julius Lester. Dial, 1998.

Fever Dream. By Jane Yolen. HarperCollins, 1998.

Journeys with Elijah: Eight Tales of the Prophet. By Barbara Diamond Goldin. Gulliver, 1999.

The Ugly Duckling. By Hans Christian Andersen. HarperCollins, 1999.

Uncle Remus: The Complete Tales. By Julius Lester. Dial, 1999.

Albidaro and the Mischievous Dream. By Julius Lester. Phyllis Fogelman Books, 2000.

Goin' Someplace Special. By Patricia McKissack. Atheneum/Anne Schwartz, 2001.

In the Forest of Your Remembrance. By Gloria Jean Pinkney. Dial, 2001.

Noah's Ark. Seastar Books, 2002.

The Nightingale. By Hans Christian Andersen. Dial, 2002.

Fabulas de Esap (Cucana) Vicens Vives. (Reprint—Spanish), 2003.

God Bless the Child. By Billie Holiday. Amistad, 2004.

Read to Me: Recommended Literature for Children Ages Two through Seven. Diane Publishing Company, 2004.

Music from Our Lord's Holy Heaven Book. By Gloria Jean Pinkney. Amistad, 2005.

The Old African. By Julius Lester. Dial, 2005.

Half Moon and One Whole Star. By Crescent Dragonwagon. Simon & Schuster, 2006.

The Little Red Hen (unauthored). Dial, 2006.

Pinkney, Myles C.

(1963–)

ILLUSTRATOR

E-mail: mylescp@aol.com

Web site: www.MylesStudio.com

"Creating children's books is very rewarding for me for several reasons. I believe that children are a gift from God. I also see that there are so many negative images that they are exposed to every day. I wanted for them to be able to see positive images of themselves, especially for Black children. I hope that our books are able to build them up, and let them feel good about themselves. I always hope to not just photograph children, but capture that quality in every child that makes them special. I learned early on, the impact that a photograph could have on its viewer. Any emotion that a person can have, can be evoked from a single image. A good photograph will capture the essence of a person. I hope the viewer will sense the personality, the emotion, and the uniqueness that each individual possesses."

Myles was born in Boston, Massachusetts, in 1963, but grew up in Croton-on-the-Hudson, New York, with a family of artists ... his father, illustrator Jerry Pinkney, his mother, author Gloria Jean Pinkney, his two brothers, illustrator Brian Pinkney, and artist Scott Pinkney, and his sister, Troy Ragsdale. He is married to Sandra L. Pinkney. Together they have three children, Leon, Charnelle, and Rashad, who appear in their books.

Myles first became interested in photography at the age of twelve, when he received his first camera as a birthday gift from his father. He was involved in as many activities involving photography as he could find. In 1993 Myles graduated from Marist College with a BA in communications. It was during this time that he opened his studio, *Myles Studio*, located in Poughkeepsie, New York. He continues his education, through the Professional Photographers Society of New York, and Professional Photographers of America.

At his studio Myles works as a portrait and wedding photographer with his wife, Sandra.

Not only do they work in the studio together, but they also have completed two highly acclaimed books, "*Shades of Black*" and "*A Rainbow All Around Me.*" He has commercial and noncommercial clients. His commercial clients include album producers, musicians, business professionals, models, magazine publishers, and newspapers. Myles has illustrated additional books by authors such as Nikki Grimes and Patricia McKissick. He also has had his work exhibited in galleries, museums, and colleges. When he is not taking pictures or working in his studio, he enjoys doing presentations and workshops at schools and during community events.

Myles has a distinct style to his work. He creates natural looking images that capture the personality of his subject. *Shades of Black* won the 2001 NAACP Image Award for Outstanding Children's Literacy Work, the 2001 Notable Book for a Global Society Award, and the Parents Guide to Children's Media Award. SeeSaw's Top Picks selected *A Rainbow All Around Me* and the book was also nominated for the NAACP Image Award in 2003.

He and his family live in Poughkeepsie, New York.

BIBLIOGRAPHY

Can You Imagine? By Patricia McKissack. Richard Owens Publishing, 1997.

It's Raining Laughter. By Nikki Grimes. Dial Books for Young Readers, 1997.

Shades of Black. By Sandra Pinkney. Scholastic, 2000.

Sitting Pretty. By Dinah Johnson. Henry Holt, 2000.

Learning How to Appreciate Differences. By Susan Kent. Rosen Publishing Group, 2001.

Learning How to Feel Good About Yourself. By Susan Kent. Rosen Publishing Group, 2001.

Let's Talk About Feeling Confused. By Melanie Ann Apel. Rosen Publishing Group, 2001.

Let's Talk About Feeling Worried. By Melanie Ann Apel. Rosen Publishing Group, 2001.

Meet Shel Silverstein. By S. Ward. Rosen Publishing Group, 2001.

A Rainbow All Around Me. By Sandra Pinkney. Scholastic, 2002.

In the Forest of Your Remembrance. By Gloria Pinkney. Penguin Putnam, 2002.

Read and Rise By Sandra Pinkey. Cartwheel Books, 2006.

Pinkney, Sandra L.

AUTHOR

E-mail: SandraPinkney@aol.com

Web site: www.mylesstudio.com

Pinkney is a free-lance writer. She lives and works with her husband, Myles, a photographer, in Poughkeepsie, New York. They have three children, Leon, Charnelle-Rene, and Rashad.

Sandra was born and raised in Ossining, New York, located an hour away from New York City. She was born into a large family and had eleven siblings. Sandra found her love for writing early while writing creative stories in her elementary school. During her early years, she overcame many difficulties, including a learning disability caused by lead poisoning, and racial discrimination by her peers.

In 1995, Sandra opened her own business, Lil' Praiser's Christian Daycare. It was during this time that she teamed up with her husband, Myles, to produce their first book together, *Shades of Black*. In this book, Sandra uses vivid text to describe the various skin tones, hair textures, and eye colors of African American children. This book invites all children and adults of different nationalities to embrace their differences and their beauty, in their own culture and the cultures around them, by helping them to realize that they themselves are unique. Much of her inspiration for this book came from her childhood, as well as her three children, who also appear in the book.

Sandra received her AS degree in Early Childhood Education from Duchess Community College in Poughkeepsie, New York. She has also received many awards for her work with children. Her most notable is the 2001 NAACP Image Award for Outstanding Children's Literary Work for *Shades of Black — A Celebration of our Children.* Other awards for *Shades of Black* include 2001 Charlotte Zolotow Highly Commended, 2001 Notable Book for a Global Society, 2001 Parents Guide to Children's Media, and the 2001 Skipping Stone Honor. She was also invited to the White House to participate in the National Book Festival and performed as one of the speakers of the day. She appeared on many news shows, including the *Today Show* on NBC. Her biography appears in the periodical *Something About the Author.*

She later joined forces with her husband again with a second book, *A Rainbow All Around Me.* This book was nominated for the 2003 NAACP Image Award for Outstanding Children's Literary Work and was on the list for See-Saws Top Pick for September 2003.

She is working on a number of new manuscripts. Sandra's favorite time to write is in the early morning before the birds get up. This is when she feels that God inspires her the most. Sandra believes that with God anything is possible. Her future is wide open.

BIBLIOGRAPHY

Shades of Black. Illustrated by Myles Pinkney. Scholastic, 2002.
A Rainbow All Around Me. Illustrated by Myles Pinkney. Scholastic, 2002.
Read and Rise Illustrated by Myles Pinkney. Cartwheel Books, 2006.

Porter, A.P.

(1945–)

AUTHOR

E-mail: himself@anthonypeytonporter.com

Web site: www.anthonypeytonporter.com

A native Chicagoan, Anthony Peyton Porter does voice-overs professionally, is an oral essayist on KZFR radio in Chico, California, and writes a column for the *Chico News & Review*.

    Jump at de Sun: The Story of Zora Neale Hurston was selected by the Young Adult Library Services Association of the American Library Association as a Recommended Book for Reluctant Young Adult Readers and was a Notable Children's Trade Book in the Field of Social Studies. *Kwanzaa* won a Chicago Reading Round Table Award.

    He was the founding President of SASE: The Write Place, a Minnesota organization for writers.

    Porter has had more than fifty jobs including a factory trained bicycle mechanic and is the only person known to have subscribed to, written for, and delivered the *Minneapolis Star Tribune*. Porter rode alone from South Dakota to Chicago on a bicycle.

    He is the author of seven books and lives in Chico, California with his wife and two of three sons.

BIBLIOGRAPHY

Greg LeMond: Premier Cyclist. Lerner, 1990.

Kwanzaa. Illustrated by Janice Lee Porter. Carolrhoda, 1991.

Nebraska. Lerner, 1991.

Zina Garrison: Ace. Lerner, 1991.

Jump at de Sun: The Story of Zora Neale Hurston. Carolrhoda, 1992.

Minnesota. Lerner, 1992.

Can He Say That? Porter Publishing, 1999.

Purnell, Gerald H.

ILLUSTRATOR

E-mail: gpurnell@comcast.net

Web site: www.geraldpurnell.com

"I wish to inform young people with a sense of their own self worth through my work. Using inner city kids as subjects and showing the dignity in everyday life, I am compelled to produce positive images which reflect and inspire our youth. All of my art work points to my love of God."

Purnell was born in West Philadelphia, received a BFA from Cheyney University and he has done graduate work at the University of the Arts in Philadelphia. In 1988 he won the Bell Atlantic Award of Excellence. In that same year he was inducted into the Bell Atlantic Hall of Fame. He is the original designer of Verizon's "Talking Telephone Book" used in national and international ad campaigns. In March 2000, he won first and second place in a logo design contest at Verizon.

In 2001, *Boy with Skateboard* was featured along with Normal Rockwell and Henry O'Tanner in the book *Tell All the Children Our Story* authored by Tonya Bolden.

In 2002, Gerald received a Letter of Accommodation from the City of Philadelphia for an art presentation he gave at the Youth Study Center. He has also presented his art work at junior and senior high schools in New Jersey, Maryland, and Philadelphia.

In 2002, he also held his first one-man show art exhibit at the Atlantic/Cape University campus. His art work has won a blue ribbon at the Virtua Memorial Pavilion Gallery Group Show.

To date he has illustrated twelve book covers for Townsend Press and continues to produce exclusive cover art for the Bluford series.

Am I a Color Too? is illustrated by Gerald and published by Illumination Arts as his first children's hardback picture book which has won the Christopher Award for 2006.

He is also a photographer and musician playing the flute and tenor sax.

Gerald married his college sweetheart thirty-one years ago and has two children. He lives in Philadelphia, Pennsylvania.

BIBLIOGRAPHY

Lost & Found. By Anne Schraff. Townsend Press, 1999.

A Matter of Trust. By Anne Schraff. Townsend Press, 1999.

Secrets in the Shadows. By Anne Schraff. Townsend Press, 1999

Someone to Love. By Anne Schraff. Townsend Press, 2000

The Bully. By Anne Schraff. Townsend Press, 2000.

Until We Meet Again. By Anne Schraff. Townsend Press, 2001.

Tell All the Children Our Story. By Tonya Bolden. Harry Abrams, 2001.

The Gun. By Paul Langan. Townsend Press, 2002.

Shattered. By Paul Langan. Townsend Press, 2002.

Brothers in Arms. By Paul Langan and D. M. Blackwell. Townsend Press, 2003.

Blood is Thicker. By Paul Langan and Ben Alirez. Townsend Press, 2004.

Summer of Secrets. By Paul Langan. Townsend Press, 2004.

The Fallen. By Paul Langan. Townsend Press, 2006.

Miracle at Monty Middle School. By Mary A. Monroe. Self Published, 2005.

Am I a Color Too? By Heidy Cole & Nancy Vogl. Illumination Arts, 2005.

Ransome, James

(1961–)

ILLUSTRATOR

E-mail: JRANSOMEILLUSTR@aol.com

Web site: www.JAMESRANSOME.com

"Like so many children today, I grew up in a household where reading was not a priority. I lived with my Grandmother who could not go to school beyond the first grade in order to help her family sharecrop. The only book I recall being in our home was the Bible, which she would often ask me to read aloud. It was the combination of these graceful, strongly illustrated Bible stories, dramatic comic books, Mad magazine, and Disney cartoons that both sparked then captured my interest. I read because I was interested in the images that accompanied the story. These pictures also became my introduction to art, first by copying comics and later by illustrating my own books about me and my friends. It is with this realization that I understand the importance an illustration can have on a reader.

"I believe children are inspired by subjects they can relate to. One of the best ways we can encourage children to read, is to familiarize them with a subject by presenting activities outside of the book itself, such as a dialog, or a visit to a place related to the subject of the book. Parallel learning, where children can have experiences beyond reading, will capture their interest and encourage them to explore a subject in more depth. "To make each book unique, I do a lot of exploration, and experimentation. In doing so, I learn a lot about the subject of the books: African tales, New England landscape, recent or distant history, and inspirational people. I hope my artwork encourages children to do the same."

Ransome was born in 1961 in Rich Square, North Carolina. He has been illustrating children's books for over sixteen years. Winner of several awards for his illustrations, including the Coretta Scott King and NAACP Image awards, Ransome received his Bachelor of Fine Arts degree in illustration from Pratt Institute in Brooklyn, New York. His exhibit "Visual Stories" is traveling around the country. In addition to illustrating over forty children's books, he has also done pieces for children's magazines, and a number of book jackets. In 2004 he completed two commissioned murals, one for the Underground Railroad Museum in Cincinnati, Ohio, and another for the Hemphill Branch Library in Greensboro, North Carolina to commemorate the fiftieth anniversary of *Brown v. Board of Education*. Ransome's work is part of both private and public children's book art collections.

As a child, Ransome did not have access to art training or fine art galleries; however, he knew he wanted to draw, so he took his inspiration from comic books, *Mad* magazine, and the classic, color plates in the Bible. He continued improving his skill, on his own, throughout elementary school, creating his own stories in order to have something to illustrate. When he moved to Bergenfield, New Jersey, he was introduced to formal art training in high school. He also developed a warm relationship with his teacher in filmmaking, Charlie Bogasat. Ransome credits Charlie with his decision to attend college and pursue the field of art. At Pratt, Ransome chose illustration as his major, feeling he could make a more successful career working for publishers rather than relying on galleries to promote his art. It was also at Pratt that he discovered the work of Jerry Pinkney, an African American illustrator. Ransome had been under the impression that there were virtually no African Americans making a career in illustration, so meeting Jerry, attending his lectures and studying his large body of work was inspirational. He has since become Ransome's mentor and friend.

In 1995, Ransome completed a mural for the Children's Museum of Indianapolis. Original paintings from his published works have been exhibited in group and solo shows throughout the United States and Canada and also in private and public collections such as the permanent children's book collection of the North Carolina's Charlotte Library.

He lives in Rhinebeck, New York with his wife, author Lesa Cline-Ransome and their four children.

BIBLIOGRAPHY

Do Like Kyla. By Angela Johnson. Orchard, 1990.
All the Lights in the Night. By Arthur Levine. Tambourine, 1991.

Aunt Flossie's Hats (and Crab Cakes Later). By Elizabeth Fitzgerald Howard. Clarion, 1991.

How Many Stars in the Sky? By Lenny Hort. Morrow, 1991.

The Girl Who Wore Snakes. By Angela Johnson. Orchard, 1993.

The Hummingbird Garden. By Christine Widman. Macmillan, 1993.

Red Dancing Shoes. By Denise Lewis Patrick. Tambourine, 1993.

Sweet Clara and the Freedom Quilt. By Deborah Hopkinson. Knopf, 1993.

Uncle Jed's Barbershop. By Margaree King Mitchell. Simon & Schuster, 1993.

Bonesy and Isabel. By Michael J. Rosen. Harcourt, 1994.

The Creation. By James Weldon Johnson. Holiday House, 1994.

My Best Shoes. By Marilee Burton. Morrow, 1994.

Celie and the Harvest Fiddler. By Valerie and Vanessa Flournoy. Tambourine, 1995.

The Old Dog. By Charlotte Zolotow. HarperCollins, 1995.

Bimmi Finds a Cat. By Elizabeth Stewart. Clarion, 1996.

Dark Day, Light Night. By Jan Carr. Hyperion, 1996.

Freedom's Fruit. By William Hooks. Knopf, 1996.

The Wagon. By Tony Johnston. Tambourine, 1996.

Rum-A-Tum-Tum. By Angela Medearis. Holiday House, 1997.

Your Move. By Eve Bunting. Harcourt Brace, 1998.

The Jukebox Man. By Jacqueline K. Ogburn. Dial, 1998.

Let My People Go. By Patricia and Fredrick McKissack. Atheneum, 1998.

Satchel Paige. By Lesa Cline-Ransome. Simon & Schuster, 2000.

Quinnie Blue. By Dinah Johnson. Henry Holt, 2000.

The Secret of the Stones. By Robert D. San Souci. Dial, 2000.

How Animals Saved the People. By J.J. Reneaux. HarperCollins, 2001.

Building a New Land. By Jim Haskins. Jim Haskins, 2001.

Quilt Alphabet. By Lesa Cline-Ransome. Holiday House, 2001.

Under the Quilt of Night. By Deborah Hopkinson. Atheneum, 2001.

Visiting Day. By Jacqueline Woodson. Scholastic, 2002.

Quilt Counting. By Lesa Cline-Ransome. Seastar Books, 2002.

Bruh Rabbit and the Tar Baby Girl. By Virginia Hamilton. Blue Sky Press, 2003.

Major Taylor Champion Cyclist. By Lesa Cline-Ransome. Simon & Schuster, 2004.

A Pride of African Tales. By Donna L. Washington. HarperCollins, 2004.

It is the Wind. By Ferida Wolff. HarperCollins, 2005.

This is the Dream. By Diane Z. Shore. HarperCollins, 2006.

Pelé. By Lesa Cline-Ransome. Random House, 2006.

Helen Keller. By Lesa Cline-Ransome. HarperCollins, 2006.

Sky Boys: How They Built the Empire State Building. By Deborah Hopkinson. Random House, 2006.

Reed, Gregory J.

AUTHOR

E-mail: girassoc@aol.com

Web site: www.gjreedlaw.com

"I believe that young people are our key for a better world provided we supply them with the proper reading materials. I have written many books, but the joy of writing books for young people with Mrs. Parks was the highlight of my writing journey. To be able to touch many young people's hearts is fulfilling."

Educated at Michigan State University, Reed received a BS and MS in engineering. He also received a JD an LLM, in law. Reed authored twelve books, many of which are award-winning. Most notable award-winning books include two young adult books entitled *Quiet Strength* and *Dear Mrs. Parks: A Dialogue with Today's Youth* co-authored with Mrs. Rosa Parks. Reed has received an NAACP Image Award and many others. In addition, he has lectured both nationally and internationally as well as in Michigan.

Reed lives in Detroit, Michigan.

BIBLIOGRAPHY

Quiet Strength (with Rosa Parks). Zondervan, 1995.

Dear Mrs. Parks: A Dialogue with Today's Youth. Illustrated by Tania Garcia. Lee and Low, 1997.

Reid, Desmond

(1945–)

AUTHOR

Reid grew up in Jamaica, the third of nine children, and remembers seeking solace in books to keep away from the hectic doings in a household with so many children. From 1961 to 1965, he attended the Gleaner School of Printing in Jamaica, and in 1965 he moved to the United States and was employed in the printing trade with the Theo. Gaus Company until he joined the United States Air Force. It was service in the Air Force that enabled him to complete his secondary schooling. After Gaus closed, he and three other employees bought the company's printing operations. They later sold it in 1981.

At his children's school, Reid noticed that the only Black representation in the books in the library was the ink on the pages. Instead of waiting for the next PTA meeting to voice his concern, he took matters into his own hands forming Desmond A. Reid Enterprises (D.A.R.E.) to start publishing and selling African American books to the public school system and daycare centers.

His interest in writing children's books began after a brief visit to Jamaica, when he wrote his first children's book. Since then, he has occupied himself with the pursuit of advanced studies and community work in Brooklyn, New York.

BIBLIOGRAPHY

Dana Meets the Cow Who Lost its Moo. Gaus, 1984.

Ringgold, Faith (Jones)

(1930–)

AUTHOR/ILLUSTRATOR

Web site: www.faithringgold.com

A native of Harlem, New York, Ringgold received her bachelor of science and master of arts degrees from the City College of New York and then worked as an art teacher. She has taught beadwork and mask making. She began to paint professionally in 1960. After making figurative soft sculptures, she decided in 1980 to make quilts.

She had worked earlier with her mother, a fashion designer and dressmaker, who told her stories of slave ancestors making quilts incorporating a painting. Her quilt *Echoes of Harlem* was the first and last project made in collaboration with her mother. Her quilts have a central large painted image framed with a text written on the quilt. She began her artistic career more than thirty-five years ago as a painter. She is best known for her painted story quilts—art that combines painting, quilted fabric, and storytelling.

Ringgold's work is found in collections of several museums in New York City, including the Museum of Modern Art; the Studio Museum in Harlem; the Metropolitan Museum of Art; the Solomon R. Guggenheim Museum; the Fine Arts Museum in Long Island, Hempstead, New York; and the High Museum in Atlanta, Georgia. Her work can also be found in private and corporate collections throughout the United States and has been exhibited in Europe, Asia, South America, and Africa. A grant from the LaNapoule Foundation enabled her to work on a series of quilts during a four-month residence in France in 1990.

Her quilt *Tar Beach*, completed in 1988, is from her Woman on a Bridge series, now part of the Guggenheim collection. It served as the basis of Ringgold's first picture book, *Tar Beach*, which re-creates scenes of Harlem from a rooftop overlooking the George Washington Bridge in New York City. The book was a 1992 Caldecott Honor Book and won the 1992 Coretta Scott King Award for illustration.

Ringgold also received a National Endowment for the Arts Award for painting in 1989, and she has been awarded six honorary doctorates in fine arts, from the Massachusetts College of Art in Boston, Massachusetts; Moore College of Art in Philadelphia, Pennsylvania; and her alma mater, the City University of New York, among others.

Ringgold is writing her first book for an adult audience, with a working title of *We Flew Over the Bridge*, based on an unpublished manuscript written in 1979.

She is the mother of two daughters, Michele and Barbara Wallace and has three granddaughters. She is a professor of art at the University of California in San Diego, California.

Ringgold lives in Englewood, New Jersey.

BIBLIOGRAPHY

Tar Beach. Crown, 1991.

Aunt Harriet's Underground in the Sky. Crown, 1992.

Dinner at Aunt Connie's House. Hyperion, 1993.

Bonjour, Lonnie. Hyperion, 1996.

Talking to Faith Ringgold. Ransom House, 1998.

Invisible Princess. Crown, 1998.

My Grandmother's Story Quilt. Random House, 1999.

Cassie's Colorful Day. Crown, 1999.

Counting to Tar Beach. Crown, 1999.

Subway Graffiti. Galison Books, 2000.

Cassie's Word Quilt. Knopf, 2002.

O Holy Night! Christmas with the Boys Choir of Harlem. HarperCollins, 2004.

Roberts, Brenda C.

(1947)

AUTHOR

"I began writing stories when I was a second grader; it's as much a part of my life as breathing. When I encounter young people who have that same love of the written word, it gives me great joy. I want to keep the joy coming, and I suppose that's one of the reasons I keep writing.

"Writing for young people is something special. To be a part of the sense of anticipation they feel when they open a book, to help recreate the sense of discovery I felt as a child in the presence of a good story—for me, that is thrilling.

"If our children are introduced early to libraries and bookstores as places where magic happens, if books are everywhere in their homes, if their evenings end with stories read to them, the love of reading will evolve naturally. Isn't it true that a child who is exposed to the fun of stories, who sees words as a passage to enjoyment, will become a good reader?

It is gratifying that the world of multicultural literature for children and young adults is expanding, but it should expand even more. The lives of our African American youths should be illuminated daily by stories that enrich their imaginations. I hope to be a part of it always."

Roberts wrote for a Northern California newspaper before earning her master's degree in English from the University of California. She continued her career in journalism at a daily newspaper in Southern California, after which she joined the staff of Los Angeles Mayor Tom Bradley as a media relations representative.

Roberts worked for a number of years as Bradley's news deputy before marrying and raising two children. She served as media relations director for a state university, branched out as a writing consultant, and later became managing editor at a Los Angeles area university.

Though Roberts earlier had won the Gwendolyn Brooks Award for Literature from the Johnson Publishing Company for a group of short stories, she had not published for young people before 1993, when Scholastic Inc. brought out *Sticks and Stones, Bobbie Bones*, a novel for readers ages seven to ten.

Roberts' first picture Book, *Jazzy Miz Mozetta*, was published in 2004. For his work on the book, illustrator Frank Morrison won the Coretta Scott King/John Steptoe New Talent Award.

A member of the Society of Children's Book Writers and Illustrators, Friends of Children and Literature, the Children's Literature Council of Southern California, and other groups for booklovers, Roberts worked for years with The Wonder of Reading, a Los Angeles-based library and reading advocacy organization she enthusiastically supports.

The author, living in Los Angeles, California, is a frequent presenter at schools, libraries, and organizations in the Los Angeles area.

BIBLIOGRAPHY

Sticks and Stones, Bobbie Bones. Scholastic, 1993.

Jazzy Miz Mozetta. Illustrated by Frank Morrison. "Farrar, Straus & Giroux, 2004.

Robinet, Harriette Gillem

(1931–)

AUTHOR

Web site: www.hgrobinet.com

Robinet was born and reared in Washington, D.C. She spent her childhood summers across the Potomac in Arlington, Virginia, where her mother's parents had been slaves under General Robert E. Lee. Robinet received a bachelor's degree from the College of New Rochelle in New Rochelle, New York, in 1953 and graduate degrees from the Catholic University of America in Washington, D.C., in 1957 and 1962.

For thirty-five years a freelance writer, she has published many magazine articles in addition to her children's books. She completed the Famous Writers Correspondence Course and is a member of the Society of Children's Book Writers and Illustrators, the Children's Reading Roundtable, and the Black Literary Umbrella.

Her book *Ride the Red Cycle* is based on personal observations of her son, disabled by cerebral palsy, and many other disabled youngsters she met. It is in Houghton Mifflin's fifth-grade reader and Scott Foresman's fourth-grade reader. *Children of the Fire* and *Mississippi Chariot* were named Notable Books in Social Studies by the Children's Book Council and the National Council of Social Studies, and *Children of the Fire* was awarded the 1991 Young People's Literature Award by Friends of American Writers. She writes historical fiction for children eight to twelve years old. As a writer of multicultural historical fiction, Robinet enjoys reaching pivotal moments in American History, moments which, she says, "have been either ignored or not appreciated." She believes that "children who read historical fiction not only learn history, they experience history." Knowing challenges of the past can give children courage for challenges of the present.

Robinet lives in Oak Park, Illinois, with her husband, McLouis Robinet, a health physicist at Argonne National Laboratory. They have six children and four grandchildren.

BIBLIOGRAPHY

Jay and the Marigold. Illustrated by Gertrude Scott. Children's Press, 1976.

Ride the Red Cycle. Illustrated by David Brown. Houghton, 1980.

Children of the Fire. Atheneum, 1991.

Mississippi Chariot. Atheneum, 1994.

If You Please, President Lincoln. Atheneum, 1995.

Washington City is Burning. Atheneum, 1996.

The Twins, the Pirates and the Battle of New Orleans. Illustrated by Keinyo White. Atheneum, 1997.

Forty Acres and Maybe a Mule. Atheneum, 1998.

Walking to the Bus Rider Blues. Atheneum, 2000.

Missing from Haymarket Square. Atheneum, 2001.

Twelve Travelers, Twenty Horses. Atheneum, 2003.

Robinson, Adjai

(1932–)

AUTHOR

Robinson was born in Freetown, Sierre Leone, Africa, and studied at Columbia University. He began collecting folktales from Nigeria and his native country for storytelling on radio in Sierra Leone. His folktale collection and storytelling skills helped him with his studies at Hunter College in New York City and the United States International School.

He has a bachelor's degree from Fourah Bay and a master's degree from Columbia University.

BIBLIOGRAPHY

Femi and Old Grandaddie. Illustrated by Jerry Pinkney. Coward, 1972.
Kasho and the Twin Flutes. Illustrated by Jerry Pinkney. Coward, 1973.
Singing Tales of Africa. Illustrated by Christine Price. Scribner, 1974.
Three African Tales. Illustrated by Carole Byard. Putnam, 1979.

Robinson, Aminah Brenda Lynn

(1940–)

AUTHOR/ILLUSTRATOR

Robinson is a nationally and internationally acclaimed artist whose skills, acquired in a formal art-school setting, through family, and those she taught herself, include painting, drawing, sewing, weaving, and papermaking. She has created more than 25,000 paintings, drawings, books, sculptures, prints, quilts, and mixed-media assemblages. Her subjects derive from her research of family and friends and her own sensitive experience of the world.

Born in Columbus, Ohio, Robinson is a graduate of the Columbus College of Art and Design in Columbus, Ohio. Robinson has done postgraduate work at Ohio State University and the University of Puerto Rico. She has taught as a visiting artist at all levels in public and private schools, churches, museums, and colleges. Her work is promoted by the Printmaking Workshop in New York City, the Carl Solway Gallery in Cincinnati, Ohio, and Winning Images and the Art Exchange, both in Columbus.

Robinson has had solo and group shows throughout the United States and Europe. In Ohio, she has exhibited in, and/or has work in the permanent collections of the Columbus Museum of Art, the Wexner Center at Ohio State University, the Carl Solway Gallery, the Dunlap Gallery in Otterbein, the Concourse Gallery in Upper Arlington, the Martin Luther King Center, the Columbus Foundation, the Columbus Metropolitan Library, Capital University, the Columbus College of Art and Design, the Akron Art Museum, and others.

Beginning in 1992, she turned her talents to writing and illustrating published books in addition to her other work. Robinson authored, illustrated, and published *The Teachings* and has illustrated *Elijah's Angel, Sophie, A School for Pompey Walker,* and *No Place Like Home.*

Robinson, also a fiber artist, received a MacArthur Fellows Grant in 2004. The grant provided $500,000 to "talented individuals who have shown extraordinary originality and dedication in their creative pursuits and a marked capacity for self-direction."

She celebrates and memorializes the neighborhood of her children, Poindexter Village, in Columbus, Ohio.

Robinson was the first living artist to be the subject of a major Columbus Museum of Art exhibition ("Pages in History: The Art of Aminah Robinson"). Commissioned murals by Robinson are permanently installed in the Columbus Metropolitan Library.

Robinson lives in Columbus, Ohio.

BIBLIOGRAPHY

Elijah's Angel, A Story of Chanokah and Christmas. By Michael J. Rosen. Harcourt, 1992.

No Place Like Home. With Mimi Bradsky Chenfield. Harcourt, 1992.

Teachings. Harcourt, 1992.

Sophie. By Mem Fox. Harcourt, 1994.

A School for Pompey Walker. By Michael J. Rosen. Harcourt, 1995.

A Street Called Home. Harcourt, 1997.

To Be a Drum. By Evelyn Coleman. Albert Whitman, 2000.

Ross, Andrea

(1959–)

AUTHOR/ILLUSTRATOR

E-mail: StorybookP@aol.com

"I've always felt the need to tell stories. As I grew older that need became a voice I heard deep inside children with behavioral problems. It is now the underlying force behind everything I write for children—their real-life personal challenges. The stories jump-start kids' creativity with an abundance of charm, courage and wit. The stories also draw from their strengths for an inspiring journey of self-discovery."

Ross was born in New York City and spent her early childhood, from age four, watching her grandfather, Rev. S. E. Churchstone Lord D.D., a foreign missionary and scholar, write books on philosophy and religion. She's been telling stories ever since.

At seven she launched her writing career by writing down her stories for her grandfather, who published them in his church newspaper. She pretended her dolls were the characters in her stories—they acted out their parts and wore clothes Ross designed and made.

She continued writing, acting, and designing in the intern program at the Playhouse in the Park in Cincinnati, Ohio, working with costume designers, directors and actors from across the country. Two of her adult plays and one of her children's plays were produced there. *Princess Forgetful Remembers*, another children's play, was performed and produced at the University of Cincinnati's Drama Department.

She moved on to the American Conservatory Theatre in San Francisco, John Houseman's Acting Company in New York City, Dance Theatre of Harlem, Broadway, television, film, and commercials. She juggles three successful careers as writer, costume designer, and performer.

Her first Chester Earth Ant children's books were published for kids in homeless shelters, cancer care kids in hospitals, slow learners in the New York City public schools. He has become a popular character, encouraging children from ages five to eight to read—as part of the New York City School Authors Read-Aloud Learning Leaders Program.

Many children wanted to read "Chester books" but they were published by small publishers and were not in bookstores. Chester's adventures were about "believing in what you want and going after it.".Not being satisfied, the children went to every bookstore in their neighborhoods several times and asked the book buyers where they could get Chester's books. Ross got a call from the book buyer at Barnes and Noble telling her that Chester had many readers and that his books needed to be made available for all children to read and that they wanted to put all of the Chester Earth Ant Books and all of Ross' other books on their Web site. Chester's books can be found on barnesandnoble.com and also on chesterearthant.com.

She received the Veterans of Foreign Wars Broadcast Script-writing Award and was chosen The Outstanding Spokesman for Freedom; also the Time Warner Cable Television Award for Best Achievements in Children's Television for writing her original children's television show, *Storybook Castle*.

Some of her television, theater, and film credits include *Ghostwriter*, *Reading Rainbow/Children's Television Workshop*, Dance Theatre of Harlem, *Malcolm X* (Denzel Washington), *Lean On Me* (Morgan Freeman), Daytime Emmy Awards (Dick Clark), *Saturday Night Live*, *Good Fellas* (Robert DeNiro), *Raw* (Eddie Murphy), Cosby Show (Bill Cosby) and has also appeared in and written TV and print commercials.

She's been published in *Spider Magazine* and can be found on SIRS DISCOVERER©, an interactive reference tool available online and on CD-ROM for young readers to develop research, reading, writing, language, and computer skills. Her biography of *The Boy King* can also be found in the Thompson/Herlie student book, *Visions*, and accompanying CD. A recorded excerpt is available at www.visions@Herlie.com.

Her books have been featured on The Dolan's *Money Talk on* CNN. She has appeared as special guest on *Martha Stewart Living*

Television. Ross is currently head of Wardrobe for CBS Television Network in New York City.

She lives in New York City.

BIBLIOGRAPHY

Chester, The Little Black Earth Ant. Exposition Press, 1980.

Comic Tale Easy Reader. May Davenport Publishers, 1984.

Comic Tale Easy Reader: Seymour The Turtle. May Davenport Publishers, 1984.

Poenisha. Winston-Derek Publishers, 1986.

Oscar Crab and Rallo Car. May Davenport Publishers, Aegina Press, 1987.

Comic Tale Easy Reader #1. May Davenport Publishers, 1987.

All About Turtles. May Davenport Publishers, 1990.

Chester Goes to the Valley. May Davenport Publishers, 1991.

Comic Tale Easy Reader. May Davenport Publishers, 1991.

Chester Earth Ant. Storybook Productions, 1996.

Chester Earth Ant Visits Margaret. Storybook Productions, 1996.

Littlest Ballerina. Storybook Productions, 1996.

Chester Earth Ant/ Alphabets. Storybook Productions, 1999.

Smiles are For Morning. Scythe Publications, 1999.

Chester Earth Ant/ Right Choice. Storybook Productions, 2000.

The Boy King. Spider, 2000.

I'm Bear: How Chester Got His Name. Author's House, 2001.

Chester Earth Ant/ Fire!Fire! Xlibris, 2005.

To Touch The Sun. May Davenport Publishers, 2006.

Roy, Lynette Edwina

(1942–)

AUTHOR

Roy was born in Trinidad, West Indies, and grew up with two cousins and a vivid imagination. As a young reader, she enjoyed fiction. One of her favorite characters was Jane Eyre, in the book of the same name by Charlotte Brontë. After completing high school in Trinidad, Roy studied nursing in Surrey, England, and she immigrated to Canada in 1972. She completed a bachelor of arts degree (with honors) in sociology at York University in 1987. A professor at York University encouraged her to write professionally, describing her writing as sensitive. One of her hobbies is coordinating clubs for children, so writing for children became her focus.

Her first book, *Brown Girl in the Ring*, a biography on Rosemary Brown, the first Black woman to be elected to a provincial-government post in Canada, was published in 1992. The book cover wears a gold seal of approval from the Canadian Children's Book Center, a recommendation for schools and libraries as required reading for children.

Professional memberships include the Canadian Society for Authors, Illustrators, and Performances; the Ontario Black History Society; and the Writers Union of Canada.

Roy enjoys visiting junior and senior high schools, doing book reading, lectures, and workshops to encourage students in their education.

She is single and lives in Uxbridge, Ontario, Canada.

BIBLIOGRAPHY
Brown Girl in the Ring. Sister Vision, 1992.
Cancer: Challenging the Disease. Umbrella, 1996.
Lincoln Alexander. Fitzhenry & Whiteside, 1992.
Four Courageous Black Women. National Heritage/Natural History, 1997.

Saint James, Synthia

(1949–)

AUTHOR/ILLUSTRATOR

E-mail: kikusaintjames@aol.com

Web site: www.synthiasaintjames.com

Self-taught artist Saint James was born in Los Angeles, California. Her professional career as an artist began in 1969 in New York City, where she sold her first commissioned oil painting. Today she has an international following. Her work is not only on canvas and limited-edition prints and posters, but on more than thirty book covers, which include books by Alice Walker, Terry McMillan, Iyanla Vanzant, and Julia A. Boyd, and more than eighty greeting cards, including UNICEF's (United National Children's Fund) card line. She has also licensed her images on T-shirts, magnets, boxes, gift bags, deck cards, puzzles, and mugs.

She has completed numerous commissions for major organizations and corporations, including the House of Seagram; Brigitte Matteuzzi's School of Modern Jazz Ballet in Geneva, Switzerland; the Mark Taper Forum; the National Bar Association; *Essence* magazine's twenty-fifth anniversary; UNICEF; the Children's Institute International, and the first Kwanzaa stamp for the United States Postal Service. She has received several awards for her books: the 1996 Parents Choice Silver Honor for her book *Sunday* and a 1997 Coretta Scott King Honor Book Award for illustrating *Neeny Coming ... Neeny Going.*

Saint James was honored with the 2004 Woman of the Year Award in Education by the Los Angeles County Commission for Women. She is also one of the women included in Dr. Cynthia Jacobs

Carter's recent National Geographic book *Africana Woman: Her Story Through Time*.

She is currently traveling nationally for exhibitions, book signing and keynote speaking engagements, while working on newly commissioned art, writing her autobiography, and completing a book of affirmations.

The New York City Solo Exhibition of Renowned Artists presented KALEIDOSCOPE from the Nafrissah Art Collectibles by Saint James in October of 2005.

She lives in Los Angeles, California.

BIBLIOGRAPHY

The Gifts of Kwanzaa. Whitman, 1994.

Snow on Snow on Snow. By Cheryl Chapman. Dial, 1994.

Tukama Tootles the Flute. By Phyllis Gershator. Orchard, 1994.

How Mr. Monkey Saw the Whole World. By Walter Dean Myers. Doubleday, 1996.

Neeny Coming ... Neeny Going. By Karen English. BridgeWater, 1996.

Sunday. Whitman, 1996.

Girls Together. By Sherley Anne Williams. Harcourt, 1998.

Greetings, Sun. By Phyllis Gershator. DK, Inc., 1998.

No Mirrors in My Nana's House. By Ysaye Barnwell. Harcourt, 1999.

Salkey, (Felix) Andrew

(1928–1995)

AUTHOR

Salkey was born in Colon, Panama, and grew up in Jamaica. He attended St. George's College in Kingston and Munro College in St. Elizabeth and earned his bachelor's degree in English from the University of London. He received the Thomas Helmore Poetry Prize in 1955 and a Guggenheim fellowship in 1960. Salkey taught English in a London comprehensive school and in 1952 became a radio interviewer and scriptwriter for BBC External Services.

He lived in London from the early 1950s until 1976.

Salkey received an honorary doctorate from Franklin Pierce College in 1981 and was a professor of creative writing at Hampshire College at Amherst, Massachusetts when he died in 1995.

BIBLIOGRAPHY

Earthquake. Illustrated by William Papas Roy. Oxford, 1968.

Jonah Simpson. Oxford, 1969.

Hurricane. Oxford, 1979.

Brother Anancy and Other Stories. Longman, 1993.

Smalls, Irene

(1950–)

AUTHOR

E-mail: ISmalls107@aol.com

Web site: www.irenesmalls.com

"I never thought I would be a writer. I think I first became a writer in kindergarten before I even knew it. I had a wonderful kindergarten teacher, who never read us stories with us sitting still. We sang the stories, we danced the stories, or we played games to the stories. I fell in love with the sounds of language, the music that I heard. My teacher read to us the poetry and stories of (Paul Laurence) Dunbar, James Weldon Johnson, (and others).

I always tell young children that all of my ideas come from the tip of my nose. There, right at the tip of my nose, was my young son, Jonathan, running and at the tip of my nose was my baby daughter, Dawn, who always woke up early in the morning. My first stories were about my children and growing up in Harlem. Writing is hard for me. I struggle. But I have found that I can write. I have become fascinated with the enslavement of African Americans."

The author was born in Harlem, New York, the oldest of four children. She was reared by her godmother, whom she credits with much of her success. That is one of the reasons she uses "I love you, Black Child" as one of the dedications in all of her books.

She attended New York public schools and graduated from Cornell University with a bachelor's degree in Black studies and was active in the Black student movement. She also attended New York University and received a master's degree in marketing and behavioral science.

Irene and the Big, Fine Nickel, her first book, was reviewed in the *New York Times*. Her second book, *Jonathan and His Mommy*, was a Junior Literary Guild main selection and was televised on the Public Broadcasting System (PBS) reading show *Storytime*. *Dawn and the Round To-It* received a pointer review in *Kirkus Reviews*. The author of more than a dozen books, Smalls is also a former Miss Black New York State and Young Ambassador to Europe.

In 1997 *Irene Jennie and the Christmas Masquerade: The JOHNKANKUS* won the Global Society Award given by the International Reading Association. Smalls signed a contract with WGBH Public Broadcasting Television to write four African American picture books about slavery to accompany the television series *Africans in America* broadcast in 1998. She lives in Boston, Massachusetts, and has three children, Dawn, Kevin Logan, and Jonathan.

BIBLIOGRAPHY

Irene and the Big, Fine Nickel. Illustrated by Tyrone Geter. Little Brown, 1991.

Jonathan and His Mommy. Illustrated by Michael Hays. Little Brown, 1992.

Dawn's Friends. Illustrated by Tyrone Geter. D.C. Heath, 1993.

Dawn and the Round To-It. Illustrated by Tyrone Geter. Simon & Schuster, 1994.

Alphabet Witch. Illustrated by Kevin McGovern. Longmeadow, 1995.

Ebony Sea. Illustrated by Jon O. Lockard. Longmeadow, 1995.

Father's Day Blues. Illustrated by Kevin McGovern. Longmeadow, 1995.

Beginning School. Illustrated by Toni Goffe. Silver Press, 1996.

Irene Jennie and the Christmas Masquerade: The JOHNKANKUS. Illustrated by Melodye Rosales. Little Brown, 1996.

Jenny Reen and the Jack Muh Lantern on Halloween. Illustrated by Keinyo White. Atheneum, 1996.

Louise's Gift: Or What Did She Give Me That For? Illustrated by Colin Boorman. Little Brown, 1996.

Jonathan and Kevin Are Lucky. Little Brown, 1997.

Kevin and His Dad. Little Brown, 1998.

Because You're Lucky. Illustrated by Michael Hays. Little Brown, 1997.

A Strawbeater's Thanksgiving. Illustrated by Melodye Rosales. Little Brown, 1998.

I Can't Take a Bath. Illustrated by Aaron Boyd. Scholastic, 2004.

My Nana & Me. Illustrated by Cathy Johnson. Little Brown, 2005.

Pop Pop and Me and a Recipe. Illustrated by Cathy Johnson. Little Brown, 2006.

Steptoe, Javaka

(1971–)

AUTHOR/ILLUSTRATOR

E-mail: info@javaka.com

Web site: www.javaka.com

"I want my audience, no matter what their background, to be able to enter into my world and make connections with comparable experiences in their own lives."

Once a model and inspiration for his late father, award-winning author/illustrator John Steptoe, Steptoe has established himself as an outstanding illustrator in his own right. Utilizing everyday objects, from aluminum plates to pocket lint, and sometimes illustrating with a jigsaw and paint, he delivers reflective and thoughtful collage creations filled with vitality, playful energy, and strength. For Steptoe, "collage is a means of survival. It is how Black folks survived four hundred years of oppression, taking the scraps of life and transforming in their own lives."

Having earned his Bachelor of Fine Arts from The Cooper Union for the Advancement of Science and Art, Steptoe is very committed to children's education, making appearances at various schools libraries, museums, and conferences across the country, including the American Library Association, the International Association, and Reading Is Fundamental, Inc.

His debut work, *In Daddy's Arms I Am Tall: African American Celebrating Fathers*, earned him the Coretta Scott King Illustrator Award, a nomination for Outstanding Children's Literature Work at the 1998 NAACP Image Awards, a finalist ranking for the Bluebonnet Award for Excellence in Children's Books, and countless other honors. *Do You Know What I'll Do authored by Charlotte Zolotow* and *A Pocketful of Poems* authored by Nikki Grimes received starred reviews from both Publishers Weekly and the ALA Booklist.

BIBLIOGRAPHY

In Daddy's Arms I Am Tall: African Americans Celebrating Fathers. Lee & Low, 1997.

Do You Know What I'll Do? By Charlotte Zolotow. HarperCollins, 2000.

A Pocketful of Poems. By Nikki Grimes. Clarion, 2001.

The Scream. Hyperion, 2002.

Jones Family Express. Lee & Low, 2003.

Hot Day on Abbott Avenue. By Karen English. Clarion, 2004.

Sweet , Sweet Baby! Scholastic, 2005.

All of the Above. By Susan Pearson. Little Brown, 2006.

Steptoe, John (Lewis)

(1950–1989)

AUTHOR/ILLUSTRATOR

Steptoe was born in Brooklyn, New York. From early childhood he drew pictures and told stories to go along with them. He attended the New York High School of Art and Design, and studied with painter Norman Lewis. Recognition of his talents began with his first published book, *Stevie*, written and published when he was sixteen years old. It received outstanding critical acclaim for depicting a Black inner city child's experiences in Black dialog and simple illustrations. It appeared in its entirety in *Life* magazine, hailed as "a new kind of book for Black children."

Steptoe also studied at the Vermont Academy and was instructed by the African American oil painter, Norman Lewis. He went on to a twenty year career. His *Mufaro's Beautiful Daughters* has been proclaimed as a breakthrough for African American storytelling for children.

Among his awards are the Society of Illustrators Gold Medal in 1970, the Coretta Scott King Award in 1982 and 1988, the Irma Simonton Black Award from Bank Street College in New York City in 1975, Caldecott Honor Book Awards in 1985 and 1988, and the Boston Globe-Horn Book Award in 1987.

Steptoe died at age thirty-nine, after a long illness.

BIBLIOGRAPHY

Stevie. Harper, 1969.
Uptown. Harper, 1970.
Train Ride. Harper, 1971.
All Us Come Cross the Water. By Lucille Clifton. Holt, 1973.
My Special Best Words. Viking, 1974.

She Come Bringing Me That Little Baby Girl. By Eloise Greenfield. Lippincott, 1974.

Marcia. Viking, 1976.

Daddy is a Monster ... Sometimes. Lothrop, 1980.

Mother Crocodile = Maman-Caiman. By Birago Diop. Translated and adapted by Rosa Guy. Delacorte, 1981.

OUTside/INside: Poems. By Arnold Adoff. Lothrop, 1981.

All the Colors of the Race: Poems. By Arnold Adoff. Lothrop, 1982.

Jeffrey Bear Cleans Up His Act. Lothrop, 1983.

The Story of Jumping Mouse: A Native American Legend. Lothrop, 1984.

Mufaro's Beautiful Daughters: An African Tale. Lothrop, 1987.

Baby Says. Lothrop, 1988.

Birthday. Holt, 1991.

Creativity. Illustrated by E.B. Lewis. Clarion, 1997.

Strickland, Michael R(aymond)

(1965–)

AUTHOR

Web site: www.michaelstrickland.com

"I've wanted to be a writer since I was old enough to understand what writing was. I remember teaching myself to write in my parents' basement. Our house was full of these wonderful things called books. My mother and father and older brothers were always very excited about books. I was literally tripping over them. I wanted to be able to do this myself—this thing called reading and writing. As a preschooler, I would run my fingers across pages of books. I would draw letters, words, and figures on a green chalkboard. Today, as a scholar of English education, I know that when I scribbled and when I turned pages, I was reading and writing. I was literate. It was the start of a process that has developed me into the writer I am now. I don't believe there is enough literature for African American children that is written by males, young and old. I hope I can be an inspiration to other men to break into the field. Women are well represented, and there are many great, Black male illustrators. But we have a huge dearth of male writers."

The author was born in Newark, New Jersey. His first book, the critically acclaimed *Poems That Sing to You*, is an anthology of fifty-five poems. Michael collaborated with his mother, Dorothy S. Strickland, a professor of reading at Rutgers University, on another anthology, *Families: Poems Celebrating the African American experience.*

Strickland was a Paul Robeson Fellow of the Institute for Arts and Humanities Education in 1993–1994. He is a poetry consultant to Literacy Place, the first core reading program of Scholastic, and he is a trustee of the Maurice R. Robinson Fund, a foundation that provides grants to grass-roots projects that directly affect the lives of children. Strickland holds a bachelor's degree in communications from Cornell University and earned a master of arts degree in corporate and public communications from Seton Hall University. He works closely with Bernice Cullinan of New York University, a widely influential scholar in children's literature, and he teaches writing at Jersey City State College.

An international traveler, Strickland conducts school presentations that focus on multicultural poetry as material for language instruction as a means of self-expression.

Strickland lives in West Orange, New Jersey.

BIBLIOGRAPHY

Poems That Sing to You. Illustrated by Alan Leiner. Edited by Michael R. Strickland. Boyds Mills, 1993.

Families: Poems Celebrating the African American Experience. Edited with Dorothy Strickland. Illustrated by John Ward. Boyds Mills, 1994.

African American Poets: Guardians of a Culture. Enslow, 1996.

Encyclopedia of African American Literature. ABC-CLIO, 1996.

My Own Song: And Other Poems to Groove To. Illustrated by Eric Sabee. Selected by Michael Strickland. Boyds Mills, 1997.

Another Haircut at Sleepy Sam's. Illustrated by Keaf Holliday. Boyds Mills, 1998.

Stroud, Bettye

AUTHOR

E-mail: bjstroud@bellsouth.net

Web site: www.bettyestroud.com

Stroud is a native of Athens, Georgi,a where she still resides. She developed a love of books and reading at an early age from a great-uncle who read to her. Opting to become a Library Media Specialist, she acquired both master's and education specialist degrees from the University of Georgia.

Her work in elementary schools provided Stroud with a rewarding career: bringing children, quality books and reading together. She received grants from The Advocates of Literature for Children and The Georgia Council for the Arts to help further her work.

Stroud has served on several education and library committees and has helped to shape the future of media centers in her state. She reviews children's books for the journal *Multicultural Review* and publishes in magazines and newspapers.

Stroud teaches classes in Writing for Children at the University of Georgia. She serves as a Contact Person for the Society of Children's Book Writers and Illustrators and has taught on its faculty at the Conference of the Southern Breeze Region. She has taught at the nationally acclaimed Harriette Austin Writers Conference as well as at Southeastern Writers. She presents workshops at such forums as the University of Georgia's Children's Literature Conference, among others. However, she finds her greatest joy in presenting book programs and writing residencies in schools.

Stroud lives in Georgia.

BIBLIOGRAPHY

Down Home at Miss Dessa's. Illustrated by Felicia Marshall. Lee & Low, 1996.

Dance Y'All. Illustrated by Ying-Hwa Hu/Cornelious Van Wright. Cavendish, 2001.

The Leaving. Illustrated by Cedric Lucas. Cavendish, 2001.

The Patchwork Path: A Quilt Map to Freedom. With Erin Susanne Bennett , Candlewick Press,2005.

Sutherland, Efua
(Theodora Morgue)

(1924–1996)

AUTHOR

"What we cannot buy is the spirit of originality and endeavor which makes a people dynamic and creative."

Born in Cape Coast, Ghana, Sutherland, whose middle and maiden names were Theodora Morgue, was a native of Ghana, a founder of the Ghana Society of Writers, the Ghana Drama Studio, Ghana Experimental Theater, and a community project called the Kodzidan (the story house). She studied at St. Monica's College, Cambridge, England, and the School of Oriental and African Studies at the University of London. She was a research fellow in literature and drama at the Institute of African Studies, University of Ghana, and was a cofounder of *Okyeame* magazine.

Sutherland published widely in her native land, and her work has been included in short-story anthologies in the United States. She taught school from 1951 to 1954 and in 1954 married African American William Sutherland. They had three children and lived in Ghana. Sutherland, best known for her work as a cultural visionary, was living in Ghana when she died in 1996.

BIBLIOGRAPHY

The Voice in the Forest. Philomel, 1983.
Playtime in Africa. Photographs by Willis E. Bell. Atheneum, 1962.
Vulture! Vulture!. Atheneum, 1968.
Tahinta. Atheneum, 1968.
The Roadmakers. Atheneum, 1961.

Tadgell, Nicole

(1969–)

ILLUSTRATOR

E-mail: nic.art@verizon.net

"Illustrating for children has been my life's goal and joy. Since I was a child, I knew there was a need for more picture books with kids that looked like me, and more stories that featured Black kids in typical childhood situations. Many books for Black children are filled with weighty issues that African Americans face. It's my goal to supplement those with stories of fantastic tales, adventures, daily life, or the joys and sorrows that all children face, regardless of race. My family moved frequently, living in Michigan, Texas, New York, and Massachusetts."

In Texas, when it was too hot to play outside, she and her older sister would spend hours playing with dolls, reading, and their favorite activity, drawing. "We wrote our own stories and made paper dolls with elaborate paper costumes, and even a swimming pool!" Nicole recalls. "I loved being a kid, and somehow I never let go of that feeling. Sometimes I pretend I'm the kid in the book, and do the things they do in the story to really get a feel for each book."

Tadgell was born near Detroit, Michigan. While at Wheaton College in Norton, Massachusetts, Tadgell studied studio art and education, hoping to become an art teacher, but she recalled how much fun it was to draw her own stories, and concluded that illustrating children's books could be the right path. Today, she has eight books and numerous educational pieces published and loves working on children's books.

Nicole met Mark Tadgell, a student at WPI, while at Wheaton College. They married after graduation, and now live in Spencer with their two Boston terriers, Brandy and Boomer. She is a member of the Society of Children's Book Writers and Illustrators and does workshops and school visits in her area. She is assistant art director at Davis Advertising in Worcester, Massachusetts.

Her other interests include bird-watching, hiking, canoeing, quilting, knitting and, of course, reading.

Fatuma's New Cloth by Leslie Bulion was awarded the Children's Africana Book Award in 2003. Nicole received a Merit Award for a 1998 First Night Worcester illustration presented by the AdClub of Worcester's Holland Awards. She was part of a gallery exhibition in 2002 at the Huntington House in Windsor, Connecticut, along with eight published children's illustrators. She also participated in an exhibit at Quinsigamond Community College, Worcester, Massachusetts, in 1999 featuring illustrations for children.

Tadgell resides in Spencer, Massachusetts.

BIBLIOGRAPHY

Just Call Me Joe Joe. By Jean Alicia Elster. Judson Press, 2001.

Fatuma's New Cloth. By Leslie Bulion. Moon Mountain, 2002.

I Have a Dream Too. By Jean Alicia Elster. Judson Press, 2002.

Moving Day Surprise. By Tina Stolberg. Bebop Books, 2002.

I'll Fly My Own Plane. By Jean Alicia Elster. Judson Press, 2002.

I'll Do the Right Thing. By Jean Alicia Elster. Judson Press, 2003.

A Day With Daddy. By Nikki Grimes. Color-Bridge Books, 2004.

Lights Out! By Angela Shelf Medearis. Color-Bridge Books, 2004.

Josias, Hold the Book. By Jennifer Elvgren Reismeyer. Boyds Mills Press, 2005.

Tadjo, Véronique

(1955–)

AUTHOR/ILLUSTRATOR

"I follow the African tradition of story telling which gives me a great freedom of interpretation of our myths and legends. I am interested in preserving the richness of our cultural heritage for the generations to come. Black children in big cities are increasingly losing contact with the oral tradition. One after the other, our stories and mythical characters are disappearing. Instead of lamenting this phenomenon, I feel it is my role as an artist to fight against alienation and amnesia."

Tadjo is a writer, painter, and illustrator from the Ivory Coast (West Africa). Born in Paris, she grew up in Abidjan where she attended local schools. She earned a BA in English from the University of Abidjan and a doctorate from the Sorbonne, Paris, in African American literature and civilization. In 1983, she went to Howard University in Washington, D.C, on a Fulbright research scholarship. She subsequently became a lecturer at the University of Abidjan until 1993 when she took up writing full time. She has written two collections of poems and five novels.

She began writing and illustrating books for children in 1988 with her first book, *Lord of the Dance, an African Retelling*. She said that she wanted to contribute to the development of literature for children in Africa. Her next book, *Mamy Wata and the Monster*, won the Unicef Award in 1993 and has subsequently been translated into eight dual language editions. It is also on the list of the 100 Best African Books of the Century. In the past few years, she has facilitated workshops on writing and illustrating children's books in Mali, the Benin Republic, Chad, Haiti, Mauritius, French Guyana, Burundi, Rwanda, and South Africa.

She has lived in several countries and is currently based in Johannesburg with her husband and their two sons.

BIBLIOGRAPHY

Lord of the Dance. A&C Black, 1988.

The Song of Life (La Chanson de la Vie). Hatier-Ceda (France), 1989.

Le bel oiseau et la pluie (French only edition). Nouvelles Editions Ivoiriennes, 1998.

Mamy Wata and the Monster. Nouvelles Editions Ivoiriennes, 1997, Milet Publishing, 2000.

Grandma Nana. Milet Publishing, 2000.

The Lucky Grain of Corn. Nouvelles Editions Ivoiriennes, 1997, Milet Publishing, 2000.

If I Were a King, If I Were a Queen. Milet Publishing, 2002.

Masque, Raconte-Moi (French only edition). NEI/EDICEF, 2002.

Talking Drums. A&C Black, 2000; Bloomsburg, 2004.

Tate, Eleanora (Elaine)

(1948–)

AUTHOR

E-mail: ablessing@members.authorsguild.net

Web site: www.eleanoraetate.com

Tate was born in Canton, Missouri, and raised by her grandmother. She graduated from Roosevelt High School in Des Moines, Iowa, and received a bachelor's degree in journalism with a news-editorial specialty from Drake University in 1973.

Her first poem was published when she was sixteen years old. She started her career as a news reporter and news editor in Des Moines and Jackson, Tennessee. In 1981, Tate received a fellowship in children's literature for the Bread Loaf Writers Conference in Middlebury, Vermont, and in 1982 she completed five weeks' travel and research in selected ethnic folk and fairy tales in West Germany, France, and Florence and Collodi, Italy.

The Secret of Gumbo Grove, the first of her Carolina trilogy of books set in the Carolinas, was named a Parent's Choice Gold Seal Award winner. The second book, *Thank You Dr. Martin Luther King, Jr.!*, was named NCSSCBC Notable Children's Trade Book and a Children's Book of the Year, and the third book, *A Blessing In Disguise*, was named an American Bookseller Pick of the List. Her book *Just an Overnight Guest* became the basis for a film of the same name produced by Phoenix Films of New York, starring Richard Roundtree and Rosalind Cash. It was named to the Selected Films for Young Adults 1985 List by the Youth Services Committee of the American Library Association. It also aired on PBS's Wonderworks series and on the Nickelodeon Children's Television Network.

Tate is also a journalist and publicist. With her husband, noted photographer Zack E. Hamlet, III, she was co-owner for ten years of Positive Images, Inc., a small award-winning public relations company in Myrtle Beach, South Carolina.

She is a former national president of the National Association of Black Storytellers, Inc. and a former president of the Horry County (South Carolina) Arts Council. She helped to design and implement its Arts in Education program.

Tate has spoken widely on children's literature and has been a frequent speaker in elementary schools, libraries, and conferences around the country over the years of her long career, including the International Black Writers Conference, Chicago, Illinois, the Broadside Press Festival of Poets in Detroit, Michigan, the National Council of Teachers of English National Conference and was the keynote speaker at the Fifth Regional Caribbean Conference of the International Reading Association (IRA) in Hamilton, Bermuda.

Memberships include the North Carolina Writers Network, the Society of Children's Book Writers and Illustrators, the Author's Guild and others. Tate is honorary chairperson of the 2004 BCALA — Wiley Black Books Galore National Contest for Librarians.

Tate and her husband live in Knightdale, North Carolina. They have one daughter, Gretchen.

BIBLIOGRAPHY

The Secret of Gumbo Grove. Watts, 1987.

Thank You, Dr. Martin Luther King, Jr.! Watts, 1990.

Front Porch Stories at the One-Room School. Bantam, 1992.

Retold African Myths. Perfection Learning Corporation, 1993.

A Blessing In Disguise. Delacorte, 1995.

Don't Split the Pole. Delacorte, 1997.

Just an Overnight Guest. Just Us Books, 1997.

African American Musicians. Wiley, 2000.

The Minstrel's Melody (An American Girl History Mystery). Pleasant Co.

To Be Free. Steck-Vaughn, 2004.

Taylor, Debbie

(1955–)

AUTHOR ?

E-mail: dpoet@umich.edu

"We must encourage children to cultivate their analytical skills and their inner lives through reading books. It's never too late to encourage good reading habits. Parents, relatives, siblings, and friends can encourage reading by giving books as gifts, establishing a reading list for the summer months and sharing their favorite books. Parents and grandparents should consider establishing a tradition of sharing and writing family stories to enhance reading in the home.

"My first responsibility as an author is to tell an engaging, compelling story. The goal of each story is to engage, comfort, inspire, and satisfy a reader. The stories I write are certainly influenced by recollections of my childhood, but I use those ideas as springboards for my tales. I wrote my first story when I was six years old, but my mother gave me a tremendous gift by teaching me to read. My foundation as a writer was laid by being read to and, later, by reading independently. My mother made books accessible to me, and in so doing opened up worlds far beyond my hometown of Columbus, Ohio. Books from the library, thrift shop or supermarket provided answers to my endless questions and also prompted me to ask new ones."

Taylor was born in Columbus, Ohio.

Debbie Taylor's stories have delighted readers for the past five years. She has published in a regional magazine and in national magazines such as *Spider, Pockets,* and *New Moon.* Her work has appeared in an educational workbook, been reprinted in SIRS® and staged as a play at Ardis Renaissance Academy in Ypsilanti, Michigan.

Her first book, *Sweet Music in Harlem*, published in 2004, was reviewed by *Booklist*, *Publisher's Weekly*, and *Kirkus Review*. She holds an undergraduate degree in English from Case Western Reserve University and a graduate degree with a Creative Writing concentration from Cleveland State University. Her passion for literature spills over into her volunteer life as a board member of a literacy organization, the Family Book Club. She is a member of the Society of Children's Book Writers and Illustrators.

Her most recent engagements include readings, signings or presentations at libraries, schools, jazz festivals, and state reading conferences.

She and her husband, Charles, live in Ann Arbor, Michigan.

BIBLIOGRAPHY

Sweet Music in Harlem. Illustrated by Frank Morrison. Lee & Low, 2004.

Thomas, Joyce Carol

(1938–)

AUTHOR ?

E-mail: jctauthor@aol.com

Web site: www.joycecarolthomas.com

Books by Thomas celebrate family life in all of its rich variety. Her many titles include: the National Book Award winner *Marked by Fire; Hush Songs; Joy; Brown Honey and Broomwheat Tea; I have Heard of a Land; Crowning Glory* and *The Gospel Cinderella*. In addition, she is a contributor in, as well as editor of, two anthologies: *A Gathering of Flowers: Stories About Being Young in America* and *Linda Brown, You Are Not Alone: The Brown v Board of Education Decision*.

Her works include short stories, dramatic plays, musicals, and many poetry books.

In the wake of her remarkable productivity, her books have won many prizes and awards: The National Book Award, the American Book Award, three Coretta Scott King Honors, two Governor's Awards, American Library Association Awards, the International Reading Association Award, an Oklahoma Lifetime Achievement Award, and many more.

Thomas is a native of Ponca City, Oklahoma (the setting for some of her fictional works). In 1948, Thomas and her family moved to the California Bay area, where she has lived for more than fifty years.

A graduate of Stanford University, fluent in Spanish and French, she has traveled to Australia, China, Ecuador, Guam, Italy, Mexico, New Zealand, and Nigeria. She has taught from grade school to the university level, including the University of California at Santa Cruz and Purdue University. Her last teaching appointment was as Full Professor in the English Department at the University of Tennessee, Knoxville, where she taught Creative Writing courses in poetry, drama, and fiction.

Thomas presently lives in Berkeley, California, near her children and grandchildren.

BIBLIOGRAPHY

Marked by Fire. Avon, 1982.

Bright Shadow. Avon, 1983.

The Golden Pasture. Scholastic, 1986.

Water Girl. Avon, 1986.

Journey. Scholastic, 1989.

A Gathering of Flowers: Stories About Being Young in America. Harper, 1990.

When the Nightingale Sings. Harper, 1992.

Gingerbread Days. Illustrated by Floyd Cooper. HarperCollins, 1993.

Brown Honey in Broomwheat Tea. Illustrated by Floyd Cooper. HarperCollins, 1993.

The Blacker the Berry: Poems. Illustrated by Brenda Joysmith. HarperCollins, 1997.

Crowning Glory. Illustrated by Brenda Joysmith. HarperCollins, 1998.

I Have Heard of a Land. Illustrated by Floyd Cooper. HarperCollins, 1998.

Cherish Me. HarperCollins, 1998.

You Are My Perfect Baby. HarperCollins, 1999.

Hush Songs: African-American Lullabies. Disney Press, 2000.

The Bowlegged Rooster and Other Tales that Signify. HarperCollins, 2000.

The Angel's Lullaby. Hyperion, 2001.

A Mother's Heart/A Daughter's Love: Poems for Us to Share. HarperCollins, 2001.

Linda Brown, You Are Not Alone: The Brown vs. Board of Education Decision. Illustrated by Curtis E. James. Hyperion/Jump at the Sun, 2003.

What's the Hurry, Fox? And Other Animal Stories. HarperCollins, 2004.

The Gospel Cinderella. HarperCollins, 2004.

The Skull Talks Back and Other Haunting Tales. HarperCollins, 2004.

Tokunbo, Dimitrea

(1966–)

AUTHOR/ILLUSTRATOR

E-mail: dimitrea@yahoo.com

"I want to represent the beauty of all children. I feel that growing up biracial, having a direct connection to two different cultures in the American context, gives my art a spirit and spark that speaks to the children who were overlooked when I was a child."

Educated at Moore College of Art for Women in Philadelphia, Tokunbo interned at WDAS Radio and the African American History Museum of Philadelphia.

Tokunbo illustrated two children's books for Boyds Mills Press, *Sidewalk Chalk: Poems of the City* by Carole Boston Weatherford, and *Has Anybody Lost a Glove?* by G. Francis Johnson. Tokunbo has written one children's book for Orchard Books (a Scholastic Imprint), *Together*, illustrated by Jennifer Gwynne Oliver. Tokunbo has both written and illustrated stories for *Read and Rise* Magazine, published by Scholastic, Inc. and the Urban League to encourage literacy for inner city children. Tokunbo has also illustrated for *Cricket* magazine and did the cover art for the February 2005 issue.

Tokunbo is a member of the Children's Book Writers and Illustrators Society. She enjoys visiting schools and libraries to share her stories with children. Tokunbo lives in New York City with her two daughters.

BIBLIOGRAPHY

Sidewalk Chalk: Poems of the City. By Carole Boston Weatherford. Boyds Mills Press, 2001.

Has Anybody Lost a Glove? By G. Francis Johnson. Boyds Mills Press, 2004.

Together. Illustrated by Jennifer Gwynne Oliver. Scholastic, 2005.

Tucker, Ezra N.

(1955–)

ILLUSTRATOR

Web site: www.ezratucker.com

"It is important for human beings, young and old, to imagine."

Tucker has created some of America's most enduring images over the past two and a half decades. The appeal for his artwork has been recognized through numerous awards and his extensive and prestigious commercial and private clientele. Tucker's original artworks are included in many major corporate and private collections.

His career as a commercial artist/illustrator has facilitated his working with individuals and corporations to conceptualize and execute artwork that conveys a myriad of messages from the subtle to bold, striking imagery. Devotion to creatively explore ideas with clients has resulted in images that capture a viewer's imagination of exotic lands, myth, legend, or adventure to promote or sell products. Tucker describes his versatile style as "Nouveau Victorian Realism" where people, animals, and landscapes are realistically depicted in fantastic settings, reminiscent of Victorian period painters.

Among Tucker's most recognizable subjects are the animals, particularly horses, he has painted for both commercial and private commissions. Tucker was honored to illustrate a children's pop-up book of horses, *Album of Horses*, written by the world renowned author on horses, Marguerite Henry. He has also illustrated many books, including *Star Wars/Dark Forces-Rebel Agent* by Bill Dietz, Cheryl Ladd's children's book *The Adventures of Little Nettie Windship*, and most recently *Big Friends* by Margery Cuyler.

Tucker's distinctive style has been selected for exhibition at the 1982 World's Fair in Knoxville, Tennessee; the Kennedy Center in Washington, D.C.; the Texas Rangers Historical Museum in Austin, Texas; the Canton Museum of Art in Canton, Ohio; the Bruce Watkins Center in Kansas City, Missouri; and a One-Man Show at the Institute of Southern California in Laguna Beach, California. He has also won medals and awards for his artwork displayed in both the New York and Los Angeles Society of Illustrators exhibitions. Ezra is a long-term member of the Graphic Artists Guild and the Los Angeles Society of Illustrators.

Tucker is a graduate of the Memphis Academy of Arts where he earned a BFA in Advertising Design. Ezra is a father of three children and has lived with his wife of twenty-two years in picturesque settings in California and, more recently, Colorado.

Ezra's original artwork is available through the Elliott Yeary Gallery in Aspen, Colorado (www.elliottyeary.com) and his personal Web site.

BIBLIOGRAPHY

Marguerite Henry's Album of Horses. By Marguerite Henry. Aladdin Books, 1993.

The Adventures of Little Nettie Windship. By Cheryl Ladd. Dove Kids, 1996.

Star Wars/Dark Forces-Rebel Agent. By Bill Dietz. G.P. Putnam, 1998.

Big Friends. By Margery Cuyler. Walker Publishing Co., Inc., 2004.

Turner, Glennette Tilley

(1933–)

AUTHOR

Web site: www.ugrr-illinois.com

Turner was born in Raleigh, North Carolina. Growing up, she loved to read and listen to stories—especially family stories and stories about people who overcame obstacles. She majored in English at Lake Forest College in Illinois. While there, she entered a nationwide college competition and her poem was selected for publication in an anthology. Later, she earned a master's degree in history and juvenile literature from Goddard College in Vermont.

An elementary school teacher in the Chicago area for almost twenty-five years, she has written for such publications as *Ebony Jr.*, *Scholastic Scope*, and *Black Child Journal*. She served as consulting and contributing editor for an issue of *Cobblestone* magazine. She has stories or articles in *Open Court*, *Scott Foresman*, *Encyclopedia Britannica*, Simon & Schuster, and *Scholastic*, and *Scholastic* educational materials.

Recalling what a deep impression stories of people who had overcome obstacles had had on her as a child, inspired her to publish biographies. She wrote the life story of inventory Lewis Howard Latimer. Her collective biographies, *Take a Walk in Their Shoes* and *Follow in Their Footsteps* profile the lives of African American achievers and include do-it-yourself kits.

Turner has had a longtime fascination with the Underground Railroad in U.S. history, which helped Black slaves escape to freedom, and is a recognized authority on its operation in the Midwest. She was an adviser to the National Park Service on the subject and discussed it during an interview on the Lincoln-Douglas Debates on the C-SPAN cable network. She has been a consultant on such projects as the Underground Railroad and produced a film by the Illinois Bureau of Tourism and programming shown at museums throughout the Chicago area. She also served as a consultant to NBC News on a special that featured Harriet Tubman, an escaped Black slave who was one of the major "conductors" on the Underground Railroad. Turner conducts Underground Railroad tours for the Newberry Library and led a private tour for the host of the PBS *Globe Trekkers* series.

Turner's work has been reviewed in numerous publications, including the *New York Times Book Reviews*, the *Christian Science Monitor, Publishers Weekly, Booklist*, and *School Library Journal*. She is a Road Scholar for the Illinois Humanities Council and often speaks on the Underground Railroad and the people she has profiled in her writings. Retired from public school teaching in 1988, she presents discussions and workshops for students of all ages, teachers, and members of historical societies and other organizations. She participates in the authors-in-the-schools program of the Near South Planning Board and Open Book. Her honors in this field include being named Outstanding Woman Education in DuPage County, Illinois, and being cited by the Illinois General Assembly for excellence in teaching. She continues in the field of education as a supervisor of student teachers at National-Louis University and served on the Illinois Brown vs. Board of Education Commission. She is a past president of Children's Reading Roundtable of Chicago and the Black Literary Umbrella.

Turner contributed an essay "Nana" to *In Praise of Our Fathers and Mothers*, a biographical sketch of Bessie Coleman in the Women Building Chicago 1790–1990, the Underground Railroad entry in the Encyclopedia of Chicago and in Stephen Marc's Passage on the Underground Railroad.

She serves on the boards of the Grove Mill and Museum, the DuPage Historical Society, Wheaton Media Commission and Northern Illinois Children's Literature Conference. She has been recognized as a writer by Illinois Reading Association, International Black Writers Conference, Illinois Young Authors Conference, the Friends of Amistad, and in a file produced for the Illinois State Library. She is the recipient of the Studs Terkel and Margaret Landon awards. She was interviewed by the History Makers and inducted into the International Literary Hall of Fame for Writers of African Descent at the Gwendolyn Brooks Center, Chicago State University, and Phi Beta Kappa at Lake Forest College for scholarly work done since graduation.

Turner lives in Wheaton, Illinois.

BIBLIOGRAPHY

Surprise for Mrs. Burns. Illustrated by Dan Siculan. Whitman, 1971.

The Underground Railroad in DuPage County, Illinois. Newman, 1981, 1984.

Take a Walk in Their Shoes. Illustrated by Elton C. Fax. Cobblehill, 1989.

Lewis Howard Latimer. Silver Burdett, 1990.

Make and Keep Family Memories. Newman, 1990.

Running for Our Lives. Illustrated by Samuel Byrd. Holiday House, 1994.

Follow in Their Footsteps. Cobblehill, 1997.

The Underground Railroad in Illinois. Newman, 1998.

Running our Our Lives. Illustrated by Shayla Johnson. Newman, 2004.

An Apple for Harriet Tubman. Albert Whitman, 2006.

Turner, Morrie

(1923–)

AUTHOR/ILLUSTRATOR

E-mail: karolt@csus.edu

Web site: www.clstoons.com/paoc/morrie.htm

Turner was born December 11, 1923, in Oakland, California, the youngest of four sons to James "George" and Nora Turner, living through the Depression years in West Oakland.

He served in the Air Force during World War II, at one point taking the test to become a pilot (Tuskegee Airman), but washed out in the final testing. Joining the all Black 477th Bomber Group, he became the group's newspaper cartoonist.

He returned to civilian life and marriage to his lifetime sweetheart, Letha, and the birth of their son, Morris. He took a job as a police clerk at the Oakland Police Department, while continuing to freelance cartoons to magazines and trade publications including *Black World* and *Ebony*.

Meeting Charles Schulz, creator of the popular *Peanuts* cartoon, had a great influence on him, leading to the creation of an all Black comic strip titled *Dinky Fellas*, which was sold to the *Chicago Defender*, a Black daily newspaper.

The Lew Little Syndicate discovered the strip and contracted it as the nation's first truly integrated strip, launching it February 15, 1965.

At the time, introducing Black characters on the comics pages was no easy task. *Wee Pals* was in only five major newspapers, when Martin Luther King, Jr. was assassinated in 1968. Within three months of King's death, the strip was appearing in over one hundred newspapers.

The success of the strip led to dozens of books and an animated television series, *Kid Power* in 1972. Turner coined the phrase "rainbow power" which, to him, means the power of all colors working together.

Turner is the recipient of the Anti-Defamation League's Humanitarian Award, the Boys' and Girls' Club Image Award, the B'nai Brith Humanitarian Award, the California Educator's Award, the Sparky Award, given by the Cartoon Art Museum, and the Milton Caniff Lifetime Achievement Award, presented by the National Cartoonist Society. He is also the subject of a documentary called *Keeping the Faith with Morrie.*

He published his first children's book, *Nipper*, in the late 1960s, followed by *Nipper's Secret Power*, from the same publisher, Westminster. Many other books followed, including the most recent *Super Sistahs*, Bye Publishing, 2004.

Turner lives in Berkeley, California.

BIBLIOGRAPHY

Nipper. Westminster Publishing Company, 1960.
Nipper's Secret Power. Westminster Publishing Company, 1960.
All God's Chillun Got Soul. Judson Press, 1980.
Wee Pals. Signet, 1970.
Discover Black History with Wee Pals. Just Us Books, 1999.
African Americans in the Military. Self Published, 2000.
Super Sistahs. Bye Publishing Service, 2004.

Velasquez, Eric

(1961–)

AUTHOR/ILLUSTRATOR

E-mail: eric@ericvelasquez.com

Web site: www.ericvelasquez.com

"As a child I never saw realistic images of African Americans or Latinos in children's books. I remember being deeply offended by the stereotypical images that I would see in print and film. As an author/illustrator my goal is to present real characters that would allow the reader to identify with the characters. I believe that if a character is presented truthfully, free of stereotypes, its appeal will then be universal, allowing everyone to see aspects of themselves in my books."

Velasquez attended The High School of Art and Design in New York where he majored in cartooning. In his senior year he was introduced to painting and illustration. He also attended The School of Visual Arts where he majored in illustration and earned his BFA in 1983. He also studied at The Art Students League for a year.

Velasquez did his first book cover in 1984 for Houghton Mifflin. His first chapter book, *Journey to Jo'Burg*, won the Bank Street College Child Study Book Award. He illustrated book covers and chapter books for the first twelve years of his career before illustrating his first children's book, *The Piano Man*, by Debbi Chocolate, which won a Coretta Scott King/John Steptoe award. He has illustrated over twelve children's books.

He teaches a course on Book Illustration at the Fashion Institute of Technology (FIT) and also visits numerous schools throughout the year, sharing his stories with children of all ages.

He and his wife Deborah live in Hartsdale, New York.

BIBLIOGRAPHY

Journey to Jo'burg. By Beverly Naidoo. HarperCollins, 1985.

The Piano Man. By Debbi Chocolate. Walker and Company, 1988.

Chain of Fire. By Beverly Naidoo. HarperCollins, 1990.

The Terrible Wonderful Tellin at Hog Hammock. By Kim Siegelson. Harper-Collins, 1996.

Escape. By Sharon Shavers Gale. Soundprints, 1999.

The Sound That Jazz Makes. By Carole Boston Weatherford. Walker and Company, 2000.

Grandma's Records. Walker and Company, 2001.

David Gets His Drum. By Bob Reiser and David "Panama" Franis. Marshall Cavandish, 2002.

Champion: The Story of Muhammad Ali. By James Haskins. Walker and Company, 2002.

Liberty Street. By Candice Ransom. Walker and Company, 2004.

A Sweet Smell of Roses. By Angela Johnson. Simon and Schuster, 2005.

Houdini: World's Greatest Escape Artist and Man of Mystery. By Kathleen Kroll. Walker and Company, 2005.

A Season for Mangoes. By Regina Hanson. Clarion Books, 2005.

Rosetta, Rosetta, Sit By Me. Marshall Cavandish, 2005.

Jesse Owens: The Fastest Man Alive. By Carole Boston Weatherford. Walker and Company, 2005.

Walker, Gregory (Brother G.)

(1963–)

AUTHOR

E-mail: brotherg@hotmail.com

Web site: www.shadesofmemnon.com

"The Shades of Memnon books have been used in dozens of reading, history, and social studies classrooms all over the United States. Years ago I set out to create an adventure series with the African Village in mind. I wanted to present work that could be shared across all ages from ten to one hundred and be inspirational and entertaining to all. The reception of this book series, along with the teaching guides and related hip hop music, have fulfilled my ambitions and inspired me to continue providing much needed literature featuring African themes and history. Shades of Memnon, the African Hero of the Trojan War, is just the first series in a genre called African Legends that presents African history and legend as a major part of world culture.

"After fifteen years, I have neither sold out, slowed down, nor copped out in my quest to present an authentic adventure genre that places people of African descent on par with all other people of the world. I have chosen to do this by entertaining and uplifting through powerful stories from African History."

Walker is a Chicago-based journalist, poet, historian, and author. While working part-time for the Associated Press news service, he spent ten years conducting research for the African Legends genre, writing "Shades of Memnon" and developing contacts in archeology, anthropology, and linguistics worldwide. Known for his uncompromising quest for the historical truths about African history, Walker is the mastermind behind the African Legends genre and creator of the *Shades of Memnon* books. While standing on the shoulders of scholars and historians of the past, he has introduced work designed for the twenty-first century. Animation, illustrated strips, artwork, and movies are in the works for lovers of adventure everywhere.

Walker won the Best New Author of the Year Award in 2000 for *Shades of Memnon Book 1*. He is single and lives in the south suburbs of Chicago.

BIBLIOGRAPHY

Shades of Memnon. Seker Nefer Press, 2000.

Shades of Memnon Book 2: Ra Force Rising. Seker Nefer Press, 2002.

Shades of Memnon Book 3: African Atlantis Unbound. Seker Nefer Press, 2005.

Walton, Darwin McBeth

(1926–)

AUTHOR

E-mail: JDWalton@aol.com

Walton believes that ordinary people can do extraordinary things. She has been called a pathfinder in the field of education and a social activist for most of her career. She was elected Outstanding Woman Leader in the Field of Racial Justice in Dupage County in 1998.

Walton brings twenty-five years of public school teaching experience to her writing for children, and is dedicated to the belief that *acceptance* is the first law of teaching and learning. "Children who are excluded for *any* reason—by teachers *or* peers—fail to maximize their learning potential." Her landmark book, *What Color Are You?* published by Johnson Publishing Co., is celebrating its thirtieth year and was one of the first books about America's diversity to be used in public schools.

Since 1978 Walton has designed and facilitated five courses in teacher education for National-Louis University and remains in the education arena as student teacher supervisor at NLU. In 2003 she was honored with the Distinguished Alumni Humanitarian Award at National.

She grew up during the Great Depression—one of five girls—in Charlotte, North Carolina. She always loved to sing and started writing stories in grade school. She attended Johnson C. Smith University in Charlotte and Howard University in Washington, D.C., while working full time. She came to Chicago with a scholarship to study music at the Chicago Conservatory of Music where she received her Bachelor of Music degree. Racism was covert but as prevalent as in the south. As one of three African American women studying at the conservatory she remembers being denied nonacademic experiences such as dancing or singing duets with white students or other on stage activities critical to a professional career in classical music. It also required *acceptance* of the fact that she was Black and there were no laws to protect her rights at that time.

Much of Walton's writing is about acceptance and inclusion in the multicultural and diverse society where our children are growing up today. It's about family relationships and social challenges. Her book, *Overcoming Challenges,* is the story of Astronaut Major General Charles F. Bolden, one of the first four Black astronauts in the United States and the challenges he faced in his quest for education during the 1960s. Her middle-grade novel, *Dance Kayla*, was chosen one of the best books of 1999 by the Banks Street Selection Committee.

In a typical workshop, Make Your Characters Come Alive, Walton guides students through drama, music, and dance. They read and dramatize skits, then change behaviors and/or dialogues of existing characters or add new characters they believe will enhance the skit. They learn that writers reveal their character types through dialogue. And then they write. Tip: She always has a microphone. A portable karaoke works miracles when working with teens.

She lives in Lombard, Illinois.

BIBLIOGRAPHY

What Color Are You? Illustrated by Hal Franklin (photographer). Johnson Publishing Company, 1973.

Dance Kayla! Illustrated by Richard Stewart. Albert Whitman, 1998.

Kwanzaa — A World of Holidays. Raintree Steck-Vaughn, 1999.

Overcoming Challenges: The Life of Charles F. Bolden, Jr. (Photos by NASA and the Bolden Family) Steck-Vaughn, 2000.

Nana's Kitchen. Illustrated by Pauline Rodriguez Howard. Steck-Vaughn, 2001.

A Family is Special (Selected Photography). Steck-Vaughn, 2002.

A Part of our Family. Illustrated by Maurie Manning. Steck-Vaughn, 2002.

Jetty's Journey to Freedom. Illustrated by Angelo. Steck-Vaughn, 2003.

Journeys of Courage (On the Underground Railroad). With Glennette Turner. Steck-Vaughn, 2003.

Washington, Donna

(1967–)

AUTHOR

E-mail: Qbot5@aol.com

Web site: www.donnawashington.com

"Every story I tell is true ... except for the parts I make up! Whether I'm performing live on stage or writing for an unknown reader, I believe that my primary responsibility to my audience is to share a good story. For many years there were few good books starring African American characters. Today, there are more, but still not enough. Books open worlds by letting readers see themselves in the pages. We must endeavor to make sure that our children and grandchildren have a plethora of exciting, beautiful engaging stories starring people who look just like them."

Washington was born an army brat in Colorado Springs, Colorado. She traveled all over the world with her parents. Attending Northwestern University, she was involved with numerous theatrical productions and it was at this time that storytelling emerged as something she wanted to learn more about. In the four years she was there, she began to make storytelling a central part of her performance life.

Her first recording work was done with Warren Coleman Productions. She provided the talent on a storytelling tape that was so successful for Children's Press that the tape was used to make four wordless picture books. It was at this time that she began writing books. Her first writing project was an anthology. *A Pride of African Tales* was released in December 2003. Award-winning illustrator James Ransome provided the lush watercolor pictures for the book. It received rave reviews from the American Library Association (ALA) Booklist and the School Library Journal. *Pride* has been nominated for the Pennsylvania 2005 Children's Book of the Year. Donna's second book, *The Story of Kwanzaa*, has been in print for eleven years. It is a wonderful primer for kids about the African-American celebration of Kwanzaa. Washington's third book, *A Big Spooky House*, is a wonderful book to read aloud at Halloween.

She is also an award-winning recording artist, receiving a 2002 Parent's Choice Award for her first independent recording, "Live and Learn: *The Exploding Frog* and Other Stories." The October 2004 edition of the ALA Booklist gave her second CD, "A Little Shiver," a recommended review. It also won the 2004 Parents' Choice Silver Honor Award. The third CD, "Fun, Foolery and Folktales," also won the 2004 Parents' Choice Silver Honor Award and her fourth CD, "The Sword and the Rose," won a Parenting Media 2005 Excellent Product Award and a 2005 Parents' Choice Silver Honor Award.

Washington has performed at numerous storytelling festivals throughout the country, including being a featured teller at the 2004 National Storytelling Festival. She is a professional storyteller who also offers workshops in storytelling, writing, education, and creative drama for librarians and educators as well. She lives in Durham, North Carolina, with her husband Dave, their son Devin and daughter Darith.

BIBLIOGRAPHY

Double Dutch and the Voodoo Shoes. Children's Press, 1991.
How Anansi Obtained the Sky God's Stories. Children's Press, 1991.
The Baboon's Umbrella. Children's Press, 1991.
The Story of Kwanzaa. HarperCollins, 1996.
The Big Spooky House. Hyperion Books for Children, 2000.
A Pride of African Tales. HarperCollins, 2004.

Weatherford, Carole Boston

(1956–)

AUTHOR

E-mail: weathfd@aol.com

Web site: www.caroleweatherford.com

Weatherford was born in Baltimore, Maryland, the first of two children. As a first grader, she dictated her first poem to her mother. Her father, a teacher, printed many of her early poems on the press in his industrial arts classroom. Today, she continues to write poetry for both children and adults. An avid reader, Weatherford is an amateur history buff.

Her first children's picture book, *Juneteenth Jamboree*, brings to life the emancipation holiday marking the freeing of the Texas slaves, the last to be freed. Illustrated by Yvonne Buchanan, the book captures the sights, sounds, smells, and tastes of a Juneteenth celebration.

Over the years, Weatherford has returned again and again to the Maryland farm her great great grandfather bought during Reconstruction. There, she not only revels in the past but gains inspiration.

Weatherford holds an MFA in creative writing from the University of Baltimore. She is the recipient of a 1995 North Carolina Arts Council writers fellowship and the inaugural Furious Flower Poetry Prize, awarded to promising new poets. Her manuscript, *The Tan Chanteuse*, won publication through the North Carolina Writers' Network's 1995 Harperprints Chapbook Competition. She has four preschool board books forthcoming (Black Butterfly Books). She was chosen to participate in the 1992 North Carolina Writers'

Network's Blumenthal Writers & Readers Series and was a winner of the Network's 1991 Black Writers Speak competition.

Beyond the printed page, her work has appeared on radio, on stage and in museums. For example, her poem "Basketweavers" was included in a Chicago Children's Museum exhibit honoring grandparents. And in 1993 the James Diggs Gallery at Winston-Salem State University commissioned her to write poems for a folk artist exhibit. That same year, she received an Arts-in-Education grant to conduct multicultural writing workshops in Winston-Salem/Forsyth County schools.

Weatherford is an arts education consultant and business writer. Her essays, editorials and articles have appeared in publications such as *The Washington Post, Christian Science Monitor* and *Essence.* Her picture book *The Sound That Jazz Makes* won the 2001 Carter G. Woodson Award from National Council for the Social Studies and was an NAACP Image Award finalist. Her poetry collection, *Remember the Bridge: Poems of a People,* won the 2002 Juvenile Literature Award from American Association of University Women-North Carolina, and has made several short lists: International Reading Association/Children's Book Council Teachers Choice; NCTE (National Council of Teachers of English) Notables; NCSS (National Council for the Social Studies) Notables and Voices of Youth Advocates Poetry Picks. Weatherford has received two North Carolina Arts Council fellowships, the Furious Flower Poetry Prize from James Madison University, and several honors from the North Carolina Writer's Network and North Carolina Poetry Society. Formerly a columnist for the Greensboro *News & Record,* she was appointed in 2002 as Distinguished Visiting Professor at Fayetteville State University.

The mother of a daughter and son, she lives in High Point, North Carolina.

BIBLIOGRAPHY

Juneteenth Jamboree. Illustrated by Yvonne Buchanan. Lee & Low, 1995.

Grandma and Me. Illustrated by Michelle Mills. Black Butterfly, 1996.

Me & My Family Tree. Illustrated by Michele Mills. Black Butterfly, 1996.

Mighty Menfolk. Illustrated by Michelle Mills. Black Butterfly, 1996.

My Favorite Toys. Black Butterfly, 1996.

Sink or Swim: African American Lifesavers of the Outer Banks. Coastal Carolina Press, 1999.

The Sound that Jazz Makes. Illustrated by Eric Velasquez. Walker, 2000.

The African-American Struggle for Legal Equality. Enslow, 2000.

Princeville: The 500 Year Flood. Illustrated by Douglas Alvard. Coastal Carolina Press, 2001.

Sidewalk Chalk: Poems of the City. Illustrated by Dimitrea Tokunbo. Boyds Mills Press, 2001.

Remember the Bridge: Poems of a People. Philomel, 2002.

Raising the Bar of Freedom: Great African American Lawyers. Enslow, 2003.

Jazz Baby. Illustrated by Laura Freeman. Lee & Low, 2002.

Freedom on the Menu. Illustrated by Jerome Lagarrigue. Dial, 2005.

A Negro League Scrapbook. Boyds Mills Press, 2005.

Webb, Charlotte Riley

ILLUSTRATOR

E-mail: cwebbart@bellsouth.net

Website: www.charlotterileywebb.com

"My childhood memories are segmented, but the little glimmers of light, reflections, and influences are very evident in my work as I recaptured genre from my past and that of my migrated family."

An Atlanta native, Webb moved with her family to Cleveland, Ohio as a toddler, where she was educated in the public school system and earned her degree from The Cleveland Institute of Art. She has also studied painting at Georgia State University, screen printing at The Atlanta College of Art, mono-printing and abstract art at Tougaloo, Mississippi.

Webb visually documented the essence of her migrating family in her three year traveling exhibition From Stories of My America, which she also used as a springboard in The High Museum workshop where she was asked to compare her work to that of Jacob Lawrence. Premiering at Atlanta's Hammonds House, the Stories exhibition has shown in nine different museums and fine art galleries, traveling to the Historic Beach Institute in Savannah, The Rosa Parks Museum in Montgomery, and The Penn Center at St. Helena Island, among them. *Gullah Rhythms*, from the tour, was also displayed as a part of the Kente' exhibition at The Marco Carlos Museum in Atlanta.

Webb's artwork was recently viewed on Comcast Cable TV's *A Woman's Place*. The program featured three different women artists' exhibitions.

Over the years her venues extended across the country and beyond the states to include Surinam, South America and Anguilla, British West Indies. Webb's work is included in numerous private, business and corporate collections. The most recent public works installations were *Faces and Phases of Fulton*, a painting installed in the Fulton County Public Service office in Atlanta and the installation of her collaborative new medium, "sculpted paintings," which she creates with her husband, Lucious. The couple installed an outdoor public work in the concert district of downtown Hampton, Virginia, for which they were awarded The Hampton Arts Commission Award of Excellence and the piece was recently voted as the city's People's Choice Purchase Award for their permanent collection.

"The uniqueness of the Webb style has left art critics with varying opinions of her associations. Hers has been compared to the works of the Impressionists, Old Masters and the Harlem Renaissance artists, yet different enough to be recognized for her own unique style," wrote art critic Richard Powell. Among her many awards and accomplishments, Charlotte has been the recipient of several Georgia Council and Bureau of Cultural Affairs grants which she used primarily to fund her thirteen year volunteer art classes and installation of an art gallery for the work of her senior citizen artists. Charlotte was one of fourteen artists nationally to receive the Absolut Vodka's Heritage Award resulting in the commission and six city national tour. She was recently paired with Actor Taurean Blacque of *Hill Street Blues*. Their collaborative painting was sponsored by Stars in the Arts Georgia, and used to benefit Prevent Child Abuse Georgia during the gala auction.

She began working in abstract art with premier abstract artist and 2004 Vander Zee award winner, Moe Brooker of Philadelphia a few years ago and again in "encaustic" the summer of 2004. She also learned John T. Scott's, of New Orleans, hand-made wax paper printing process after studying with him in 2003. These opportunities aided her in finding her "abstract niche" and helped propel the career which she had been hinging on for many years even in her figurative works.

Webb lives in Stockbridge, Georgia.

BIBLIOGRAPHY

Rent Party Jazz. By William Miller. Lee & Low, 2001.
Sweet Potato Pie. By Kathleen Lindsey. Lee & Low, 2003.

Wells, Daryl Elaine

AUTHOR/ILLUSTRATOR

E-mail: darylwells@asl.org

"Through years of involvement in both public art and children's art education, I have come to realize the power of children's books to engage young readers and help them develop a passion for art and literature. Both have the potential to help students grasp the importance of having a creative inner life, through imaginative storytelling and vibrant illustration. Though I was mainly trained as a visual artist, I am currently in the process of writing and illustrating several works for children which focus on the experience of inner city youth as well as the rich variety of contemporary urban existence."

Raised in Los Angeles, Wells was educated at the Rhode Island School of Design (BFA 1992) and the Slade School of Fine Art, University College London (MA/MFA 1997). After working as a scenic artist in Los Angeles, she became involved in community arts activities, first as a mural designer and supervisor for at-risk youth through the city's Department of Cultural Affairs, and subsequently as an art educator.

After working on large public projects at the National Association of Negro Women and the National Association of Jewish Women, she was asked to illustrate *Two Mrs. Gibsons* for Children's Book Press, and her work was also featured in *Just Like Me* by the same publisher. *Two Mrs. Gibsons* was a winner of a PEN-West award, and was also featured on PBS' *Storytime*.

Currently living in London, and teaching visual art at the American School in London, Wells continues to pursue her interest in children's literature. Current project include *The Subway Lullabye* and *What am I?*, and she has also published her creative non-fiction in *Calabash* (spring 2005), a publication of London's Centreprise Literature Development Project.

BIBLIOGRAPHY

Two Mrs. Gibsons. By Toyomi Igus. Children's Book Press, 1996.

Just Like Me. (various additional illustrators). Children's Book Press, 1997.

Wesley, Valerie Wilson

(1947–)

AUTHOR

E-mail: valwilwes@aol.com

Web site: www.TamaraHayle.com

Wesley served as artist-in-residence in the fiction department at Columbia College in Chicago for the spring semester of 2005. She is formerly executive editor of *Essence* magazine. Her fiction and nonfiction for both adults and children have appeared in many publications, including *Essence*, *Family Circle*, *TV Guide*, *Ms*, *Creative Classroom*, the *New York Times,* and *Weltwoche*, a Swiss weekly newspaper. She is a 1993 recipient of the Griot Award from the New York Chapter of the National Association of Black Journalists.

She has received awards from several book groups and community organizations, including 2004 Author of the Year from the Amigirls Book Club and 1996 Author of the Year from the Go On Girls Book Club. She is a former board member of Sisters in Crime, a professional organization committed to fighting discrimination against women writing mysteries.

She was on the board of directors of the Newark Arts Council from 2002 to 2004 and was the chair and former trustee of the Montclair Art Museum. She serves presently on the board for the Newark Literary Campaign. Wesley is also the author of several award-winning adult novels, mystery stories, and short stories..

Wesley's latest adult novel is *Playing My Mother's Blues*. She is also the author of several other novels and mystery stories and short stories for adults which have received many awards.

Wesley is a graduate of Howard University and holds masters degrees from both the Bank Street College of Education and the Columbia Graduate School of Journalism.

She is married to noted screenwriter and playwright Richard Wesley and has two adult daughters.

BIBLIOGRAPHY

Afro-Bets Book of Black Heroes. With Wade Hudson. Just Us Books, 1988.

Where Do I Go From Here? Scholastic, 1993.

Freedom's Gift: A Juneteenth Story. Simon & Schuster, 1997.

Juneteenth. Illustrated by Sharon Wilson. Simon & Schuster, 1997.

Afro-Bets Book of Black Heroes from A to Z: An Introduction to Important Black Achievers for Young Readers. With Wade Hudson. Just Us Books, 1999.

Willimena Rules! How to Lose Your Class Pet. Illustrated by Maryn Ross. Hyperion/Jump at the Sun, 2003.

Willimena Rules! How to Fish for Trouble. Illustrated by Maryn Ross. Turtleback Books, 2004.

Willimena Rules: How to Almost Ruin Your School Play. Hyperion, 2005.

Willimena Rules: How to Lose Your Cookie Money. Illustrated by Sharon Wilson. Scholastic, 2005.

White, Edgar Nkosi

(1947–)

AUTHOR

White was born in the British West Indies and came to the United States when he was five years old. He has lived both in the United States and England. He received his bachelor's degree at New York University and completed graduate study at Yale University. His *Underground: Four Plays* and *Crucificardo: Plays* were published by William Morrow and have been performed at theaters including the New York Shakespeare Festival Public Theater and the Eugene O'Neill Foundation. He has written for magazines and the *Yardbird Reader*.

BIBLIOGRAPHY
Omar at Christmas. Illustrated by Dindga McCannon. Lothrop, 1973.
Sati the Rastefarian. Illustrated by Dindga McCannon. Lothrop, 1973.
Children at Night. Illustrated by Dindga McCannon. Lothrop, 1974.

Williams, Maiya

(1962–)

AUTHOR

E-mail: maiyamv@aol.com

Web site: maiyawilliams.com

"My objective is to tickle the young reader's imagination. By injecting familiar situations with fantasy I try to convince them that there truly is magic in the world, you just have to know where to look. I love writing for young people. They are blissfully unencumbered by that veneer of cynicism that so afflicts older people. They also participate fully in a book in a way that adults don't; they consume new ideas for sustenance, it feeds their souls. I don't think of my writing as being 'Black literature' so much as being adventure stories that include people of all walks of life. If I succeed at anything I hope it is to impress upon all readers that kids with brown skin can have fun adventures too, and that stories featuring minority children aren't always about struggling with racism. I've been influenced by all the good books I read as a child and I try to follow their example. Never condescend to the reader. Never be boring. Always challenge the reader; force him to think and feel. Always have fun. Most importantly, always leave the reader with hope."

Born in Corvallis, Oregon, Williams grew up in New Haven, Connecticut, and Berkeley, California. She attended Harvard University, earning a Bachelor of Arts in History and Literature and graduating with honors. While at Harvard she was an editor of the Harvard Lampoon for four years, and became vice president of the organization for one year.

Williams moved to Hollywood, California directly after college and immediately began writing and producing television shows such as *Roc*, *Amen*, *Fresh Prince of Bel-Air*, *Rugrats*, and *Mad-TV*. Her first novel for children, *The Golden Hour*, received high praise and won several awards, among them the Southern California Booksellers Association award for Best Children's Middle Grade novel of 2004, the International Readers Association award for Best Children's novel of 2004, the National Parenting Association Honor, and inclusion in the Amazon top ten list for middle-grade books of 2004. She has currently written the manuscript for the second book in the Golden Hour Series entitled The Hour of the Cobra was published In 2006 and she is researching the third.

She is a member of the Writers Guild of America and the Society of Children's Book Writers and Illustrators and continues to write in the entertainment industry. She is married, with three children, and lives in Pacific Palisades with a white Labrador Retriever, a rabbit, a hamster, and a variety of fish.

BIBLIOGRAPHY

The Golden Hour. Amulet Books, 2004.
The Hour of the Cobra. Amulet Books, 2006.

Williams-Garcia, Rita M.

(1957–)

AUTHOR

E-mail: ritawg@aol.com

Web site: www.ritawg.com

"My first novel, Blue Tights, was written more than twenty years ago because I couldn't find a book about a black urban girl's life. Since then, writing stories for young people has become my passion and my mission. There is not a story that I'll shy away from, if it haunts me long enough. Our teens will read. They hunger for stories that engage them and reflect their images and experiences."

Author of award-winning novels, one picture book, and short stories that have appeared in numerous anthologies, Williams-Garcia continues to break new ground in young people's literature. Known for their realistic yet humorous portrayal of teens of color, Williams-Garcia's works have been recognized by the Coretta Scott King Award committee, PEN Norma Klein, American Library Association, and Parents' Choice, among others.

Her writing career began at age twelve, by reading The Writer's Market and submitting short stories to magazines. She sold her first story, "Benji Speaks," to *Highlights* magazine at age fourteen, and later sold a short story to *Essence* magazine while in college.

She earned her BA degree in Liberal Arts at Hofstra University, then received her MA in Creative Writing from Queens College in 1997. She recently served on the National Book Award Committee for Young People's Literature, and is on the faculty at the Vermont College MFA program for Children's Literature.

Williams-Garcia is the mother of two daughters, and lives in Jamaica, Queens, New York. After twenty-five years of employment with a media software company, she has resigned her position to write stories and teach writers.

She lives in New York City.

BIBLIOGRAPHY

Blue Tights. LodeStar/Dutton, 1987.

Fast Talk on a Slow Track. LodeStar/Dutton, 1991.

Like Sisters on the Home Front. LodeStar/Penguin, 1995.

Catching the Wild Waiyuuzee. Simon and Schuster, 2000.

Every Time a Rainbow Dies. Amistad/HarperCollins, 2001.

No Laughter Here. Amistad/HarperCollins, 2004.

Wilson-Max, Ken

(1965–)

AUTHOR/ILLUSTRATOR

E-mail: Kenwilsonmax@max.com

Web site: www.ideasforchildren.com

"I come from a very large mixed and diverse family and all of us know that people are more similar than they are different. Being away from my own home has made it somewhat easier to observe daily life and find similar close moments between children and adults of every color and creed. Every one of my books and ideas is based on this belief."

Wilson-Max was born and educated in Zimbabwe. He took a graphic design apprenticeship under Chaz Maviyane Davies. In 1986 he traveled to The United Kingdom to study, but ended up working instead as a book designer in 1987 at Orchard Books, learning for the next two years how to design books for children while studying part time. In 1990 he went to work for the BBC for another ten years, after which he decided to try to tell his own stories and started working on a book called *Big Yellow Taxi*. He also traveled back and forth to Zimbabwe. Book success came in 1995 when *Big Yellow Taxi* was published, quickly followed by *Little Red Plane*, *Big Blue Engine*, and eventually all seven books in the series.

Wilson-Max has worked on over forty books since then, and been published in ten languages worldwide. He lives in London with his wife, Manja Stojic, also a children's books illustrator-graphic designer, and their daughter Luba.

BIBLIOGRAPHY

The Sun is a Bright Star (with Sue Hendra). Bloomsbury, 1995, 1997.

Big Yellow Taxi. Cartwheel Books, 1996.

Big Blue Engine (Small Format Vehicle Books). Chrysalis Children's Books, 1996.

Great Day Out: African Life, African Words (Learning About Our World). With Audra Wilson-Max. Chronicle Books, 1997.

Let's Play: African Life, African Words with Audra Wilson-Max. Chronicle Books, 1997.

K is for Kwanzaa: A Kwanzaa Alphabet Book. By Juwanda G. Ford. Scholastic, 1997.

Dexter Gets Dressed. Larousse Kingfisher Chambers, 1998.

Max. Jump at the Sun (Hyperion), 1998.

Max's Amazing Circus Performers. Cartwheel Books, 1998.

Wake Up, Sleep Tight. Cartwheel Books, 1998. (Board Book – September 1, 1998)

Wake Up, Sleep Tight. Cartwheel Books, 1998 (Board Book – September 1, 1998).

Halala Means Welcome: A Book of Zulu Words. (Jump at the Sun) Hyperion, 1998.

Big Silver Space Ship (Small Format Vehicle Books). Chrysalis Books, 1999.

L is for Loving. (Paperback – January 1999). Scholastic, 1999.

Max Loves Sunflowers. Jump at the Sun (Hyperion), 1999.

Max's Letter. Jump at the Sun (Hyperion), 1999.

Max's Money. Jump at the Sun (Hyperion), 1999.

Numbers. Bloomsbury Publishing, 1999.

Opposites. Bloomsbury Publishing, 1999.

Shapes. Bloomsbury Publishing, 1999.

Sizes. Bloomsbury Publishing, 1999.

Tic-Tac-Toe: Three in a Row. By Judith Bauer Stamper. Sagebrush, 1999.

Flush the Potty! With Liza Baker. Cartwheel, 2000. (Board Book, November 1, 2000).

La Carta de Max. Ediciones B, 2000.

La Moneda de Max. Ediciones B, 2000.

La Moneda de Max, La. (Rebound by Sagebrush – Spanish), 2000.

Little Green Tow Truck. Cartwheel, 2000. (Board Book).

Little Red Plane. Cartwheel, 2000. (Board Book).

Mon Taxi Jaune. Albin Michel, 2000.

Zelda in the City. Dial Books, 2000.

Big Red Fire Truck. Cartwheel Books, 2001.

Furaha Means Happy: A Book of Swahili Words. Turtleback Books, 2001.

Happy Cat, Me: A Slide-the-Spot Book of Animals. Illustrated by Manya Stojic. Cartwheel, 2001.

Little Orange Submarine. Cartwheel, 2001. (Board Book).

Monsters Round the Corner. By Ian Whybrow. Macmillan, 2001.

A Book of Letters. Illustrated by Manya Stojic. Cartwheel, 2002.

Best Friends in the Snow. By Angela Shelf Medearis. Cartwheel, 2002.

Blue Sky Blue. With Manya Stojic. Chrysalis Books, 2002.

Diamonds and Squares. With Manya Stojic. Chrysalis Books, 2002.

Goodnight, Little Monster. By Ian Whybrow. Macmillan, 2002.

Goodnight, Monster. By Ian Whybrow. Knopf Books for Young Readers, 2002.

Kwanzaa Kids. With Joan Holub. Puffin Books, 2002.

Sunny and *Cloudy.* With Manya Stojic. Chrysalis Books, 2002.

Ten Fingers. With Manya Stojic. Chrysalis Books, 2002.

Tickle Tickle. By DaKari Hru. Bloomsbury, 2002.

Wake Up, Buttercup. By Alison Inches. Red Wagon Books, 2002.

101 Trucks. By Sam Williams. Cartwheel, 2003.

Baby Goes Beep, The. By Rebecca O'Connell. (Hardcover, September, 2003) Roaring
Brook Press, 2003.

Big Red Fire Engine. Chrysalis Books, 2003. (Hardcover, August, 2003).

Big Silver Spaceship. Chrysalis Books, 2003. (Hardcover, August, 2003).

I Can Do It Too! By Karen Baicker. (Hardcover, April, 2003), Handprint Books, 2003.

House That Max Built, The. By Susanna Leonard Hill. Simon & Schuster, 2003.

Max Paints the House. (Hardcover) Chrysalis Books, 2003.

Max's Starry Night (Hardcover). Chrysalis Books, 2003.

Catch! By Trish Cooke. Scholastic (Hippo), 2004.

Just For You! I Hate To Be Sick. By Aamir Bermiss. Turtleneck Books, 2004.

Setting the Turkeys Free. By W. Nikola-Lisa. Jump at the Sun (Hyperion), 2004.

Splash, Joshua, Splash! By Malachy Doyle. Bloomsbury, 2004.

Crocodiles Don't Brush Their Teeth. By Colin Fancy. Scholastic, 2005.

I Can Do It Too. By Karen Baicker. Handprint Books, 2005.

Just Like You Did. Marjorie Newman. Bloomsbury, 2005.

Motorcycle Police. Abrams Books or Young Readers, 2005.

Red Light, Green Light. By Anastasia Suen. (Hardcover, October, 20050. Gulliver Books, 2005.

You Can Do It Too. By Karen Baicker. Handprint Books, 2005.

Can You Hear The Sea? By Judy Cumberbatch. Bloomsbury USA Children's Books, 2006.

Just Like Me. By Marjorie Newman. Walker Books for Young Readers, 2006.

Woods, Brenda

(1952–)

AUTHOR

"*My goal as a writer is to allow our children to examine not only the past but the present as well. By doing this, we allow them to impact the future in a positive and thoughtful manner. I enjoy making a reader think and to perhaps have that moment when everything becomes crystal clear. The power of words astounds me. The beauty of our language encourages me. To be able to write is a gift, but to be able to read is something to be cherished. My years of public service have prepared me to be a writer who understands my people. In fact, it is they who have given me not only the stories but the dialects, allowing me to write authentically.*"

Woods was born in Cincinnati, Ohio, but grew up in Los Angeles, California. When approached by an English professor, during her sophomore year of college, who encouraged her to pursue a career in writing or English, she declined. Instead, she chose a career in the health sciences and holds a BS in community health from California State University, Northridge and a certificate in physical therapy from the same institution. She has worked as a physical therapist for nearly twenty-seven years.

Her first short story was published in 1999 and her first novel, *The Red Rose Box*, won a Coretta Scott King Honor in 2002. It was also a PEN Center USA finalist, and received the Judy Lopez Memorial Award. Her second novel, *Emako Blue*, received the award for the best YA novel from the International Reading Association as well as being named by the ALA as one of the top ten quick picks for reluctant readers.

She is affiliated with SCBWI and PEN CENTER USA. She often presents at schools in the Los Angeles area.

Woods is the mother of two adult sons and recently became a grandmother.

BIBLIOGRAPHY

The Red Rose Box. G.P. Putnam's Sons, 2002.
Emako Blue. G.P. Putnam's Sons, 2004.
My Name is Sally Little Song. G.P. Putnam's Sons, 2006.

Wyeth, Sharon Dennis

(1948–)

AUTHOR

Web site: www.sharondenniswyeth.com

"I learned to write my first word in kindergarten. The word was 'beautiful.' I remember running home, waving the paper with my word on it in the air. To make a word, by myself, to make it come out of the end of my pencil—what a joyous sensation! At five years old, I already was a big sister with three little brothers at home, but my mother made time to read that word 'beautiful' over and over again, expressing her pride in me.

I was in a classroom in the Bronx where I volunteer a few times a year to acquaint children with the writing process and to inspire them to read more. I shared my book, Something Beautiful. After I'd finished reading, the children were very quiet. The story is about a child living in a dense urban environment—like I did, like those children in the classroom do. 'What do you think?' I asked the children. One little voice piped up: 'I am in that book! I am in that book!' That's enough for me. In my ear, I have the memory of that child's little voice, saying 'I am in that book!'"

Wyeth is a picture book author as well as a novelist. Her fiction spans contemporary themes as well as historical; she writes for middle grade as well as young adult readers. Her protagonists are often children at risk grappling with such issues as broken homes, poverty, and identity. In some instances she draws upon her own childhood experiences. Her books have received multiple awards from the Children's Books Council, *Parents* magazine, Reading Rainbow, and the New York Public Library. She is the recipient of the Stephen Crane Literary Award presented annually by the Newark Public Library. A frequent guest lecturer at schools and Conferences, she has been the closing keynote speaker at the annual conference of the International Reading Association and a guest lecturer at the National Library of Iceland. Wyeth also has a background in the theater. A few years after graduating from Harvard University cum laude, she opened her own off-off Broadway theater in New York City where she engaged in writing and producing plays as well as acting. For twelve years she was on the faculty of The New School, teaching voice and public speaking. During this period, she also worked as a family counselor on the Lower East Side of Manhattan. Television credits include a script for "Reading Rainbow" as well as long story projections and scripts for daytime television. Her story, "A Family for Baby Grand," is currently touring symphony orchestras (accompanying the music of Brad Ross) in concerts for younger audiences.

BIBLIOGRAPHY

The World of Daughter McGuire. Delacorte, 1994.

Always My Dad. Illustrated by Raoul Colon. Knopf, 1995.

Ginger Brown: Too Many Houses. Illustrated by Cornelius Van Wright and Ying-Hwa. Random House, 1996.

Vampire Bugs: Stories Conjured from the Past. Illustrated by Curtis E. James. Delacorte, 1995.

Once On This River. Knopf, 1998.

Something Beautiful. Random House, 1998.

Corey's Underground Railroad Diary (Books 1, 2 and 3). Scholastic, 2001.

A Piece of Heaven. Knopf, 2001.

Orphea Proud. Delacorte Press, 2004.

Yancey, Antronette (Toni)

(1957–)

AUTHOR

"My involvement in clinical care of adolescents in foster care in New York City introduced me to the challenges to positive ethnic identity and self image for African-American youth. In developing the program for these teens that led me to a career in public health, I discovered the opportunity for engaging them in reading and writing presented by hip hop culture's embrace of poetry/spoken word. Since I've been writing poetry since I was eight years old, this is a natural communication vehicle for me. The feelings and memories of my own youthful experiences during the political and social turbulence of the 1960s and 70s 'populate' my poems, and often, I'm told, speak to their own struggles and shifting world view. While An Old Soul with a Young Spirit: Poetry in the Era of Desegregation Recovery was not specifically intended for young audiences, many of my youth-targeted poems were inspired by my observations of and dialogues with my own godson. This is complemented by my artist-collaborator's capturing of several of his children and grandchildren in the paintings illustrating our book."

A native of Kansas City, Kansas, Yancey completed her bachelor of arts degree in biochemistry and molecular biology at Northwestern University and her medical degree at Duke. For five years, she juggled her work as a general practitioner in clinics and emergency rooms. She subsequently returned to residency training, completing her specialty in preventive medicine and master's degree in public health at UCLA. Currently a professor in the Department of Health Services at the UCLA School of Public Health, she recently returned to academia full time after five years in public health practice, first as Director of Public Health for the city of Richmond, Virginia, and then as Director of Chronic Disease Prevention and Health Promotion for the Los Angeles County department of Health Services.

Yancey began reciting her poetry publicly to punctuate her medical lectures in 1994. In addition to her many scientific publications in health and medical journals, her poetry has been published in several newspapers and in the *American Journal of Preventive Medicine.*

Yancey lives with her partner of four years and two dogs in Los Angeles, California.

BIBLIOGRAPHY

Wilma Rudolph's Legacy (poem/commentary). *American Journal of Preventive Medicine* 1996;12(6):448–449.

An Old Soul with a Young Spirit: Poetry in the Era of Desegregation Recovery. Imhotep Publishing, 1997.

Recapturing Recess (poem). *American Journal of Preventive Medicine* 1998;15(4):iv.

Renaissance Woman/Race Woman (spoken word/music CD). Imhotep Publishing, 2001.

Ain' Like There's Hunger (commissioned poem/commentary). *American Journal of Preventive Medicine* 2003;25(3Si).

Zephaniah, Benjamin

(1958–)

AUTHOR

Web site: www.benjaminzephaniah.com

"I think if the curriculum is too rigid it can be very dangerous. Reading, writing and arithmetic are necessary to get on in the world but can also be used as tools for creativity. Pupils should also be seen, not just as people who should absorb knowledge but also as creative beings. I was one of those kids who kept asking, 'Why?' Once I received some of the answers, I realized that those in authority were not always right, so I could not always go along with them.

"I always felt that there wasn't literature that I identified with. So I started writing children's literature by simply asking myself: 'What would I have liked to read when I was young?'"

Zephaniah was born in 1958 and raised in Birmingham, England. His poetry is strongly influenced by the music and poetry of Jamaica. His first real public performance was in church when he was ten years old. By the time he was fifteen he had developed a strong following and gained a reputation as a young poet who was capable of speaking on local and international issues. At the age of twenty-two, he headed south to London to have his first poetry book, *Pen Rhythm*, published.

He has read all around the world, from Argentina to Palestine, in prisons, theaters, youth clubs, demonstrations—taking poetry to those who don't read books. His poetry was musical, radical, relevant—and on TV. It was once said of him that he was Britain's most filmed and identifiable poet.

A revolutionary poet that injected new life into the British poetry scene, he attracted the interest of many mainstream publishers and turned his hand to writing novels for young people. He has been awarded ten honorary doctorates in recognition of his work in literature, arts, and humanities.

He is from a family of eight brothers and sisters and currently resides in London, England.

BIBLIOGRAPHY

Talking Turkeys. Puffin/Penguin (London), 1994.

Funky Chickens. Puffin/Penguin (London), 1996.

School's Out. Edinburgh, AK Press, 1997.

Face. Bloomsbury (London), 1999.

Wicked World. Puffin/Penguin (London), 2000.

Refugee Boy. Bloomsbury (London), 2001.

Gangsta Rap. Bloomsbury (London), 2004.

Appendix I
Bookcovers and Jackets

Cover from *Hot Day On Abbott Avenue* by Karen English.
Jacket illustrations copyright © 2004 by Javaka Steptoe.
Reprinted by permission of Clarion Books, an imprint of Houghton
Mifflin Company. All rights reserved.

Cover from *The Sun's Daughter* by Pat Sherman,
illustrated by R. Gregory Christie.
Jacket illustrations copyright © 2005 by R. Gregory Christie.
Reprinted by permission of Clarion Books, an imprint of Houghton
Mifflin Company. All rights reserved.

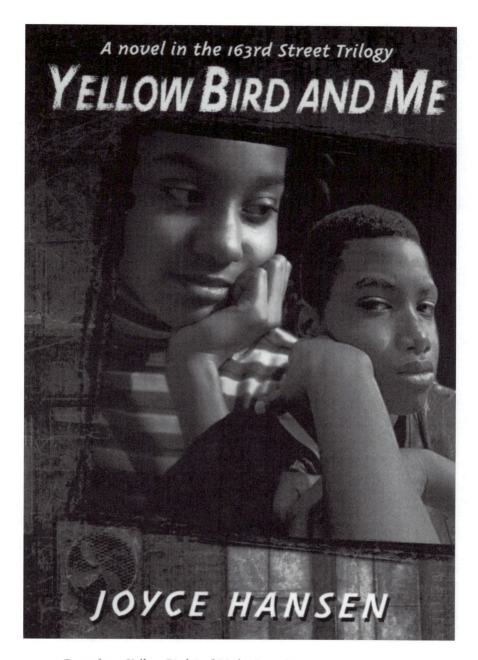

Cover from *Yellow Bird And Me* by Joyce Hansen.
Copyright © 1986 by Joyce Hansen.
 Reprinted by permission of Clarion Books, an imprint of Houghton
Mifflin. All rights reserved.

Cover from *One True Friend* by Joyce Hansen.
Jacket illustration copyright © 2001 by James Ransome.
Reprinted by permission of Clarion Books, an imprint of Houghton
Mifflin Company. All rights reserved.

A novel in the 163rd Street Trilogy

THE GIFT-GIVER

JOYCE HANSEN

Cover from *The Gift-Giver* by Joyce Hansen.
Copyright © 1980 by Joyce Hansen.
Reprinted by permission of Clarion Books, an imprint of Houghton
Mifflin Company. All rights reserved.

Cover from *This Our Dark Country* by Catherine Reef.
Copyright © 2002 by Catherine Reef.
Reprinted by permission of Clarion Books, an imprint of Houghton
Mifflin Company. All rights reserved.

Cover from *Slave Spirituals And The Jubilee Singers* by Michael L. Cooper.
Copyright © 2001 by Michael L. Cooper.
Reprinted by permission of Clarion Books, an imprint of Houghton Mifflin Company. All rights reserved.

Cover from *Gugu's House* by Catherine Stock.
Jacket illustration copyright © 2001 by Catherine Stock.
Reprinted by permission of Clarion Books, an imprint of Houghton
Mifflin Company. All rights reserved.

Cover from *Fight On!: Mary Church Terrell's Battle For Integration*
by Dennis Brindell Fradin and Judith Bloom Fradin.
Copyright © 2003 by Dennis Brindell Fradin and Judith Bloom Fradin.
Reprinted by permission of Clarion Books, an imprint of Houghton
Mifflin Compnay. All rights reserved.

Cover from *A Season For Mangoes* by Regina Hanson,
illustrated by Eric Velasquez.
Jacket illustration copyright © 2005 by Eric Velasquez.
Reprinted by permission of Clarion Books, an imprint of Houghton
Mifflin Company. All rights reserved.

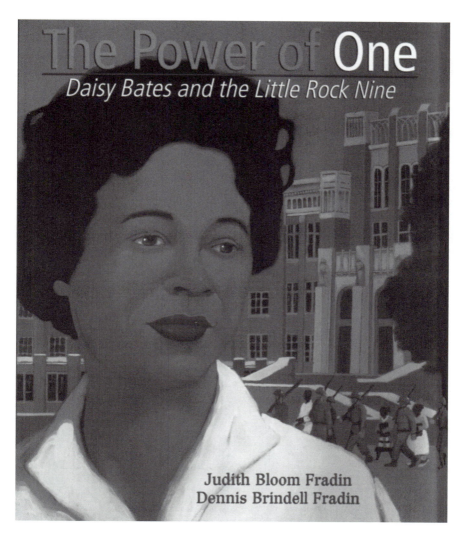

Cover from *The Power Of One: Daisy Bates And The Little Rock Nine*
by Dennis Brindell Fradin and Judith Bloom Fradin.
Jacket illustration copyright © 2004 by Jim Burke.
Reprinted by permission of Clarion Books, an imprint of Houghton
Mifflin Company. All rights reserved.

TOLOLWA M. MOLLEL

MY ROWS AND PILES OF COINS

illustrated by E. B. LEWIS

Cover from *My Rows And Piles Of Coins* by Tolowa M. Mollel.
Jacket illustrations copyright © 1999 by E.B. Lewis.
Reprinted by permission of Clarion Books, an imprint of Houghton
Mifflin Company. All rights reserved.

From *Shades Of Black* by Sandra L. Pinkney,
photographs by Myles Pinkney.
Photographs copyright © 2000 by Myles Pinkney.
Reprinted by permission of Scholastic Inc.

Cover from *Big Rain Coming* by Katrina Germein,
illustrated by Bronwyn Bancroft.
Jacket illustration copyright © 1999 by Bronwyn Bancroft.
Reprinted by permission of Houghton Mifflin Company. All rights
reserved.

Dust jacket from *Carver: A Life In Poems* by Marilyn Nelson
(Front Street, an imprint of Boyds Mills Press, Inc., 2001).
Designed by Helen Robinson. Reprinted with permission.

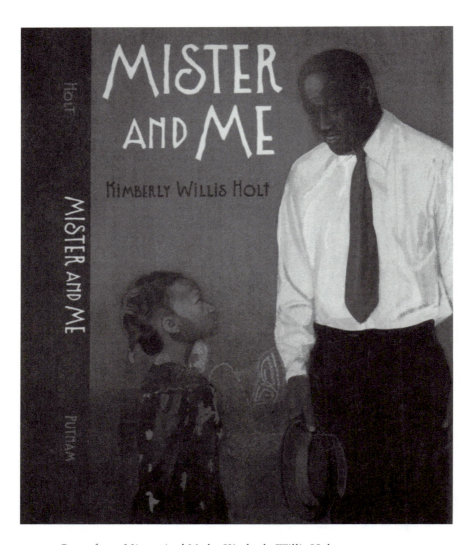

Cover from *Mister And Me* by Kimberly Willis Holt.
Reprinted by permission of Penguin Young Readers Group.

Cover from *Hot City* by Barbara Joosse,
illustrated by R. Gregory Christie.
Reprinted by permission of Penguin Young Readers Group.

Cover from *Sing-Along Song* by JoAnn Early Macken,
illustrated by LeUyen Pham.
Reprinted by permission of Penguin Young Readers Group.

Cover from *Trembling Earth* by Kim L. Siegelson.
Reprinted by permission of Penguin Young Readers Group.

Cover from *Emako Blue* by Brenda Woods.
Reprinted by permission of Penguin Young Readers Group.

Cover from *The Red Rose Box* by Brenda Woods.
Reprinted by permission of Penguin Young Readers Group.

Cover from *Behind You* by Jacqueline Woodson.
Reprinted by permission of Penguin Young Readers Group.

Cover from *Hush* by Jacqueline Woodson.
Reprinted by permission of Penguin Young Readers Group.

Cover from *If You Come Softly* by Jacqueline Woodson.
Reprinted by permission of Penguin Young Readers Group.

Cover from *Locomotion* by Jacqueline Woodson.
Reprinted by permission of Penguin Young Readers Group.

Dust jacket from *Fortune's Bones: The Manumissian Requiem*
by Marilyn Nelson
(Front Street, an imprint of Boyds Mills Press, Inc., 2004)
Designed by Helen Robinson. Reprinted with permission.

Every Man Heart Lay Down.
Text copyright © 1946, renewed 1970 by Lorenz Graham;
Illustrations copyright © 1970 by Colleen Browning.
Published by Caroline House, Boyds Mills Press, Inc.
Reprinted by permission.

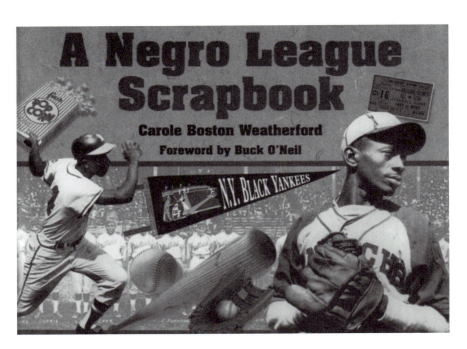

A Negro League Scrapbook.
Text copyright © 2005, by Carole Boston Weatherford.
Published by Boyds Mills Press, Inc. Reprinted by permission.

Has Anybody Lost A Glove?
Text copyright © 2004 by G. Francis Johnson;
Illustrations copyright © 2004 by Dimitrea Tokunbo.
Published by Boyds Mills Press, Inc. Reprinted by permission.

America, My New Home.
Text copyright © 2004 by Monica Gunning;
Illustrations copyright © 2004 by Ken Condon.
Published by Boyds Mills Press, Inc. Reprinted by permission.

Sidewalk Chalk: Poems Of The City.
Text copyright © 2001 by Carole Boston Weatherford;
Illustrations copyright © 2001 by Dimitrea Tokunbo.
Published by Wordsong, Boyds Mills Press, Inc.
Reprinted by permission.

Bear Hug. Text copyright © 2003 by Laurence Pringle;
Illustrations copyright © 2003 by Kate Salley Palmer.
Published by Boyds Mills Press, Inc. Reprinted by permission.

JUST FOR YOU!

Shop Talk

by Juwanda G. Ford

Illustrated by Jim Hoston

SCHOLASTIC

Cover illustration copyright © 2004 by Jim Hoston from *Shop Talk*
by Juwanda G. Ford. A Just for You!
Book published by Scholastic, Inc. Reprinted by permission.

Cover illustration copyright © 2004 by Nicole Tadgell from *A Day With Daddya* by Nikki Grimes. A Just for You!
Book published by Scholastic, Inc. Reprinted by permission.

JUST FOR YOU!™

Only the Stars

by Dee Boyd
Illustrated by Anna Rich

■ SCHOLASTIC

Cover illustration copyright © 2004 by Anna Rich from *Only The Stars* by Dee Doyd. A Just for You!
Book published by Scholastic, Inc. Reprinted by permission.

Cover illustration copyright © 2004 by Marjorie Borgella from *Never Finished, Never Done!* by Regina Brooks. A Just for You! Book published by Scholastic, Inc. Reprinted by permission.

Cover illustration copyright © 2004 by Nancy Devard from *The Mystery Of The Missing Dog* by Gwendolyn Hooks. A Just for You! Book published by Scholastic, Inc. Reprinted by permission.

Cover illustration copyright © 2004 by Randy DuBurke from *The Bravest Girl In The World* by Olivia George. A Just for You!
Book published by Scholastic, Inc. Reprinted by permission.

Cover illustration copyright © 2004 by mark *Page from The Two Tyrones*
by Wade Hudson. A Just for You!
Book published by Scholastic, Inc. Reprinted by permission.

Cover illustration copyright © 2004 by Gary Grier from *Don't Hit Me!* by Bernette Ford. A Just for You! Book published by Scholastic, Inc. Reprinted by permission.

From the dust jacket for *Under The Breadfruit Tree: Island Poems* by Monica Gunning,
illustrated by Fabricio Vanden Broeck (Boyds Mills Press, Inc., 1998).
Reprinted with the publisher's permission.

A Story from West Africa

Vacation in the Village

by Pierre Yves Njeng

From the dust jacket for *Vacation In The Village: A Story From West Africa* by Pierre Yves Njeng (Boyds Mills Press, Inc., 1999). Reprinted with the publisher's permission.

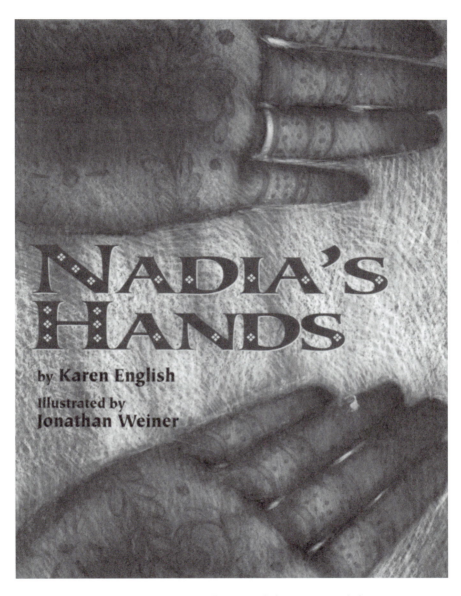

From the dust jacket for *Nandia's Hands* by Karen English, illustrated by Jonathan Weiner (Boyds Mills Press, Inc., 1999). Reprinted with the publisher's permission.

From the cover of *Madoulina: A Girl Who Wanted To Go To School* by Joël Eboueme Bognomo (Boyds Mills Press, Inc. 1999). Reprinted with the publisher's permission.

From the dust jacket for *Haircuts At Sleepy Sam's* by Michael R. Strickland,
illustrated by Keaf Holliday (Boyds Mills Press, Inc., 1988).
Reprinted with the publisher's permission.

From the cover of *It's Raining Laughter* by Nikki Grimes, photograph by Myles C. Pinkney (Boyds Mills Press, Inc., 2005). Reprinted with the publisher's permission.

Appendix 2
Coretta Scott King Awards and Honor Books

This award was established in 1969 designed to commemorate the life and work of the late Dr. Martin Luther King, Jr. and to honor Mrs. Coretta Scott King for her courage and determination in continuing to work for peace and world brotherhood. The award is presented annually by the American Library Association Social Responsibilities Round Table and the Coretta Scott King Task Force. The award was established to recognize and honor African American authors and illustrators of children's books who create outstanding books for children and young adults. For the first time, in 1974, the award's jury honored an illustrator.

Later in 1995 the John Steptoe Award for New Talent was given to a Black author and to a Black illustrator for an outstanding book, designed to bring visibility to a writer or artist at the beginning of his/her career as a published book creator. These awards are not necessarily presented each consecutive year.

2006

AUTHOR AWARD AINNER
Julius Lester, *Day of Tears: A Novel in Dialogue* (Hyperion)

HONOR BOOKS
Tonya Bolden, *Maritcha: A Nineteenth-Century American Girl* (Harry N. Abrams)
Nikki Grimes, *Dark Sons* (Hyperion)
Marilyn Nelson, *A Wreath for Emmett Till* (Houghton Mifflin)

Jaime Adoff, *Jimi & Me* (Hyperion)

ILLUSTRATOR AWARD WINNER
Bryan Collier, *Rosa,* by Nikki Giovanni (Henry Holt)

HONOR BOOK
R. Gregory Christie, *Brothers in Hope: The Story of the Lost Boys of Sudan* by R. Gregory Christie and Mary William (Lee & Low)

JOHN STEPTOE NEW TALENT ILLUSTRATOR AWARD
No award presented.

2005

AUTHOR AWARD WINNER
Toni Morrison, *Remember: The Journey to School Integration* (Houghton Mifflin)

HONOR BOOKS
Sharon Flake, *Who Am I Without Him?* (Hyperion)
Shelia P. Moses, *The Legend of Buddy Bush* (Simon & Schuster)
Marilyn Nelson, *Fortune's Bones: The Manumission Requiem* (Front Street)

JOHN STEPTOE NEW TALENT AUTHOR AWARD
Barbara Hathaway, *Missy Violet and Me* (Houghton Mifflin)

ILLUSTRATOR AWARD WINNER
Kadir Nelson, *Ellington Was Not a Street*, by Ntozake Shange (Simon & Schuster)

HONOR BOOKS
Jerry Pinkney, *God Bless the Child*, by Billie Holiday and Arthur Herzog Jr. (HarperCollins)
Leo Dillon and Diane Dillon, *The People Could Fly: The Picture Book*, by Virginia Hamilton (Knopf)

JOHN STEPTOE NEW TALENT ILLUSTRATOR AWARD
Frank Morrison, *Jazzy Miz Mozetta*, by Brenda Roberts (Farrar Straus Giroux)

2004

2003

Leo and Diane Dillon, Rap A Tap Tap: Here's Bojangles – Think of That (Scholastic)
Bryan Collier, Visiting Langston by Willie Perdomo (Henry Holt)

JOHN STEPTOE NEW TALENT ILLUSTRATOR AWARD
Randy DuBurke, *The Moon Ring* (Chronicle Books)

2002

AUTHOR AWARD WINNER
Mildred D. Taylor, *The Land* (Penguin/Putnam)

HONOR BOOKS
Sharon G. Flake, *Money-Hungry* (Hyperion)
Marilyn Nelson, *Carver: A Life in Poems* (Front Street)

ILLUSTRATOR AWARD WINNER
Jerry Pinkney, *Goin' Someplace Special* by Patricia McKissack (Atheneum)

HONOR BOOKS
Bryan Collier, *Martin's Big Words* by Doreen Rappoport (Hyperion)

JOHN STEPTOE NEW TALENT ILLUSTRATOR AWARD
Jerome Lagarrigue, *Freedom Summer* by Deborah Wiles (Atheneum)

2001

AUTHOR AWARD WINNER
Jacqueline Woodson, *Miracle's Boys* (Putnam)

HONOR BOOKS
Andrea Davis Pinkney, *Let It Shine! Stories of Black Women Freedom Fighters* (Harcourt)

JOHN STEPTOE NEW TALENT AUTHOR AWARD
No award presented

ILLUSTRATOR AWARD WINNER
Bryan Collier, *Uptown* (Henry Holt)

HONOR BOOKS

Bryan Collier, *Freedom River* by Doreen Rappaport (Hyperion)

R. Gregory Christie, *Only Passing Through: The Story of Sojourner Truth* by Anne Rockwell (Random House)

E.B. Lewis, *Virgie Goes to School with Us Boys* by Elizabeth Howard (Simon & Schuster)

JOHN STEPTOE NEW TALENT ILLUSTRATOR AWARD
No award presented

2000

AUTHOR AWARD WINNER
Christopher Paul Curtis, *Bud, Not Buddy* (Delacorte)

HONOR BOOKS

Karen English, *Francie* (Farrar, Straus and Giroux)

Patricia C. and Fredrick McKissack, *Black Hands, White Sails: The Story of African-American Whalers* (Scholastic)

Walter Dean Myers, *Monster* (HarperCollins)

JOHN STEPTOE NEW TALENT AUTHOR AWARD
No award presented

ILLUSTRATOR AWARD WINNER
Brian Pinkney, *In the Time of the Drums* by Kim L. Siegelson (Hyperion)

HONOR BOOKS

E.B. Lewis, *My Rows and Piles of Coins* by Tololwa M. Mollel (Clarion)

Christopher Myers, *Black Cat* (Scholastic)

JOHN STEPTOE NEW TALENT ILLUSTRATOR AWARD
No award presented

1999

AUTHOR AWARD WINNER
Angela Johnson, *Heaven* (Simon & Schuster)

HONOR BOOKS
Nikki Grimes, *Jazmin's Notebook* (Dial)

Joyce Hansen and Gary McGowan, *Breaking Ground, Breaking Silence: The Story of New York's African Burial Ground* (Holt)

Angelia Johnson, *The Other Side: Shorter Poems* (Orchard)

Sharon Flake, *The Skin I'm In* (Hyperion)

Michele Wood, I *See the Rhythm* by Toyomi Igus (Children's Book Press)

Floyd Cooper, *I Have Heard of a Land* by Joyce Carol Thomas (HarperCollins)

E.B. Lewis, *The Bat Boy and His Violin* by Gavin Curtis (Simon & Schuster)

Brian Pinkney, *Duke Ellington: The Piano Prince and His Orchestra* by Andrea Davis Pinkney (Hyperion)

Eric Velasquez, *The Piano Man* by Debbie Chocolate (Walker)

1998

Sharon M. Draper, *Forged by Fire* (Atheneum)

Joyce Hansen, *I Thought My Soul Would Rise and Fly: The Diary of Patsy, A Freed Girl* (Scholastic)

James Haskins, *Bayard Rustin: Behind the Scenes of the Civil Rights Movement* (Hyperion)

No award presented

Javaka Steptoe, *In Daddy's Arms I am Tall: African Americans Celebrating Fathers* by Alan Schroeder (Lee & Low)

Ashley Bryan, *Ashley Bryan's ABC of African American Poetry* (Atheneum)

Baba Wagué DiaKité, *The Hunterman and the Crocodile: A West African Folktale* (Scholastic)

Christopher Myers, Harlem by Walter Dean Myers (Scholastic)

JOHN STEPTOE NEW TALENT ILLUSTRATOR AWARD
No award presented

1997

AUTHOR AWARD WINNER
Walter Dean Myers, *Slam!* (Scholastic)

HONOR BOOKS
Patricia C. and Fredrick McKissack, *Rebels Against Slavery: American Slave Revolts* (Scholastic)

JOHN STEPTOE NEW TALENT AUTHOR AWARD
Martha Southgate, *Another Way to Dance* (Delacorte)

ILLUSTRATOR AWARD WINNER
Jerry Pinkney, *Minty: A Story of Young Harriet Tubman*, by Alan Schroeder (Dial)

HONOR BOOKS
R. Gregory Christie, *The Palm of My Heart: Poetry by African American Children*, edited by Davida Adedjouma (Lee & Low)

Reynold Ruffins, *Running the Road to ABC*, by Denizé Lauture (Simon & Schuster)

Synthia Saint James, *Neeny Coming, Neeny Going*, by Karen English (Bridge Water)

JOHN STEPTOE NEW TALENT ILLUSTRATOR AWARD
No award presented

1996

AUTHOR AWARD WINNER
Virginia Hamilton, *Her Stories: African American Folktales, Fairy Tales and True Tales* (Scholastic)

HONOR BOOKS
Christopher Paul Curtis, *The Watsons Go to Birmingham – 1963* (Delacorte)

Rita Williams-Garcia, *Like Sisters on the Homefront* (Dutton)
Jacqueline Woodson, *From the Notebooks of Melanin Sun* (Scholastic)

JOHN STEPTOE NEW TALENT AUTHOR AWARD
No award presented

ILLUSTRATOR AWARD WINNER
Tom Feelings, *The Middle Passage: White Ships, Black Cargo* (Dial)

HONOR BOOKS
Leo Dillon and Diane Dillon, *Her Stories: African American Folktales, Fairy Tales and True Tales*, by Virginia Hamilton (Scholastic)
Brian Pinkney, *The Faithful Friend, by Robert San Souci* (Simon & Schuster)

JOHN STEPTOE NEW TALENT ILLUSTRATOR AWARD
No award presented

1995

AUTHOR AWARD WINNER
Patricia C. and Fredrick McKissack Jr., *Christmas in the Big House, Christmas in the Quarters* (Scholastic)

HONOR BOOKS
Patricia C. and Fredrick McKissack Jr., *Black Diamond: The Story of the Negro Baseball Leagues* (Scholastic)
Jacqueline Woodson, *I Hadn't Meant To Tell You This* (Delacorte)
Joyce Hansen, *The Captive* (Scholastic)

JOHN STEPTOE NEW TALENT AUTHOR AWARD
Sharon Draper, *Tears of a Tiger* (Atheneum)

ILLUSTRATOR AWARD WINNER
James Ransome, *The Creation*, by James Weldon Johnson (Holiday House)

HONOR BOOKS
Floyd Cooper, *Meet Danitra Brown*, by Nikki Grimes (Lothrop)

Terea Shaffer, *The Singing Man*, by Angela Shelf Medearis (Holiday House)

JOHN STEPTOE NEW TALENT ILLUSTRATOR AWARD
No award presented

1994

AUTHOR AWARD WINNER
Angela Johnson, *Toning the Sweep* (Orchard)

HONOR BOOKS
Joyce Carol Thomas, *Brown Honey in Broomwheat Tea* (HarperCollins)
Walter Dean Myers, *Malcolm X: By Any Means Necessary* (Scholastic)

ILLUSTRATOR AWARD WINNER
Tom Feelings, *Soul Looks Back in Wonder*, Edited by Phyllis Fogelman (Dial)

HONOR BOOKS
Floyd Cooper, *Brown Honey in Broomwheat Tea*, by Joyce Carol Thomas (HarperCollins)
James E. Ransome, *Uncle Jed's Barbershop*, by Margaree King Mitchell (Simon & Schuster)

1993

AUTHOR AWARD WINNER
Patricia C. McKissack, *The Dark-Thirty: Southern Tales of the Supernatural* (Knopf)

HONOR BOOKS
Mildred Pitts Walter, *Mississippi Challenge* (Bradbury)
Patricia C. and Fredrick McKissack, *Sojourner Truth: Ain't I a Woman?* (Scholastic)
Walter Dean Myers, *Somewhere in the Darkness* (Scholastic)

ILLUSTRATOR AWARD WINNER
Kathleen Atkins Wilson, *The Origin of Life on Earth: An African Creation Myth*, by David A. Anderson. (Sights)

Wil Clay, *Little Eight John*, by Jan Wahl (Lodestar)

Brian Pinkney, *Sukey and the Mermaid*, by Robert San Souci (Four Winds)

Carole Byard, *Working Cotton*, by Sherley Anne Williams (Harcourt)

1992

AUTHOR AWARD WINNER

Walter Dean Myers, Now Is Your Time! The African-American Struggle for Freedom (HarperCollins)

HONOR BOOKS

Eloise Greenfield, Night on Neighborhood Street (Dial)

ILLUSTRATOR AWARD WINNER

Faith Ringgold, *Tar Beach* (Crown)

HONOR BOOKS

Ashley Bryan, *All Night, All Day: A Child's First Book of African-American Spirituals* (Atheneum)

Jan Spivey Gilchrist, *Night on Neighborhood Street*, by Eloise Greenfield (Dial)

1991

AUTHOR AWARD WINNER

Mildred D. Taylor, *The Road to Memphis* (Dial)

HONOR BOOKS

James Haskins, *Black Dance in America: A History Through Its People* (HarperCollins)

Angela Johnson, When I Am Old with You (Orchard)

ILLUSTRATOR AWARD WINNER

Leo Dillon and Diane Dillon, *Aida*, by Leontyne Price (Harcourt)

1990

AUTHOR AWARD WINNER

Patricia C. and Fredrick McKissack, *A Long Hard Journey: The Story of the Pullman Porter* (Walker)

Eloise Greenfield, *Nathaniel Talking* (Black Butterfly)

Virginia Hamilton, *The Bells of Christmas* (Harcourt)

Lillie Patterson, *Martin Luther King, Jr. and the Freedom Movement* (Facts on File)

ILLUSTRATOR AWARD WINNER

Jan Spivey Gilchrist, *Nathaniel Talking*, by Eloise Greenfield (Black Butterfly)

HONOR BOOKS

Jerry Pinkney, *The Talking Eggs*, retold by Robert D. San Souci (Dial)

1989

AUTHOR AWARD WINNER

Walter Dean Myers, *Fallen Angels* (Scholastic)

HONOR BOOKS

James Berry, *A Thief in the Village and Other Stories* (Orchard)

Virginia Hamilton, *Anthony Burns: The Defeat and Triumph of a Fugitive Slave* (Knopf)

ILLUSTRATOR AWARD WINNER

Jerry Pinkney, *Mirandy and Brother Wind*, by Patricia C. McKissack (Knopf)

HONOR BOOKS

Mr. Amos Ferguson, *Under the Sunday Tree*, by Eloise Greenfield (Harper)

Pat Cummings, *Storm in the Night*, by Mary Stolz (HarperCollins)

1988

AUTHOR AWARD WINNER

Mildred D. Taylor, *The Friendship* (Dial)

HONOR BOOKS

Alexis De Veaux, *An Enchanted Hair Tale* (Harper)

Julius Lester, *The Tales of Uncle Remus: The Adventures of Brer Rabbit* (Dial)

John Steptoe, *Mufaro's Beautiful Daughters: An African Tale* (Lothrop)

HONOR BOOKS

Ashley Bryan, *What a Morning! The Christmas Story in Black Spirituals*, selected and edited by John Langstaff (McElderry)

Joe Sam, *The Invisible Hunters: A Legend from the Miskito Indians of Nicaragua*, compiled by Harriet Rohmer et al. (Children's Press)

1987

AUTHOR AWARD WINNER

Mildred Pitts Walter, *Justin and the Best Biscuits in the World* (Lothrop)

HONOR BOOKS

Ashley Bryan, *Lion and the Ostrich Chicks and Other African Folk Tales* (Atheneum)

Joyce Hansen, *Which Way Freedom?* (Walker)

ILLUSTRATOR AWARD WINNER

Jerry Pinkney, *Half a Moon and One Whole Star*, by Crescent Dragonwagon (Macmillan)

HONOR BOOKS

Ashley Bryan, *Lion and the Ostrich Chicks and Other African Folk Tales (Atheneum)*

Pat Cummings, *C.L.O.U.D.S.* (Lothrop)

1986

AUTHOR AWARD WINNER

Virginia Hamilton, *The People Could Fly: American Black Folktales* (Knopf)

HONOR BOOKS

Virginia Hamilton, *Junius Over Far* (Harper)

Mildred Pitts Walter, *Trouble's Child* (Lothrop)

ILLUSTRATOR AWARD WINNER

Jerry Pinkney, *The Patchwork Quilt*, by Valerie Flournoy (Dial)

Leo Dillon and Diane Dillon, *The People Could Fly: American Black Folktales*, by Virginia Hamilton (Knopf)

1985

AUTHOR AWARD WINNER
Walter Dean Myers, *Motown and Didi: A Love Story* (Viking)

HONOR BOOKS
Candy Dawson Boyd, *Circle of Gold* (Scholastic)
Virginia Hamilton, *A Little Love* (Philomel)

ILLUSTRATOR AWARD WINNER
No award

1984

AUTHOR AWARD WINNER
Lucille Clifton, *Everett Anderson's Goodbye* (Holt)

HONOR BOOKS
Virginia Hamilton, *The Magical Adventures of Pretty Pearl* (Harper)
James Haskins, *Lena Horne* (Coward-McCann)
Joyce Carol Thomas, *Bright Shadow* (Avon)
Mildred Pitts Walter, *Because We Are* (Lothrop)

ILLUSTRATOR AWARD WINNER
Pat Cummings, *My Mama Needs Me*, by Mildred Pitts Walter (Lothrop)

1983

AUTHOR AWARD WINNER
Virginia Hamilton, *Sweet Whispers, Brother Rush* (Philomel)

HONOR BOOKS
Julius Lester, *This Strange New Feeling* (Dial)

ILLUSTRATOR AWARD WINNER
Peter Magubane, *Black Child* (Knopf)

John Steptoe, *All the Colors of the Race:* by Arnold Adoff (Lothrop)

Ashley Bryan, *I'm Going to Sing: Black American Spirituals* (Atheneum)

Pat Cummings, *Just Us Women,* by Jeannette Caines (Harper-Collins)

1982

AUTHOR AWARD WINNER
Mildred D. Taylor, *Let the Circle Be Unbroken* (Dial)

HONOR BOOKS
Alice Childress, *Rainbow Jordan* (Putnam/Coward)
Kristin Hunter, *Lou in the Limelight* (Scribner)
Mary E. Mebane, *Mary: An Autobiography* (Viking)

ILLUSTRATOR AWARD WINNER
John Steptoe, *Mama Crocodile, Maman-Caiman*, by Birago Diop, Translated and adapted by Rosa Guy (Delacorte)

HONOR BOOK
Tom Feelings, *Daydreamers*, by Eloise Greenfield (Dial)

1981

AUTHOR AWARD WINNER
Sidney Poitier, *This Life* (Knopf)

HONOR BOOK
Alexis De Veaux, *Don't Explain: A Song of Billie Holiday* (Harper)

ILLUSTRATOR AWARD WINNER
Ashley Bryan, *Beat the Story Drum, Pum-Pum* (Atheneum)

HONOR BOOKS
Carole Byard, *Grandma's Joy*, by Eloise Greenfield (Philomel)
Jerry Pinkney, *Count on Your Fingers, African Style*, by Claudia Zaslavsky (Crowell)

1980

1979

1978

Eloise Greenfield, *Mary McLeod Bethune* (Crowell)
James Haskins, *Barbara Jordan* (Dial)
Lillie Patterson, *Coretta Scott King* (Garrard)
Ruth Ann Stewart, *Portia: The Life of Portia Washington Pittman, the Daughter of Booker T. Washington* (Doubleday)

ILLUSTRATOR AWARD WINNER
Carole Byard, *Africa Dream*, by Eloise Greenfield (Harper)

1977

AUTHOR AWARD WINNER
James Haskins, *The Story of Stevie Wonder* (Lothrop)

HONOR BOOKS
Lucille Clifton, *Everett Anderson's Friend* (Holt)
Mildred D. Taylor, *Roll of Thunder, Hear My Cry* (Dial)
Clarence N. Blake and Donald F. Martin, *Quiz Book on Black America* (Houghton)

ILLUSTRATOR AWARD WINNER
No award

1976

AUTHOR AWARD WINNER
Pearl Bailey, *Duey's Tale* (Harcourt)

HONOR BOOKS
Shirley Graham, *Julius K. Nyerere: Teacher of Africa* (Messner)
Eloise Greenfield, *Paul Robeson* (Crowell)
Walter Dean Myers, *Fast Sam, Cool Clyde and Stuff* (Viking)
Mildred D. Taylor, *Song of the Trees* (Dial)

ILLUSTRATOR AWARD WINNER
No award

1975

AUTHOR AWARD WINNER
Dorothy Robinson, *The Legend of Africania* (Johnson)

ILLUSTRATOR AWARD WINNER
No award

1974

AUTHOR AWARD WINNER
Sharon Bell Mathis, *Ray Charles* (Cromwell)

HONOR BOOKS
Alice Childress, *A Hero Ain't Nothin' but a Sandwich* (Coward-McCann)
Lucille Clifton, *Don't You Remember?* (Dutton)
Louise Crane, *Ms. Africa: Profiles of Modern African Women* (Lippincott)
Kristin Hunter, *Guests in the Promised Land* (Scribner)
John Nagenda, *Mukasa* (Macmillan)

ILLUSTRATOR AWARD WINNER
George Ford, *Ray Charles*, by Sharon Bell Mathis (Crowell)

1973

AUTHOR AWARD WINNER
Alfred Duckett, *I Never Had It Made: The Autobiography of Jackie Robinson* (Putnam)

1972

AUTHOR AWARD WINNER
Elton Fax, *17 Black Artists* (Dodd)

1971

AUTHOR AWARD WINNER
Charlemae Rollins, *Black Troubadour: Langston Hughes* (Rand McNally)

HONOR BOOKS
Maya Angelou, *I Know Why the Caged Bird Sings* (Random)
Shirley Chisholm, *Unbought and Unbossed* (Houghton)
Mari Evans, *I Am a Black Woman* (Morrow)

Lorenz Graham, *Every Man Heart Lay Down* (Crowell)

June Jordan and Terri Bush, *The Voice of the Children* (Holt)

Barney Grossman with Gladys Groom and the pupils of P.S. 150, the Bronx, New York, *Black Means ...* (Hill and Wang)

Margaret Peters, *The Ebony Book of Black Achievement* (Johnson Publishing)

Janice May Udry, *Mary Jo's Grandmother* (Whitman)

1970

AUTHOR AWARD WINNER

Lillie Patterson, *Dr. Martin Luther King, Jr.: Man of Peace* (Garrard)

Appendix 3
National Listing of Bookstores

ALABAMA

Black Classics-Books and Gifts
2206D Airport Boulevard
Westwood Square
Mobile, AL 36606

Campus Bookstore
1013 Old Montgomery Road
Tuskegee Institute
AL 36088

Lodestar Books
2020 11th Avenue South
Birmingham, AL 35205

Mahogany Books & Gifts
37 Western Hills Mall
Fairfield, AL 35064

Ophelia's Art Gallery
1905 Bessemer Road
Birmingham, AL 35208

Roots and Wings
1345 Carter Hill Road
Montgomery, AL 36106

ARIZONA

Paradise Bookstore
9008 N. 99th Avenue
Suite #6
Peoria, AZ 85345

ARKANSAS

Africa Enterprises
707 E. Broadway
W. Memphis, AR 72301

Pyramid
The Museum Center
500 East Markham
Suite #110
Little Rock, AR 72201

CALIFORNIA

African Heritage Books & Gifts
5191 3rd Street
San Francisco, CA 94124

African Marketplace
2560 W. 54th Street
Los Angeles, CA 90043

Black Spring Books
503 Georgia Street
Vallejo, CA 94589

Books in Color
5444 Watt Avenue
Suite #900B
North Highlands, CA 95660

Bright Lights Bookstore
8461 S. Van Ness Avenue
Inglewood, CA 90305

Carol's Books & Things
5964 S. Land Park Dr.
Sacramento, CA 95822

Completely Anointed Bookstore
3854 W. Slauson
Los Angeles, CA 90043-2935

Deawah's Book Shop
4801 South Crenshaw
  Boulevard
Los Angeles, CA 90016

Education 2000+
309 Pine Avenue
Long Beach, CA 90802

Eso Won
3655 S. La Brea Avenue
Los Angeles, CA 90016

Ethnic Notions Bookstore
2070 Columbus Parkway
Bernica, CA 94510

Hanna's Ethnic Bookseller
240 Blue Mountain Way
Claremont, CA 91711-2825

Ironwood Corner
 462 Toolen Place
Pasadena, CA 91103

Kongo Square Gallery
4334 Degnan Boulevard
Los Angeles, CA 90008

Malik's Books
3650 W. Martin Luther King
  Jr.
 Los Angeles, CA.

Marcus Bookstore
1712 Filmore Street
San Francisco, CA 94115

Marcus Bookstore
3900 Martin Luther King Jr.
  Way
Oakland, CA 94610

Phenix Information Center
381 N. E. Street
San Bernardino, CA 92401

Shades of Sienna
582 Grand Avenue
Oakland, CA 94610

Smiley's
20220 S. Avalon Boulevard
Suite D.
Carson, CA 90746

The African Book Mart
2440 Durant Avenue
Berkeley, CA 94704-1611

The Book House Cafe
484 Lakepart Avenue.
Suite #1Oakland, CA 94610

Word of Life Christian Book
  Store
6321 West Boulevard
Los Angeles, CA 90043

Zahra's Books And Things
900 North La Brea
Inglewood, CA 90302

COLORADO

Africa House
1201 16th St. Mall #322
Denver, CO 80205

Black and Read
7821 Wadsworth Boulevard
Arvada, CO 80003-2107

Hue-Man Experience
911 Park Avenue
W., Denver, CO 80205

Underground Railroad Bookstore
4878 Chambers Road
Denver, CO 80239

CONNECTICUT

Black Books Galore
65 High Ridge Road
Suite #407
Stamford, CT 06905-3806

Blackprint Heritage Gallery
162 Edgewood Avenue
New Haven, CT 06511-4522

Dygnyti Books
828 Dixwell Avenue
Hamden, CT 06514

Eden Books
680 Blue Hills Avenue
Hartford, CT 06147-4338

DELAWARE

Haneef's Bookstore
911 N. Orange Street
Wilmington, DE 19801

District of Columbia
Attitude Exact
739 8th Street SE
Washington, D.C. 20003.

Drum and Spear
556 Varnum Street NW
Washington, D.C. 20011

Howard University Bookstore
2225 Georgia Avenue NW
Washington, D.C. 20059

Sisterspace and Books
1515 U Street NW
Washington, D.C. 20009

Yawa Books
2206 18th Street NW
Washington, D.C. 20009

FLORIDA

African American Heritage
Book
515 Northwood Road West
Palm Beach, FL 33407-5817

Afro-In-Books & Things
5575 NW 7th Avenue,
Miami, FL 33127

African Book Store
3600 W. Broward Boulevard
Ft. Lauderdale, FL
33312-1014

Amen-Ra's Bookstore
812 S. Macomb Street
Tallahassee, FL 32301

Books for Thought
10910 N. 56th Street
Terrace Village Plaza
Tampa, FL 33617

Ethnic Elegance
9501 Arlington Expressway
Jacksonville, FL 32225

Heritage Bookstore
2219 Fowler Avenue
Fort Myers, FL 33901

Montsho Bookfair
2009 W. Central Boulevard
Orlando, FL 32805

Nefertiti's Books
7640 Lem Turner Boulevard
Jacksonville, FL 32208

Pyramid
544-2 Gateway Boulevard
Boynton Beach, FL 33535

Tenaj Books & Gift Gallery
6085 US 1
Fort Pierce, FL 34954

Tenaj Books & Gift Gallery
47 E. Robinson Street
Suite. 201
Orlando, FL 32801

GEORGIA

Celebrate
1015 Patina Pt.
Peachtree City, GA
    30269-4013

Freedom Now Bookstore
2118 Chandler Road
Decatur, GA 30032

Heritage Bookstore
2389 Wesley Chapel Road
Suite #201
Decatur, GA 30035-2819

Medu Bookstore
2841 Greenbriar Parkway, SW
Atlanta, GA 30331

Mt. Zion Kid's Village, Little
    Angels Children's Books.
7175 Mt. Zion Boulevard
Jonesboro, GA 30236

Mutana Afrikan Warehouse
1388 Abernathy Boulevard SW
Atlanta, GA 30310

Nubian Bookstore
2445 Southlake Mall
Morrow, GA 30260

Shrine of the Black Madonna
946 Gordon
Atlanta, GA 30310

Soul Source Bookstore
118 James P. Brawley Dr. SW
Atlanta, GA 30314

The Crowning Seat of
    Wisdom
C/O Jeryl Muhammad
1130 Jackson Street
Madison, GA 30650

The Reading Room Bookstore
56 Marietta Street
NW, Atlanta, GA 30303

The Shrine Bookstore
946 Ralph Abernathy
    Boulevard
Atlanta, GA 30310

The Tree of Life Bookstore of
    Harlem,
1701 M L King Dr., SW
Atlanta, GA 30314-2227

Two Friends Bookstore
598 Cascade Road
Atlanta, GA 30310

ILLINOIS

African American Images
1909 W 95th Street
Chicago, IL 60643-1105

Afri-Ware
948 Lake Street
Oak Park, IL 60301

Afrocentric Bookstore
333 South State Street
Chicago, IL 60604

Black Expression Book Source
9500 5 Western Avenue
Evergreen Park, IL
   60805-2800

Cultural Bookstore
100 W. Randolph, Second
   Level
Chicago, IL 60601

Epicenter Bookshop-Uic
750 S. Halsted St., #M-Co48
Chicago, IL 60607-7008

Reading Room Bookstore
112 S. State Street
Chicago, IL 60603

INDIANA

Global Greetings
406 Main Street
Lafayette, IN 47901

X-Pression
5912 N. College Avenue
Indianapolis, IN 46220-2554

KANSAS

African American Gifts
2219 E. 13th Street N.
Wichita, KS 67214-1929

KENTUCKY

Nimde Books
2200 W. Chestnut Street
Louisville, KY 40211

LOUISIANA

Community Book Center
217 N. Broad Street
New Orleans, LA 10119

Reflections Books & Gifts
616 Harding Boulevard
Baton Rouge, LA 70807

MARYLAND

Arawak Books
3414 Hamilton Street
Hyattsville, MD 20783

Ascension Books
5490 Cedar Lane, Suite B3
Columbia, MD 21044

Black By Popular Demand
5711 Ager Road .
Hyattsville, MD 20782-2602

Everyone's Place
African Cultural Center
1380 W. North Avenue
Baltimore, MD 21217

Karibu
3500 East West Highway
Hyattsville, MD 20782

Masterworks Books
2703 Curry Drive
Adelphi, MD 20783

Peek A Boo Books Li
Wheaton Mall
11160 Veirs Mill Road
Wheaton, MD 20902

Sepia Sand and Sable
6796 Reisterstown Road
Baltimore, MD 21215

Sibanye
4031 West Rogers Avenue
Baltimore, MD 21215

Caravan Books & Imports
Rivertowne Commons Shopping Center
6053 Oxon Hill Road
Oxon Hill, MD 20745

MASSACHUSETTS

Black Orchid Books
105 Columbia Street
Maiden, MA 02148-3017

Cultural Collections
730 Belmont Street
Brockton, MA 02301

The Black Library
325 Huntington Avenue
Suite #83
Boston, MA 02115

MICHIGAN

Apple Book Center
7900 W. Outer Drive
Detroit, MI 48235

Bts Unlimited Books
19309 Greenfield Road
Detroit, MI 48235

Forewords Books and Gifts
1671 Plymouth Road
Ann Arbor, MI 48105

Laceter's Book Service
16345 Melrose Street
Southfield, MI 48075

Mahogany Books
15768 Biltmore
Detroit, MI 48227-1558

Shrine of the Black Madonna
13535 Livernois Avenue
Detroit, MI 48238

The Truth Bookstore
Northland Mall #476
21500 Northwestern
Highway
Southfield, MI 48075

Truth Boutique & Bookstore
Eastland Mall #823
18000 Vernier
Harper Woods, MI 48225

MINNESOTA

Faith to Faith Books
1304 E. Lake Street
Minneapolis, MN 55411

Presence of Africans in the Bible
Bookcenter
1012 26th Avenue N.
Minneapolis, MN 55411

Uhuru Books
2917 Lyndale Avenue S.
Minneapolis, MN 55407

MISSISSIPPI

The Heritage Center
1414 Washington Street
Vicksburg, MS 39180

MISSOURI

Afrocentric Books
6172 Delmar
St. Louis, MO 63112

Ujamma Ma Ktaba
4267 Manchester Avenue
St. Louis, MO 63110

Ujamma Ma Ktaba
5114 Natural Bridge Avenue
St. Louis, MO 63115

NEBRASKA

Aframerican Bookstore
3226 Lake Street
Omaha, NE 68111

NEW JERSEY

African American Bookstore
216 1st Street
Hackensack, NJ 07601-2400

Books-n-Things
Cross Keys Plaza
3501 Route 42
Turnersville, NJ 08080

Kujichagulia
150-154 Ellison Street
Paterson, NJ 07505

Mind and Soul Bookstore
449 S. Broad Street
Trenton, NJ 08611

New Jersey Books
59 Market Street
Newark, NJ 07102

Ourstory Books and Gifts
1318 South Avenue
Plainfeld, NJ 07062

Sacred Thoughts Bookstore
Newport Center Mall
Jersey City, NJ 07310

Serengeti Plains
615 Bloomfield Avenue
Montclair, NJ 07042

Tunde Dada House of Africa
Woodbridge Mall Lower Level
337 Woodbridge Center Drive
Woodbridge, NJ 07095

Tunde Dada House of Africa
356 Main Street
Orange, NJ 07050

NEW YORK

4W Circle of Arts
704 Fulton Street
Brooklyn, NY 11217-1625

A & B Distributors
146 Lawrence Street
Brooklyn, NY 11217

African Artisans
1211 Grand Avenue
Baldwin, NY 11510-1115

Black Mind Book Boutique
610 New York Avenue
Brooklyn, NY 11203-1509

Dare Books
33 Lafayette Avenue
Brooklyn, NY 11217

House of Isis
236 5B West 135th Street
New York, NY 10030

Hue-Man Bookstore
2319 Frederick Douglass
   Boulevard
New York, NY 10027

Langston Hughes Community
   Lib.
102-09 Northern Blvd
Corona, NY 11368

Liberation Bookstore
421 Malcolm X Boulevard
New York, NY 10027

Mood Makers Books & Art
  Gallery
Village Gate Square
274 N. Goodman Street
Rochester, NY 14807

Nkiru Books
76 St. Marks Avenue
Brooklyn, NY 11217

Nkiru Center for Education &
  Culture
732 Washington Avenue
Brooklyn, NY 11238

Our Black Heritage
2295 Adam Clayton Powell
  Boulevard
New York, NY 10031

Queens Borough Public Library
89-11 Merrick Boulevard
Jamaica, NY 11432-5248

Rainbow Books & Blooms
2016 Crompond Road
Yorktown Heights, NY 10598

Revolution Books
9 West 19th Street
New York, NY 10011

Schomburg Center Gift Shop
515 Malcolm X Boulevard
New York, NY 10037-1801

Sisters Uptown Bookstore
1942 Amsterdam Avenue
New York, NY 10032

Studio Museum of Harlem
144 West 125th Street

New York, NY 10027

That Old Black Magic
163 Mamaroneck Avenue
White Plains, NY 10601

Tunde Dada House of Africa
Green Acres Mall Second
  Level
2049 Green Acres Mall
Valley Stream, NY 11581

Zawadi Gift Shop
519 Atlantic Avenue
Brooklyn, NY 11217

NORTH CAROLINA

Blacknificent Books & More
2011 Poole Road
Raleigh, NC 27610

Heritage House
901 S. Kings Drive
Charlotte, NC 28204

King Solomon's Children's
  Enterprise
1308 Thurmond Street
Winston Salem, NC
  27105-5731

Special Occasions
112 N. Martin Luther King
  Jr. Drive.
Winston Salem, NC
  27101-4407

The Know Bookstore
2520 Fayetteville Street
Durham, NC 27707

W&W African American Art
417 Cross Creek Mall
Fayetteville, NC 28303

OHIO

A Cultural Exchange
12621 Larchmere Blvd
Cleveland, OH 44120-1109

African & Islamic Books
3752 Lee Road
Cleveland, OH 44128-1410

Black Arts Plus
3269 W. Siebenthaler Avenue
Dayton, OH 45406

Brighter Day Books & Gifts
5941 Hamilton Avenue
Cincinnati, OH 45224-3045

Lady Grace Bookshop
1044 Cleveland Road
Sandusky, OH 44870

People's Books and Gifts
1528 S. Yellowsprings Street
Springfield, OH 45506

The African Book Shelf
1324Q Euclid Avenue
Cleveland, OH 44112-4524

Timbuktu
5508 Superior Avenue
Cleveland, OH 44103

Ujamaa Book Store
1511 E. Livingston Avenue
Columbus, OH 43205

OKLAHOMA

Paperback Connection
5120 N. Classen Blvd
Oklahoma City, OK 73118

OREGON

Jackson's Books
320 Liberty Street
SE, Salem, OR 97301

Reflections Coffee and
   Bookstore
Walnut Park Retail Center
446 NE Killingsworth Street
Portland, OR 97211

PENNSYLVANIA

Basic Black Books
Gallery One, Mall Level
9th and Market Street
Philadelphia, PA 19107

Know Thyself
528 S. 52nd Street
Philadelphia, PA 19143

Ligorius Bookstore
Cheltenham Square Mall
Philadelphia, PA 19150

Liguorius Bookstore
2385 Cheltenham Avenue
Philadelphia, PA 19150

Robin's Book Store
108 South 13th Street
Philadelphia, PA 19107

SOUTH CAROLINA

Books in the Black
228 Somerset Drive
Columbia, SC 29223

Dorothea's African American
   Books
5410-D Two Notch Road
Columbia, SC 39204

Evans Book Outlet
4001 Highway 1008
Little River, SC 29566

Off The Shelf African American
Books
903 Elmwood Avenue
Suite C, Columbia, SC 29201

Powerhouse Books
1424 Horreil Hill Road
Hopkins, SC 29061

Tdir Books
6920 North Main Street
Columbia, SC 29203

TENNESSEE

African American Gift Gallery
114 Carr Street
Knoxville, TN 37919

Afro Books
1206 Southland Mall
Memphis, TN 38116

Alkebu-Lan Images

2721 Jefferson Street

Nashville, TN 37208

TEXAS

Babatunde & Yetunde
1102 W. Jasper Drive
Killeen, TX 76542

Black Book Discounters
4720 La Branch
Houston, TX 77004

Black Images Book Bazaar
230 Wynnewood Village
Dallas, TX 75224

Cush City
13559 Bammel N. Houston
    Road
Houston, TX 77066

Exhale African American Books
    & Gifts
5555 New Territory
    Boulevard
Suite #9102
Sugar Land, TX 77478

Jokae's African American Books
3917 W. Camp Wisdom
Suite #107
Dallas, TX 75237

Mainstreet Books
4201 Main Street
Houston, TX 77002

Nu World of Books
3250 Washington Boulevard
Beaumont, TX 77705

Out of Africa
Windsor Park Mall
7900 IH 35 N.
San Antonio, TX 78218

Shrine of the Black Madonna
5309 M. L. King Jr. Boulevard
Houston, TX 77021

The Black Bookworm
2300 Ridgeview Street
Fort Worth, TX 76119-3125

The Black Bookworm
605 E. Berry Street
Fort Worth, TX 76110-4300

Tricia's Book N Things
11975 Swords Creek
Houston, TX 77067

UTAH

Sam Weller Books
254 S. Main
Salt Lake City, UT 84101

VIRGINIA

Atlantic Bookpost
11654 Plaza America Drive
Suite #173
Reston, VA 20190-4700

WASHINGTON

Brother's Books
11443 Rainier Avenue S.
Seattle, WA 98178-3954

Carol's Essentials
1106 23rd Avenue
Seattle, WA 98122

Long Brothers Fine & Rare
Books
4811 41st Avenue
S.W., Seattle, WA 98116

WISCONSIN

Black Swan Books and Coffee
765-G Woodlake Road
Kohler, WI 53044-1321

The Cultural Connection
Bookstore
3424 W. Villard Avenue
Milwaukee, WI 53209-4710

The Reader's Choice
1950 N. Dr. Martin Luther
King, Jr. Drive
Milwaukee, WI 53212-3642

Index

Children and Young Adult Book Titles

"i" indicates cover illustration

Index

Authors and Illustrators

"i" indicates cover illustration

Dr. Barbara Thrash Murphy

ABOUT THE AUTHOR

A graduate of the University of Pittsburgh, Dr. Barbara Thrash Murphy has a bachelor's and a master's degree in elementary education and a doctorate in curriculum and supervision. She holds professional certification from the Commonwealth of Pennsylvania in the areas of early childhood supervision in elementary education, and early childhood education.

She began her professional career as a faculty member in the School of Education at the University of Pittsburgh at the laboratory school, where she trained undergraduate and graduate students while coordinating the Early Childhood Program. She has taught child development in the Pittsburgh public schools.

Presently retired, she devotes her time to volunteer work, reading to children in Head Start programs, participating in programs in the Carnegie Library of Pittsburgh, and writing children's stories.

She is a committee member of *Best Books for Babies* at the University of Pittsburgh, which identifies ten annual selections for children in infancy to 18 months of age, to assist parents, professionals, and others in selecting quality literature.

She is continuing to compile biographies of Black authors and illustrators of books for children and young adults and information of related interest in the genre of children's books.

Deborah Murphy

ABOUT THE AUTHOR

Deborah Murphy is a graduate of the University of Pittsburgh with a bachelor's degree in Sociology. She has worked in the non-profit sector for over twenty years as a training administrator for social service therapists and professionals.

An avid reader since childhood, she is also a free lance writer focusing on topics of children and literacy.